The Gen

The Genesis of Blessings

Andrew E. Walker

The Christadelphian
404 Shaftmoor Lane, Hall Green, Birmingham B28 8SZ, UK

2016

First published 2016

ISBN 978 0 85189 344 0 (print edition)
ISBN 978 0 85189 345 7 (electronic edition)

Printed and bound in Malta by
Gutenberg Press Limited

Contents

SECTION FOUR: Abraham, the friend of God

SECTION FIVE: Chosen families – Isaac and Jacob

SECTION SIX: From Haran to Canaan

Foreword

LOOKING westwards through the haze, Moses stood upon Mount Horeb. With his ancient hands gripping his staff and his eyes piercing the morning light, he gazed across the river towards the land of promise. Although he would walk no further, under God's hand he had led the nation from Egypt, and guided them in the wilderness like a flock.

It was a journey that had started long ago, its beginnings in another place and another time. It began on the distant streets of Ur, when a man and his wife turned their back on a familiar world because they believed in something better. Or perhaps it began earlier: as the flood waters receded, the rainbow shining in the sky. Or earlier still, as the Lord God formed the first man from the dust of the ground, and breathed into his nostrils the breath of life. Or even earlier: when a voice sounded in the darkness, and called out light from dark. All were moments of promise, because they spoke of what God could do with His creation.

Reading a book written by someone who loves the scriptures is always a delight. It reveals their motivations for discipleship and the foundations for their faith. It explains a thousand brief conversations and so many throwaway remarks made during Bible classes, for we find within the book the product of years of meditation and devotion. Yes, we say: this is how Bible study should be done – with an ear for the nuance of the passage, a sensitivity for the immediate context, and a certainty that greater knowledge of the scriptures draws us closer to our Lord. We may not reach the same conclusions or interpret in the same way, but we are utterly convinced that the author loves his Lord and honours the scriptures. And in reading, we are inspired to press on with our journey.

Here, Brother Andrew Walker has laid out a lifetime's love of Genesis with a unique perspective on its structure, key themes and connections. He brings us to one of the greatest books of our Old Testament: the book of beginnings. Who can fail to feel a shiver down their spine as all creation is brought to birth? Who does not wonder at the intimacy of the early fellowship in Eden, or watch – all too uncomfortably – as first Adam and then Eve protest their innocence? Who has not felt for their own families when Cain's jealousy of Abel spills over into bloodshed, or looked, open-mouthed, as Noah's call goes unheeded? Here, in *The Genesis of Blessings*, all these are ushered onto the stage. Then, as promises, passions and family politics are worked out in the lives of the patriarchs, we are reminded again of the most important of historical lessons: that times change, but people don't; that the griefs, follies and faiths of the men and women who went before us are in fact the maps of our own lives.

For a disciple, reading this book of beginnings yet longing for the conclusion of the present age, we know this: the dawn is almost within reach, and the blessings will come at break of day. Then, as once they did before, the morning stars will sing together, and all the sons of God will shout for joy.

Martyn Lawrence
September 2016

Introduction

THE book of Genesis is often described as the seedbed of the Bible. It is the book of beginnings and in it we find the teaching and purpose of the Lord God that is then expanded throughout the rest of the scriptures.

It is not the longest book in the Old Testament yet, by the time we reach its end, we are nearly two thirds of the way along the Old Testament timeline. It covers many generations of different peoples yet it is a seamless whole, knit together by the constant use of the phrase "these are the generations of", leading us from one section to the next.[1]

Most of the two and a half millennia it spans are covered in the first eleven chapters and, as we read them, we realise that they were written to bring us to one man, Abraham, to see his faith and that of all who will become his spiritual descendants through faith.

It is a book that begins with a picture of the Lord God as the great Creator of the heavens and the earth. Later in the scriptures, with the Psalmist, we see the wonder of these things for the heavens declare His glory and the skies His handiwork. The Lord is the God who made the infinite universe and the beauty of the earth on which we live. Hence, when we read of all that He has promised to do and the kingdom yet to appear, we have absolute confidence that it will come. What He has promised He is able to perform and so with David we can say:

---

1 See Digression, "The generations of ...", page 20.

> "Yours, O LORD, is the greatness, the power and the glory, the victory and the majesty; for all that is in heaven and in earth is yours; yours is the kingdom, O LORD, and you are exalted as head over all." (1 Chronicles 29:11)

Genesis is a book that tells us of this kingdom, for when God spoke to the first bridegroom and his bride He blessed them and gave them dominion; they were created to rule over all the earth. Man and woman were made for this purpose.

It tells us of sin and its consequences, the ways in which mankind turned aside from God and tried to thwart His purpose, yet repeatedly we read of faithful people who kept His way alive. It speaks of a priesthood greater than that of the one revealed to Moses and of the one who will be the head of that priestly order.

It is a book of contrasts. It speaks of the way of the Lord and the way of Cain, the sons of God and the daughters of men. It tells us of two cities, Babel and Jerusalem, of the seed of the serpent and the promised seed who will overcome sin. It is a book about the battle between righteousness and sin and about the grace of God that will provide the victory. In it, with Abraham, we see the day of the Lord Jesus Christ and when we read these chapters, we rejoice together with him for we too are Abraham's seed and heirs of the promise.

Above all Genesis tells us of the lives of the faithful and of God working through them. It speaks of those who were prophets such as Abel, Enoch, Noah and Abraham, men who were moved by the spirit of God and who looked forward to Christ. It is a book about people.

We see the ways in which the Lord communicated with them. He will speak to them directly and we find the phrase "the word of the LORD" for the first time early in the book. He will reveal His purpose through dreams and send the Angel of the Lord to guide the faithful. He will manifest Himself directly to His chosen ones, giving them a glimpse of His glory, a vital part of the message of His promises. We find that this follows a pattern: as we look at the five[2] principal characters of the book we see that the Lord spoke to each of them at the beginning of His dealings with them, sharing His purpose with them.

It is the word "promise" more than any other that we associate with Genesis. From Adam through to Jacob we find God making "exceeding great and precious promises", confirming them with an oath so that they become absolutely sure and certain. They are given with His blessing[3] and these two words are so closely linked that some writers refer to them as promise-blessings. Genesis uses the word bless (*barak*) more than any other Old Testament book. It is indeed "the Genesis of blessings" as it speaks of the blessing, given from the beginning, that the earth will be filled with God's glory, manifested in the people that He has made.

2 Noah, Abraham, Isaac, Jacob, Joseph.

3 See Appendix 1 for a study of the word 'blessing' (page 402).

SECTION ONE:
The creation record

1 | The creation of the heavens and the earth

THROUGHOUT the pages of the Bible, we often come across passages that mark special occasions in the purpose of Almighty God and which ask us to pause and think carefully about what is happening. For example, when we read of angels singing together in worship of the Lord then this must mark something exceptional.

It occurs three times in scripture and they all share a common theme.

The angels were present at the birth of the Lord Jesus Christ, a great multitude of the heavenly host, seen by the shepherds who were looking after their flocks in the fields outside Bethlehem. "Glory to God in the highest" they said as they praised the God who is above all things and acknowledged the marvellous manifestation of His glory seen in His greatest act of creation, the birth of His only Son.

> "For there is born to you this day in the city of David a Saviour, who is Christ the Lord." (Luke 2:11)

They were also present, "thousands of thousands" of them, at the events described in Revelation chapter 5. At his resurrection, the Son of God had been acknowledged by the Father and established as the heir of all of His creation.[1]

> "You are my Son, today I have begotten you. Ask of me, and I will give you the nations for your inheritance, and the ends of the earth for your possession." (Psalm 2:7,8)

1 Cf. also Acts 13:33.

The Son then ascended to his Father and took the scroll out of His hand. Of all creation, he alone was found worthy to do this and so the record of future world events leading to the fulfilment of all the promises of God was opened. In this act they were made absolutely certain, the word went forth and would never return to Him void; in the Son they became "Yes" and "Amen". No wonder the angels rejoiced.

These things were accompanied by a change in status of the Son for after his resurrection the Bible no longer describes him as "the only begotten Son" but as "the firstborn among many brethren". His resurrection is described as a new birth, a new beginning and a new creation as the Apostle Paul tells us (Colossians 1:12-18).

So the angels sang:

> "Worthy is the Lamb who was slain to receive power and riches and wisdom, and strength and honour and glory and blessing!" (Revelation 5:12)

However, it is the book of Job which tells us of the first occasion when such praise was given. When all the men involved in the drama portrayed in that book had fallen silent, the Lord finally spoke. His answer to Job emphasised the greatness of His power and majesty; He alone had laid the foundations of the earth and created the heavens and, when He did then:

> "... the morning stars sang together, and all the sons of God shouted for joy." (Job 38:7)

This first creation is also described as a birth for twice in this chapter God speaks of parts of His creation as if they came out of the womb.

There is also another description of rejoicing at this creative birth for Solomon wrote of God's wisdom that was present and active in all that He made:

> "When he prepared the heavens, I was there, when he drew a circle on the face of the deep, when he established the clouds above, when he strengthened the fountains of the deep, when he assigned to the sea its limit, so that the waters would not transgress his command, when he marked out the

foundations of the earth, then I was beside him as a master craftsman; I was daily his delight, rejoicing always before him, rejoicing in his inhabited world, and my delight was with the sons of men." (Proverbs 8:27-31)

The creation of the heavens and earth was not therefore merely a physical event brought about by the infinite power of the Lord. It was the beginning of His purpose for the future. Each day of creation, everything was done with supreme insight according to His divine plan, made according to a pattern that was necessary for the future He had in store for the world and its inhabitants.

These three events, when angels rejoiced had a common purpose:

- each was a creative act by the Almighty;
- each is described as a birth;
- each had a crucial part to play in God's purpose with the earth.

In the beginning

"In the beginning God created the heavens and the earth." (Genesis 1:1)

With these words begins the mighty word of God and immediately His uniqueness and power are established. It is not 'in the beginning God' for He is without beginning and end, from everlasting to everlasting. The One who had always existed, now began a purpose that scripture later tells us will only be complete when His glory and immortality are manifested in the people He will create.

Immediately the Bible poses a challenge: if we believe in a God whose power is such that He created all things, then whatever else He tells us He will do we must surely believe. In the words of the Apostle Paul, we can be fully persuaded that what God has promised, He is able to perform (Romans 4:21).

The writer to the Hebrews tells us that faith in the Lord as Creator is the beginning of a life of faith in a God who exists and who is a rewarder of those who seek Him. All the names that follow in that chapter are, therefore, of those who believed in the creation record:

> "By faith we understand that the worlds were framed by the word of God, so that the things which are seen were not made of things which are visible." (Hebrews 11:3)

Throughout the pages of the Bible, this is proclaimed by many people, for example:

> **David:** "Our help is in the name of the LORD, who made heaven and earth." (Psalm 124:8)
>
> **Hezekiah:** "O LORD God of Israel, the one who dwells between the cherubim, you are God, you alone, of all the kingdoms of the earth. You have made heaven and earth." (2 Kings 19:15)
>
> **The Lord Jesus Christ:** "I thank you, Father, Lord of heaven and earth, that you have hidden these things from the wise and understanding and revealed them to little children." (Matthew 11:25, ESV)

This majestic power of the Lord is emphasised in the language used to describe His act, for the exact form of the Hebrew word translated 'created' is only ever used of actions of the Lord God; He alone has such creative power.

If Biblical creation is rejected in favour of any theory of evolution, then immediately the rest of the Bible becomes irrelevant. Why should we believe what God tells us He will do if He is not the Creator He claims to be?

The foundation of the world

There is another point to ponder in the first verse of chapter 1. In the Hebrew it consists of just seven words, the first of many patterns of seven in the two opening chapters,[2] and the very first word is *reshiyth*, beginning. Elsewhere in the Old Testament, this is translated as:

- Beginning;
- Firstfruits;

2 U. Cassuto, *A Commentary on the Book of Genesis*, Part 1, pages 12-14.

- First;
- Chief;

and is particularly used of that which is offered to God as the very first of the harvest.

These are words seen in the New Testament about the new creation, for when Paul wrote about the Lord Jesus Christ he described him as the firstborn, the head, the beginning, the one with pre-eminence (Colossians 1:18). He is also the firstfruits of those who are raised from the dead, the guarantee of the resurrection of those who will be raised at his coming. The mighty power of the Lord was evident in the beginning, through His creative acts. It was also at work in the sending of His Son and also in the new, spiritual creation of men and women made that His purpose with the earth may be finally fulfilled.

This message is also found in the use of another New Testament phrase, "the foundation of the world", which is mentioned ten times. It is used to describe the creation of the heavens and the earth but constantly links this to the final outworking of the purpose of God in Christ, for example:

- Christ was foreknown before the foundation of the world, but was manifest in these last times for us (1 Peter 1:20).
- His sacrifice was foreknown by God from the beginning – the Lamb slain from the foundation of the world (Revelation 13:8).
- Yet these things were hidden until his advent for in the coming of Christ and his ministry are things kept secret from the foundation of the world (Matthew 13:35).
- From the beginning this was the path of redemption known by God for He chose us in him before the foundation of the world, that we should be holy and without blame before Him in love (Ephesians 1:4).
- At his return Christ will invite his saints to inherit the kingdom prepared for them from the foundation of the world (Matthew 25:34).
- There remains therefore a rest for the people of God for we who have believed will enter into His rest as He said –

although the works were finished from the foundation of the world (Hebrews 4:3).

The ordinances of the heavens and earth

Each day of creation began with the word of God prefaced by the phrase, "and God said" and summed up by the Psalmist in this way:

> "By the word of the LORD the heavens were made, and all the host of them by the breath of his mouth." (Psalm 33:6)

As the days unfolded, God spoke more often – four times in day six, ten times in all and the scriptures make it clear that His creative acts were accompanied by ordinances, physical laws which would sustain all that He had made. His creation speaks to us of this ongoing, immutable power:

> "The heavens declare the glory of God; and the firmament shows his handiwork. Day unto day utters speech, and night unto night reveals knowledge. There is no speech nor language where their voice is not heard. Their line has gone out through all the earth, and their words to the end of the world." (19:1-4)

In recent years, this has been shown to be true in a spectacular way. As we have learned more about the universe, and the immutability of the laws that govern it, it has become clear that all of God's creation, the whole of the heavens and earth, works in a way that is precisely right for life on earth. One writer described this as "the Goldilocks Enigma":[3] as baby bear's porridge was just right for Goldilocks, so creation is perfect for us. When the Lord had finished His creative work, He looked at it all and described it as being very good and our increasing knowledge of the world helps our understanding of His words.

We do not need to be scientists to appreciate this in awe – that God made the heavens and earth, and sustains them daily, in a way that is divinely perfect for His purpose with mankind. No wonder David, keeping the flocks long ago in the hills outside

3 P. Davies, *The Goldilocks Enigma, why the Universe is just right for life*.

Bethlehem, looked at the night sky, the moon and the stars that God had ordained, and said: "What is man that you are mindful of him?"

In the book of Job, the Almighty spoke to him about these things in a way designed to bring him to his knees before the omnipotence of his Creator. Was it His words about the night sky that would strike the deepest?

> "Can you bind the cluster of the Pleiades, or loose the belt of Orion? Can you bring out Mazzaroth in its season? Or can you guide the Great Bear with its cubs? Do you know the ordinances of the heavens? Can you set their dominion over the earth?" (Job 38:31-33)

This is important teaching for us. God has set the ordinances of the heavens and earth, they are the physical laws of nature essential for life on earth and when Jeremiah wrote of them he linked them directly to the Hope of Israel:

> "Thus says the LORD, who gives the sun for a light by day, the ordinances of the moon and the stars for a light by night, who disturbs the sea, and its waves roar (The LORD of hosts is his name): 'If those ordinances depart from before me', says the LORD, 'then the seed of Israel shall also cease from being a nation before me forever.' Thus says the LORD: 'If heaven above can be measured, and the foundations of the earth searched out beneath, I will also cast off all the seed of Israel for all that they have done, says the LORD.'"
>
> (Jeremiah 31:35-37)

> "Thus says the LORD: 'If my covenant is not with day and night, and if I have not appointed the ordinances of heaven and earth, then I will cast away the descendants of Jacob and David my servant, so that I will not take any of his descendants to be rulers over the descendants of Abraham, Isaac, and Jacob. For I will cause their captives to return, and will have mercy on them.'" (33:25,26)

Of course He will not do this. The gifts and calling of God are without repentance and the promises made to Abraham, and confirmed with the divine oath, will never be broken. He will never cast off His people Israel and one of the guarantees of this is seen in the unchanging laws that have governed all creation since the beginning. Whenever there is a glorious sunset or the majesty of the starry heavens on a clear night, we see things of beauty, the glory of God; yet, more than these for the scriptures tell of the unchangeable word of God and His ordinances in all that is seen – the same unchangeable word that unrolls from Genesis throughout the whole Bible speaking of our salvation.

Created, made and formed

In Genesis 1 and 2 God's acts are described in three different ways:

1. He *created* the heavens and the earth;
2. He *made* the firmament;
3. He *formed* man.

These three verbs are found together on only two other occasions in the Bible – both are in Isaiah:

> "Everyone who is called by my name, whom I have *created* for my glory; I have *formed* him, yes, I have *made* him."
>
> (Isaiah 43:7)
>
> "For thus says the LORD, who *created* the heavens, who is God, who *formed* the earth and *made* it, who has established it, who did not create it in vain, who formed it to be inhabited: 'I am the LORD, and there is no other ... Tell and bring forth your case; yes, let them take counsel together. Who has declared this from ancient time? Who has told it from that time? Have not I, the LORD? And there is no other God besides me, a just God and a Saviour; there is none besides me. Look to me, and be saved, all you ends of the earth! For I am God, and there is no other. I have sworn by myself; the word has gone out of my mouth in righteousness, and shall not return, that to me every knee shall bow, every tongue shall take an oath. He shall say, "Surely in the LORD I have righteousness and strength. To him men shall come, and all shall be ashamed who are incensed against Him".'" (Isaiah 45:18-24)

In the beginning, the word went forth from the Lord and He created, formed and made the universe. It was not made in vain (Hebrew, *tohu*, "without form", as in Genesis 1:2) but to be inhabited by people who are called by His name and whom He has made for His glory. The oath sworn by Yahweh to Moses in Numbers 14, that the earth would be filled with His glory, was not of something new but a reiteration of His purpose from the beginning. Israel's faithless decision to make a captain to return to Egypt would never thwart this: the word had gone out from His mouth; God had spoken and it would be so.

Forming and filling

> "The earth was without form (*tohu*), and void (*bohu*); and darkness was on the face of the deep." (Genesis 1:2)

We are not told when planet earth was made; it is simply introduced as an empty mass, without light and covered in water. One writer describes it in these words:

> "The creator first prepared for himself the raw material of the universe with a view to giving it afterwards order and life ... the whole material was an undifferentiated, unorganised, confused and lifeless agglomeration. It is this terrestrial state that is called '*tohu*' and '*bohu*' [without form and void]."[4]

What follows, therefore, in the six days of Genesis 1 is concerned with forming that which was *tohu* and filling that which was *bohu*.

These six periods[5] can be divided into two sets of three.

Forming (*tohu*)			**Filling (*bohu*)**		
Day	**Focus**		**Day**	**Focus**	
1	Light (1:3-5)	Heaven	4	Lights (1:14-19)	Heaven

4 U. Cassuto, *A Commentary on the Book of Genesis*, Part 1, page 23.

5 It is not the purpose of this book to debate whether the six days were literal days or longer periods.

2	Firmament (1:6-8) sky / seas	Heaven	5	Inhabitants (1:20-23) birds / fish	Earth
3	Dry land (1:9,10) vegetation (1:11-13)	Earth	6	Land animals (1:24,25) People (1:26-31)	Earth

And God blessed them (1)

Day after day, creative acts followed the statement "and God said", reinforcing the message of the Psalmist that "He spoke, and it was done; he commanded, and it stood fast". It was on the fifth day however that God did something different for the first time:

> "So God created great sea creatures and every living thing that moves, with which the waters abounded, according to their kind, and every winged bird according to its kind. And God saw that it was good. And God blessed them, saying, 'Be fruitful and multiply, and fill the waters in the seas, and let birds multiply on the earth.'" (Genesis 1:21,22)

It is a surprise to read that a blessing, an act of God that will be of such importance in His dealings with mankind, was first given to fish.[6]

Why was this so? Fish could not understand God's blessing, it could have no spiritual or moral impact on them whatsoever. Of all creation only man and woman were made with the capacity to understand God's purpose and their lives would not commence until the following day.

Look at what took place:

- Fish and sea creatures were the first fauna that God made.
- They were *chay nephesh*, "living souls" – the same language was used of Adam.
- God's words (His blessing) to the fish were His first words spoken directly to His creation.

6 To fish only and not to birds; cf. U. Cassuto, op. cit., page 51.

- His blessing was "be fruitful and multiply, and fill the waters in the seas".

The waters abounded with fish and this is seen today in the shoals that fill the oceans – for example, the sardine shoals that annually move south down the east coast of Africa or the mega shoals of herrings in the North Atlantic or on the Pacific coast of the USA. Such shoals are amongst the biggest swarms of living creatures seen on the planet.

In this verse there is a link to two miracles the Lord Jesus Christ performed – both involved God's power to create miraculous shoals of fish.[7] Yet both were also parables in which the fish represented people: they were given to teach the disciples, who were fishermen, for they were to be "fishers of men". This abundance of fish life is therefore a type, representing the great multitude which no one could number, of all nations, tribes, peoples, and tongues, who will stand before the Lord Jesus Christ at his return.

This link is seen in the way the key words of this blessing (fruitful, multiply, fill) are repeated elsewhere in the Bible. These are all the occasions:

> "And God blessed them, saying, 'Be fruitful and multiply, and fill the waters in the seas, and let birds multiply on the earth.'" (Genesis 1:22)
>
> "Then God blessed them, and God said to them, 'Be fruitful and multiply; fill the earth and subdue it; have dominion over the fish of the sea, over the birds of the air, and over every living thing that moves on the earth.'" (verse 28)
>
> "So God blessed Noah and his sons, and said to them: 'Be fruitful and multiply, and fill the earth.'" (9:1)
>
> "But the children of Israel were fruitful and increased abundantly, multiplied and grew exceedingly mighty; and the land was filled with them." (Exodus 1:7)

In each case after Genesis 1:22 the words "be fruitful, multiply and fill ..." are part of a blessing by God on His people

7 Luke 5:4-10; John 21:5-11.

(the words in Exodus 1 are an initial fulfilment of the blessing of Jacob in Genesis 35).

Hence:

> The fundamental purpose of blessings (*berakah*) from God is the giving of abundant life by the Creator from whom all life comes. This life is given for a purpose: it is to fill part of His creation; the fish in the sea, His chosen people, the whole earth.

2

The sixth day

CREATION came to a climax on the sixth day and both Genesis 1 and 2 tell us of events within it. It is useful to list all that happened in order to get an overall picture.

1. God made the animals.
2. There was a dialogue with the Elohim about the creation of man.
3. The Lord God formed Adam out of dust and gave him life.
4. He planted the Garden of Eden.
5. He took Adam into the Garden.
6. Adam was given the work of tending the Garden.
7. Adam was given a law to keep.
8. The Lord God decided that it was not good for the man to be alone, he needed a companion to help him in the work he had been given.
9. The Lord God brought the animals and birds He had created before the man. Adam named them and looked to see if any of them were suitable to be his helper.
10. None of the animals was suitable to help Adam so the woman was formed from Adam's side.
11. The Lord God brought the woman to Adam to be his helper; there was a formal union before Him.
12. The Lord God blessed them.
13. Their necessary food was given to them.
14. The sixth day ended.
15. The next day, the seventh, was the first Sabbath.

As we come to the creation of Adam in Genesis 2, there is a change in the record. Previously all has been made by the word of God, but now He is directly involved and His name is given for the first time. It is not until the beginning of the book of Exodus that this name will be fully revealed to us yet its introduction here, linked with the formation of man, tells us of the way in which the name of the Lord will be intimately involved in His purpose with mankind.

It begins with a dialogue involving the Lord and His angels in the court of heaven.

In His image

> "Then God said, 'Let us make man in our image, according to our likeness; let them have dominion over the fish of the sea, over the birds of the air, and over the cattle, over all the earth and over every creeping thing that creeps on the earth.' So God created man in his own image; in the image of God he created him; male and female he created them." (Genesis 1:26,27)

Adam was made in the image of the Elohim, the angels, and in some way physically like them for this act had a message for the men and women who would fill the earth.

Consider the greatness of the Lord God. He dwells in light unapproachable, no man can see Him and live. His thoughts are

Let us

Four times in scripture we find the plural "us" used in connection with the words of God and on each occasion the heavenly dialogue is about the fate of the men and women being discussed. Each of the three passages after Genesis 1:26 speaks of the Lord reflecting on the turning away of people from Him and of the consequences of their sins. When we read them one after another it gives a feeling of sadness: God made men in such a careful, special way for His purpose and that purpose was rejected by them (cf. Genesis 3:22; 11:7; Isaiah 6:8).

not our thoughts, His ways not our ways. He is spirit, far above the heavens. In His creation He is shown to be the Sovereign Lord over the whole universe and He has brought order to all He has made through the ordinances of the heavens and the earth. How can He communicate with us about these things, how can we understand a God who is so far above us?

It is true that, in creation, His eternal power and Godhead are clearly seen (Romans 1:20) and the Psalmist tells us that every morning as the sun comes over the horizon, like a bridegroom coming out of his chamber, we see the glory of God and His handiwork speaks to us. Yet now, in the creation of man, God began another way in which He would reveal Himself to people. Searching through the Old Testament we find the Lord described as possessing all of the five senses that we have:

- God can see (Genesis 1:31);
- God can smell (Genesis 8:21);
- God can hear (Genesis 17:20);
- God can touch (Psalm 104:32);
- God can taste (Leviticus 3:11; Ezekiel 44:7).

Of course, this cannot be literally true: God is a spirit being, He does not have a body but He made men and women with these senses so that He can communicate to us through His word in a way that can be understood. Consider what the Psalmist wrote:

> "He who planted the ear, shall he not hear? He who formed the eye, shall he not see?" (Psalm 94:9)

God gave people ears so that they can understand what it means when they read that He hears the cry of the afflicted. He gave eyes so that they can comprehend that He sees the plight of the pitiful.[1] People are not the product of some random evolutionary process but are so made that the Almighty Creator can communicate with them in a way that helps them understand both Him and His purpose.

1 B. Waltke, *Genesis, A Commentary*, page 65.

After His likeness

In one sense, the creation of man and the animals was similar. They were all made living souls, or living creatures, and the words simply indicate that they had life itself; that quality of existence which can come only from the Lord, the one in whom "we live and move and have our being". They were also both formed out of the ground (*adamah*) emphasising the point that, in the physical nature of flesh and blood, men and animals are similar. This is seen in the way that we are made: all living creatures have the same cell structure, all have DNA within their cells. Yet this similarity, which is acknowledged in the Bible, is wrongly used to assume that people and animals have all evolved from a common source.

However, the differences between mankind and the animal creation outweigh this similarity. The animals were to multiply after their kind, each within its species, solely for the prolongation of that species. With mankind it was not so; the Lord was much more intimately involved in his creation. He formed man of the dust of the ground and the same word is used of the potter moulding (forming) clay (Isaiah 45:9). God was closely involved and He made man and woman in a specific form and for a specific purpose:

> "And God said, Let us make man in our image, after our likeness: and let them have dominion over the fish of the sea, and over the fowl of the air, and over the cattle, and over all the earth, and over every creeping thing that creepeth upon the earth. So God created man in his own image, in the image of God created he him; male and female created he them."
>
> (Genesis 1:26,27, KJV)

These words are difficult to understand but there is some evidence that "in our image" refers to physical likeness and "after our likeness" to moral likeness or development. Consider these two passages:

> "Therewith bless we God, even the Father; and therewith curse we men, which are made *after the similitude of God*."
>
> (James 3:9, KJV)

> "And have put on the new man, which is renewed in knowledge *after the image of him* that created him."
>
> (Colossians 3:10, KJV)

Each of these passages echoes Genesis 1:26, and each of them refers to our spiritual development. Indeed Paul, talking of the new life in Christ after baptism, likens this to the development of Adam. It is through knowledge and this tells us of that which God wished of His Son at creation. An ability to develop a knowledge and understanding of his Creator was what set Adam apart from the animal creation; none of them was made with this capacity, not even the serpent. This moral quality was essential for God's purpose, for Adam and the woman were to raise their children in the nurture and admonition of the Lord. It is the Lord's avowed will that the earth be filled with His glory and therefore these offspring should have developed 'after the likeness' of God. It was the Lord's intention that they should take His word and His moral glory with them in their lives as they spread out from the Garden.

This is the principle behind both the teaching about the "godly seed" (Malachi 2:15) and that of Genesis 1:28, "be fruitful, and multiply, and replenish (fill) the earth".

All other creatures were made "after their kind" in defined, fixed species but man and woman were made 'after God's likeness'. One writer says that 'after his likeness' carries the idea that man was "granted a capacity to reflect the divine character".[2] It is this quality of our being that distinguishes us from all else that God made; this capacity that enables us to be part of the fulfilment of God's purpose with His creation. The Apostle Paul summed this up when he spoke on Mars Hill:

> "God, who made the world and everything in it, since he is Lord of heaven and earth, does not dwell in temples made with hands. Nor is he worshipped with men's hands, as though he needed anything, since he gives to all life, breath, and all things. And he has made from one blood every nation of men

---

2 Brother H. P. Mansfield, *The Book of Genesis*, page 46.

> to dwell on all the face of the earth, and has determined their pre-appointed times and the boundaries of their dwellings, so that they should seek the Lord ... for in him we live and move and have our being, as also some of your own poets have said, 'For we are also his offspring.'" (Acts 17:24-28)

Paul's words were prophetic; these things are not yet completely true for: "now we are children of God; and it has not yet been revealed what we shall be, but we know that when he (Christ) is revealed, we shall be like him."

It is in Christ that we see all that the image and likeness of God means to us. In him was all the fullness of the Godhead bodily. The Old Testament tells us that he came to do the will of God and that this will was done in the body prepared for him. He was made of flesh and blood like us yet only he has fulfilled completely the purpose for which God created mankind.

The creation account then is of vital importance to us. It tells us of God's almighty power and of the way that power was used to make a universe exactly right for the existence of men and women. We are made with a capacity to understand His purpose and develop Godly characters and we disregard this at our peril as the apostle went on to tell the Athenians in Mars Hill. If we turn our backs on our calling then we are no different from the rest of God's creation for "man who is in honour, yet does not understand, is like the beasts that perish".

The breath of life

> "And the LORD God formed man of the dust of the ground, and breathed into his nostrils the breath of life; and man became a living being." (Genesis 2:7)

Note the uniqueness of this event. Woman would be made out of Adam's side but only one man, Adam, was made in such a direct way, as the Lord God formed the earth into shape and breathed into the clay the breath of life.

Job tells us that this breath is analogous to the spirit of God and it departs at death:

> "If he should set his heart on it, if he should gather to himself his Spirit and his breath, all flesh would perish together, and man would return to dust." (Job 34:14,15)

He wrote of spirit as the life force that comes from God and returns to Him at death. Any of us who have sat by the bedside of a desperately sick and dying relative and seen them fighting with all their might to breathe can understand Job's words. There is an unmistakeable change as the last breath is taken and death comes – something has departed, of course not an immortal soul, but the spirit, the life force given by God, has returned to Him.

Yet, as always here in these early chapters of Genesis, we see past the physical to the spiritual for in the making of the first Adam, there is an echo, pointing forward to the last Adam. Consider these two passages.

> **In God's image:** "His dear son ... who is the image of the invisible God, the firstborn of every creature."
> (Colossians 1:13-15, KJV)
>
> **And after His likeness:** "Who being the brightness of his glory, and the express image of his person ..."
> (Hebrews 1:3, KJV)

In the Lord Jesus Christ we see all that man was created to be.

In the beginning, Adam alone was privileged to be given the word of God: just one commandment was entrusted to him, and he rejected it. It was the only begotten Son of the Father who took all of scripture as the totally inspired, God-breathed word and made it his life so completely that he could be described as the word made flesh.

DIGRESSION: The generations of ...

There are many theories about the age of the Book of Genesis and its writer. Moses is associated with it as with all the books of the Pentateuch. However, he must have been merely a redactor of Genesis for there is evidence that it was written many years before he became the leader of Israel. Here are some of the major clues about its age.

1. Some of the place names in Genesis 14 were so old that they had become unknown by the time of Moses and he had to add explanatory text, for example:
   - Bela (which is Zoar);
   - En-mishpat (which is Kadesh);
   - Hobah (which is on the left hand of Damascus).
2. "And the border of the Canaanites was from Sidon as you go toward Gerar, as far as Gaza; then as you go toward Sodom, Gomorrah, Admah, and Zeboiim, as far as Lasha" (Genesis 10:19). This must have been written before the destruction of Sodom and Gomorrah. They disappeared completely in the events of Genesis 19 and all trace of them was lost.
3. New Testament writers believed that Abraham had a written word (Romans 4:23; Galatians 3:8; James 2:23).

Genesis is arranged in ten sections, each separated by a phrase "the generations of". One suggestion is that these are pointers to the writers of each section and that the whole book was later compiled by Moses,[3] although there is little evidence for such a theory. A modified but similar view was given by a Christadelphian writer:

> "The book of Genesis itself is a compilation of books. Apart from the introduction (1:1 to 2:3), it is divided into ten parts, each with the heading, 'These are the generations of ...' (2:4; 5:1; 6:9, etc.). Internal evidence points to the eleven parts having been written either on scrolls or tablets by ten or eleven prophets who were near contemporaries of the events they recorded. As they accumulated, the inspired scriptures which eventually became our Genesis were handed down through the chosen line, so that by the time 'the prophet Moses' wrote Exodus they were a single complete compilation to which his new book could refer in the manner previously described. This theory is fascinating and breathtaking in its implications, especially when in practical terms it means that

3 P. J. Wiseman, *Clues to Creation in Genesis*.

every generation of the people of God 'since the world began' (Luke 1:70) have had their God-given scriptures to guide them through the life that now is to that which is to come."[4]

These are the sections.

1. "These are the generations of the heavens and of the earth when they were created, in the day that the LORD God made the earth and the heavens" (Genesis 2:4, KJV);
2. "This is the book of the generations of Adam. In the day that God created man, in the likeness of God made he him" (Genesis 5:1, KJV);
3. "These are the generations of Noah: Noah was a just man and perfect in his generations, and Noah walked with God" (Genesis 6:9, KJV);
4. "Now these are the generations of the sons of Noah, Shem, Ham, and Japheth: and unto them were sons born after the flood" (Genesis 10:1, KJV);
5. "These are the generations of Shem: Shem was an hundred years old, and begat Arphaxad two years after the flood" (Genesis 11:10, KJV);
6. "Now these are the generations of Terah: Terah begat Abram, Nahor, and Haran; and Haran begat Lot" (Genesis 11:27, KJV);
7. "Now these are the generations of Ishmael, Abraham's son, whom Hagar the Egyptian, Sarah's handmaid, bare unto Abraham" (Genesis 25:12, KJV);
8. "And these are the generations of Isaac, Abraham's son: Abraham begat Isaac" (Genesis 25:19, KJV);
9. "Now these are the generations of Esau, who is Edom" (Genesis 36:1, KJV);
10. "These are the generations of Jacob. Joseph, being seventeen years old, was feeding the flock with his brethren; and the lad was with the sons of Bilhah, and with the sons of Zilpah, his father's wives: and Joseph brought unto his father their evil report" (Genesis 37:2).

---

4 Brother E. Whittaker, *For the Study and Defence of the Holy Scripture*, page 23.

SECTION TWO:
Life inside the Garden

3

The Garden planted eastward in Eden

THE events of Genesis 2 concerning Adam and the woman take place predominantly inside the Garden of Eden and specific details are given about it:

"The LORD God planted a garden eastward in Eden, and there he put the man whom he had formed. And out of the ground the LORD God made every tree grow that is pleasant to the sight and good for food. The tree of life was also in the midst of the garden, and the tree of the knowledge of good and evil. Now a river went out of Eden to water the garden, and from there it parted and became four riverheads. The name of the first is Pishon; it is the one which skirts the whole land of Havilah, where there is gold. And the gold of that land is good. Bdellium and the onyx stone are there. The name of the second river is Gihon; it is the one which goes around the whole land of Cush. The name of the third river is Hiddekel; it is the one which goes toward the east of Assyria. The fourth river is the Euphrates." (Genesis 2:8-14)

It is difficult to identify the location of the Garden in today's world. However, the traditional views of a garden somewhere in Mesopotamia present a puzzle. Why did God change the centre of His purpose with the earth from Mesopotamia to the land of Israel? From Abraham onwards, Israel, and Jerusalem in particular, are presented as the places chosen to be the centre of God's purpose, the place of His rest.

I suggest that the Garden was planted in what later became the land of Israel and was centred on the mountains of Jerusalem.

We know the following about the rivers that are mentioned. An unnamed river arose in the land of Eden, flowed through the Garden and then parted into four, named rivers:

- **Pison:** 'increase', only found here and nowhere else in scripture. It comes from a root *puwsh* meaning 'to jump, run to and fro'.
- **Gihon:** 'bursting forth', comes from a root *giyach* meaning 'to come forth'. Gihon is mentioned as the name of the spring outside the walls of Jerusalem. It was the nearest source of living waters to Jerusalem, which had none within the city walls (Zion means a 'parched place') and hence has spiritual significance. It was where Solomon was crowned and was the spring redirected by Hezekiah to the pool of Siloam (2 Chronicles 32).
- **Hiddekel:** 'rapid', the River Tigris (as the Septuagint translates it).[1]
- **Euphrates:** 'fruitfulness'.

It is clear that the courses of these four rivers, as originally formed by God, have been radically changed at some time in history, possibly at the time of the Flood, when rain fell for the first time.

The Garden was "eastwards". The word used in Genesis 2:8, *qedem*, has its origins in a root meaning 'to be in front of'. It is used of the position of the tabernacle.

> "Those who were to camp before the tabernacle on the east (*qedem*), before the tent of meeting toward the sunrise (*mizrach*), were Moses and Aaron and his sons, guarding the sanctuary itself, to protect the people of Israel. And any outsider who came near was to be put to death."
>
> (Numbers 3:38, ESV)

Two quite different words are used, suggesting that the tabernacle faced eastwards (*qedem*) and that Moses and Aaron camped there, on the east side (*mizrach*, literally 'the place of the sunrising'). If this is the case then Genesis 2 simply tells us that

1 Mentioned only here and in Daniel 10:4.

the Garden of Eden faced eastwards (just like the tabernacle) and we know that the entrance was on this east side (Genesis 3:24).

Use of 'tabernacle language'

The language used in describing the Garden, and the events in it, is used later to describe the building and work of the tabernacle and temple. Each had three parts: the created world is described as – the earth, the land of Eden and the Garden of Eden and the Tabernacle as – the Outer Court, the Holy Place and the Most Holy Place.

- God took a rib (*tsela*) from the side of Adam and used it to make a woman. The word *tsela*, "rib", is used forty-one times in the Old Testament. Two of these are in Genesis 2; of the remainder, thirty-six describe the building of the tabernacle, the temple or Ezekiel's temple.
- Adam was placed in the Garden "to tend (*abad*) and to keep (*shamar*) it". The same language is used of the priests and Levites concerning their duties in the tabernacle:

  > "Bring the tribe of Levi near, and present them before Aaron the priest, that they may serve him. And they shall attend (*shamar*) to his needs and the needs of the whole congregation before the tabernacle of meeting, to do (*abad*) the work of the tabernacle." (Numbers 3:6,7)
- The woman was brought by the angel to Adam and given to him to help him in this work. So the Levites belonged to God who gave them to Aaron to help him with the work (cf. Numbers 8:14,19).

David and Goliath

The fight between David and Goliath ended with a remarkable victory and the strange way in which David celebrated the death of the Man of Sin – by cutting off his head and taking it to Jerusalem.

Why did he do this? The city was not yet a Jewish city, not yet called Jerusalem – it was still a Canaanite city called Jebus. It was clearly prophetic: the place where Jesus was crucified was

Golgotha, the place of the skull, the place where Goliath's head was buried. But how did David know to take it there? The answer must be that he knew Genesis 3:15. He had just killed Goliath with a stone cast at his head ("he shall bruise your head"). He now cut off the head as another sign of this victory, standing on Goliath's neck or head as he did it. He took the skull to the place where the promise was first given – back to the entrance into the Garden of Eden.

Conclusion

It is suggested that the evidence presented above supports the view that the land of Eden was in the land of Israel with its centre, the Garden, at Jerusalem, the place of God's rest from the beginning. If this is the case then the following points are probable.

- Both the altar built by Adam outside the Garden and the first Cherubim are found where the temple was situated. It is the place where David took the skull of Goliath and where Jesus was crucified. This was the sacrifice necessary to open the way into the Most Holy Place as Hebrews tells us. This was the way back into the Garden of Eden using the imagery of Genesis 4.
- There is a hint in Genesis 4 that God's respect for Abel's sacrifice included a consuming fire from the sword of the Cherubim, just as at the threshing floor of Ornan (1 Chronicles 21:26).
- It is the place where Abraham took Isaac for sacrifice.
- The altar in Solomon's temple was placed on this rock.
- The fig leaf covering, inadequately provided by Adam in the Garden, represented the law. The fig tree was cursed by Jesus, in the same place where Adam made a covering (Matthew 21:18,19).

4

In the Garden of Eden

IN Genesis 2 the creation narrative is revisited but from a different perspective. Adam and the woman are now placed at the centre of God's work and all He does concerns His relationship with them.

It was the Elohim that created the heavens and the earth in Genesis 1 and this title of God is linked to His power as the Creator. However, in the fourth verse of chapter 2 we read these words:

> "This is the history of the heavens and the earth when they were created, in the day that the LORD God made the earth and the heavens."

The divine name is now added to His title and the definition of His work is changed – the earth is mentioned before the heavens. Everything that will be revealed about the Yahweh name through the Old Testament begins here.[1] The Lord is a covenant God who now starts His work with people, the part of

1 Because of Exodus 6:3: "I appeared to Abraham, to Isaac, and to Jacob, as God Almighty, but by my name LORD I was not known to them" it has been suggested that the Yahweh name was an editorial insertion into Genesis by Moses. Whilst we could consider this in narrative sections, in Genesis eleven people directly address God as Yahweh in dialogue, beginning with Eve and ending with Rachel. The Lord Himself uses His name once in direct speech. This must be part of divine inspiration. The internal evidence therefore is that the name was widely used from the beginning but its full meaning was not revealed until the time of Moses. This interpretation is supported by the Septuagint which in Exodus 3 says, "I did not manifest [reveal, make known] my name LORD". For further comment on the use of the divine name in Genesis see Brother G. Pearce, "Yahweh the Memorial Name of God", *The Christadelphian*, Volume 124, 1987.

His creation made to fulfil His purpose, and this purpose is with both the earth and its inhabitants.

We can imagine something of the wonder Adam felt when, as a living creature, he first opened his eyes and saw the Angel of the Lord that had breathed life into his nostrils. Perhaps the angel helped him to his feet "lest he dash his foot against a stone". He was formed[2] outside the Garden of Eden, for only after his creation did God make it. In it was everything that the man needed for his natural and spiritual life. Twice it is recorded that God "put" the man there and whilst verse 8 of Genesis 2 simply means that he was placed there, a different word is used in verse 15:

> "Then the LORD God took the man and put him in the garden of Eden to tend and keep it."

Here the idea behind "put" is of settling down in a place of rest; it is the word behind the name "Noah" and it is the word used when God spoke of the place of His rest. The earth was to be filled with people but the Garden of Eden was given to "the man", Adam, as his special inheritance and he was to tend and keep it: it was to become the place of his dominion.

The Apostle Paul taught, "first that which is natural then that which is spiritual" and this principle is met here for the first time in the command given to Adam. In the Garden, God made every tree that was good for food – note how generous He was. Yet they needed tending to produce fruit; Adam had work to do as the gardener.

But, he was also to keep the Garden: he was a watchman, there to preserve it and look after it. The word "keep" (*shamar*) is found throughout the Old Testament and carries a message about man's relationship with God, seen in the Lord's words about Abraham:

> "For I have known him, in order that he may command his children and his household after him, that they keep the way of the LORD, to do righteousness and justice, that the LORD

2 The same word is used of the potter with his clay in Isaiah 45:9.

> may bring to Abraham what He has spoken to him."
> (Genesis 18:19)

In patriarchal times therefore, "keep" was used to describe the role of the head of the family to lead his household in worship of the Lord and in the teaching of His commandments.

The same responsibilities were given to the High Priest under the Mosaic covenant:

> "So you shall appoint Aaron and his sons, and they shall attend (keep) to their priesthood." (Numbers 3:10)

Adam was given both natural and spiritual work to do. He was to provide food necessary for the lives of the woman and himself and was also the spiritual guardian of his family with a responsibility to feed them spiritually so that they too would keep God's way.

The divine law

> "And the LORD God commanded the man, saying, 'Of every tree of the garden you may freely eat; but of the tree of the knowledge of good and evil you shall not eat, for in the day that you eat of it you shall surely die.'" (Genesis 2:16,17)

This verse poses a difficulty which has led to many problems of interpretation over the years. If we take it literally, when Adam sinned he should have died the same day, yet he didn't and lived on for 930 years. "You shall surely die" is a Hebraism emphasising the absolute certainty of death; literally it is, "dying you shall die". It was used, for example, by David when he threatened Shimei with death if he left Jerusalem, "on the day you go out and cross the brook Kidron, know for certain you shall surely die" (1 Kings 2:37). However, Shimei left Jerusalem, went to Gath to find his runaway servants and brought them back to Jerusalem before Solomon had him executed. The emphasis of the phrase is on the certainty of death following a specific action at a defined time but no time-frame is attached to the judgement.

God's words to Adam have been explained as follows:

> "Furthermore, the sentence 'Thou shalt surely die', is proof that the phrase 'in the day' relates to a longer period than

the day of the natural eating. This was not a sentence to be consummated in a moment, as when a man is shot or guillotined. It required time; for the death threatened was the result, or finishing, of a certain process which is very clearly indicated in the original Hebrew. In this language the phrase is *muth temuth*, which literally rendered is, 'dying thou shalt die'. The sentence, then, as a whole reads thus – 'In the day of thy eating from it dying thou shalt die'.

"From this reading, it is evident, that Adam was to be subjected to a process, but not to an endless process; but to one which should commence with the transgression, and end with his extinction. The process is expressed by *muth*, dying; and the last stage of the process by *temuth*, thou shalt die ...

"Hence, the divine interpretation of the sentence, 'In the day thou eatest thereof thou shalt surely die', is, 'In the day of thy eating all the days of thy life of sorrow, returning thou shalt return unto the dust of the ground whence thou wast taken'. Thus, 'dying', in the meaning of the text, is to be the subject of a sorrowful, painful, and laborious existence, which wears a man out, and brings him down to the brink of the grave; and, by 'die', is signified the end, or last stage of corporeal existence, which is marked by a ceasing to breathe, and decomposition into dust.

"Thus, man's life from the womb to the grave is a dying existence."[3]

This reading is supported by a number of other writers in their analyses of the text.[4]

The timing of this first commandment that God gave to mankind is significant. The Lord had made the heavens and earth, created as ideal for human life on earth; in His sight all was good. Adam had been taken into a special place, a walled garden (the meaning of the word paradise) in which he had everything he needed for his life and was protected from the world outside.

---

3 Brother J. Thomas, *Elpis Israel*, Fifteenth Edition, pages 72-75.

4 For example: V. Hamilton, *The Book of Genesis*, volume 1, page 171; G. Vos, *Biblical Theology*, pages 36-40.

He had the company of the Angel of the Lord who had brought him into the Garden and who was still present there. Only then did God impose one restriction on him.

Yet, even in the giving of this law, the denial of the fruit of the tree of the knowledge of good and evil, God's generosity is seen. Of *every* tree he could freely eat (Hebrew, "eating he could eat"); he was denied the fruit of *just one* tree but if he ate, he would surely die (Hebrew, "dying he would die").

In keeping this law Adam would acknowledge the supremacy of the divine being who had made him. God's mighty power had been shown to him in the creation of the world round about him and now he was asked to do just one thing in homage to the Lord. Although the Apostle Paul was writing about life in his day, when he wrote the following words to the ecclesia at Rome, surely he had the events of early Genesis in mind:

> "For what can be known about God is plain to them, because God has shown it to them. For his invisible attributes, namely, his eternal power and divine nature, have been clearly perceived, ever since the creation of the world, in the things that have been made. So they are without excuse."
>
> (Romans 1:19,20, ESV)

As Adam looked around at the world into which he had been brought, he saw abundant evidence of the divine nature of the God who spoke to him: it was made very clear to him, there was no lack of knowledge, he could not say that he did not understand. The evidence showed him that God was a being far above him and was superior to everything that lived. His acceptance of the Lord as his omnipotent God should have been shown in his obedience to His word. Yet the Lord asked for more, for in the verses before those quoted above, the apostle wrote that "the just shall live by faith". Obedience to God's word would show a belief that such behaviour would be rewarded with eternal life; disobedience would show a lack of faith in His promises.

Four millennia later, it was written of the last Adam that he learned obedience by the things he suffered and that he suffered being tempted. When considering all the many ways the Lord Jesus Christ was tempted, resisting unto blood and striving against sin, the testing of the first Adam seems minimal. Yet God had made Adam with free will and a nature that could be tempted. The question was, would he be obedient or would he give in to the pleasures of sin for a season?

"In the day that you eat ..."

Adam did not die in the literal day when he sinned so what did God mean? Perhaps the easiest suggestion is to take the words "dying you shall die" and see a pointer to the change in Adam when he was cursed with mortality. Would he know what dying meant when he was in the "very good" state of his creation? He would know when he experienced the change in his being that mortality brought (this would later be driven home to him in the first recorded death, that of the animal killed as a sacrifice for his sin). It is possible that the clock started ticking at the moment his nature was changed and the 930 years of his life should be counted from that day.

However, there is another possibility. A thousand years is as a day with the Lord and even though the patriarchs before the Flood lived to great ages and Methuselah, the longest lived, reached 969 years, no one reached 1,000. In the years ahead, as all those listed in Genesis 5 lived their long lives and then died, they were reminded that longevity did not mean immortality and that inevitably death came upon all men for all had sinned.

"It is not good ..."

There was one final act of creation before God would rest from His work. All He had done was good in His sight but Adam on his own could not accomplish the purpose for which he was made. He needed a help suitable for this work. "It is not good" is, in the Hebrew, highly emphatic language: God was declaring the absolute necessity of the step He would now take.

For the first time God declared in advance what He intended to do:

> "I will make a helper suitable for him." (Genesis 2:18, NIV)

What would Adam have thought about these things? All of the animal creation had been brought before him but none was suitable for his needs. They were brute beasts that would perish; none had the capacity to listen to Adam's teaching about the Lord and to develop spiritually after His likeness.

So, out of his side woman was made and brought to him. At his creation, Adam had opened his eyes to see the Angel of the Lord; now he awoke to see the woman and there was an immediate affinity with her.

> "And Adam said: 'This is now bone of my bones and flesh of my flesh; she shall be called Woman, because she was taken out of Man.' Therefore a man shall leave his father and mother and be joined to his wife, and they shall become one flesh."
> (Genesis 2:23,24)

I will

We see in Genesis 2:18 the first time God said "I will". As we read through the scriptures, we see His purpose gradually unfold through men and women, descended from Adam and Eve, those whom He chose to accomplish His will. Then, almost at the end of the Bible we meet the very last time that God, through an angel, says "I will":

> "Come, I will show you the bride, the Lamb's wife."
> (Revelation 21:9)

The way in which these statements are linked is wonderful. He is the Lord God who knows the end from the beginning; with Him was the plan for salvation through His Son from the foundation of the world.

As His angel led the first bride to the first bridegroom, all that was necessary for the fulfilment of the divine purpose was complete. All was now "very good". Even though sin would destroy the relationship between the Lord and Adam, this purpose would not be thwarted and the time will come when the true bridegroom and his bride will be united in the kingdom of God.

It is only when coming to the words of Jesus in Matthew's Gospel that we discover that the second of these two verses was not an editorial comment but was spoken by the angel:

> "And he answered and said to them, 'Have you not read that he who made them at the beginning made them male and female, and said, For this reason a man shall leave his father and mother and be joined to his wife, and the two shall become one flesh'?" (Matthew 19:4,5)

From the beginning, marriage was a solemn, formal affair and was presided over by the Angel of the Lord who declared that the union was a three-part process:

1. In marriage a new bond is formed, the man's care of his wife (both physical and spiritual) is his primary responsibility.
2. In contrast to leaving his father and mother, he is to be joined to his wife. This is not a sexual term but describes a mental and spiritual unity that should exist in a marriage; "those whom God has joined together" are the words used by Jesus. The same word is used of Israel's relationship with the Lord.

   > "You shall fear the LORD your God; you shall serve him, and to him you shall hold fast, and take oaths in his name." (Deuteronomy 10:20)
3. Only after the above steps, and after the formality of the marriage, does physical union take place.

And God blessed them (2)

God's blessing was given initially to fish. From this we understood that the fundamental purpose of blessings (*berakah*) from God is the giving of abundant life by the Creator from whom all life comes. This life is given for a purpose: it is to fill part of His creation; the fish in the sea, His chosen people in the whole earth.

Now, having put in place all that was necessary for such a blessed purpose to be fulfilled in people, the Lord spoke again to Adam and the woman:

> "Then God blessed them, and God said to them, 'Be fruitful and multiply; fill the earth and subdue it; have dominion over

> the fish of the sea, over the birds of the air, and over every living thing that moves on the earth.'" (Genesis 1:28)

But, what sort of people were to fill the world? The Lord had created mankind with the capacity to understand His word and worship Him and Malachi commented on this aspect of God's blessing. He wrote of the spiritual decline of the returned Jews who had turned away from the Lord and so He would turn their blessing into a curse (Malachi 2:1). He condemned the way they had cast off the wives of their youth and married Gentile women who worshipped strange gods. Men who did this, he said, had nothing of God's spirit, they did not understand the purpose of the Lord in giving the marriage sacrament:

> "Did he not make them one, with a portion of the Spirit in their union? And what was the one God seeking? Godly offspring." (verse 15, ESV)

The union of man and woman was to be spiritual as well as physical. They were to share the word of the Lord in their lives with their children so that they became Godly children.

Here is the revealed purpose of God. The earth was to be filled with people, they are to be men and women who have developed spiritually after His likeness and become a Godly seed. Through such people who fulfil His purpose, the earth will be filled with the glory of the Lord.

However, Adam and the woman were not just told to fill the earth, they were to subdue it and have dominion over it and this carries the idea of ruling as kings. Adam, the bridegroom, was given the spiritual responsibility for his bride and family: to him were given the priestly responsibilities. Yet the dominion, the authority to reign as kings, was given to the bridegroom and his bride together. What a marvellous foreshadowing of Christ and his saints this is, for he will come with many crowns to be given to those who have been faithful and who will live and reign with him for a thousand years (Revelation 20:4).

But, there is another aspect to this blessing:

> "And the LORD spoke to Moses, saying: 'Speak to Aaron and his sons, saying, "This is the way you shall bless the children

of Israel. Say to them: 'The LORD bless you and keep you; the LORD make his face shine upon you, and be gracious to you; the LORD lift up his countenance upon you, and give you peace.'" So they shall put my name on the children of Israel, and I will bless them.'" (Numbers 6:22-27)

It has been suggested that these words were spoken by the High Priest to the congregation on the Day of Atonement as he came out of the Most Holy Place. Priestly blessings were highly structured events. They were connected with God's covenant and purpose with His people, given by men who ministered before Him and they were always given "in his name" (Deuteronomy 10:8).

What hope there is for us in these words to Moses. Sin will separate man from God, Adam would be cast out of the Garden from God's presence and the given blessing will never be fulfilled through him but it will not be lost. Each year the High Priest went into the Most Holy Place to intercede for himself and his people, each year he came out with the message that the way back into the presence of God had not been opened up by the sacrifices of that day. Yet the Lord sent out His blessing with His minister; He would continue to keep and protect His covenant people until the way back to Him was opened.

Necessary food

The sixth day was about to come to an end and the first Sabbath would follow. Yet the Lord had not quite finished His instructions to Adam and Eve. His final act of the day was to talk to them about what they should eat. He had already told Adam about the trees of the Garden and their fruit, why did they need further instruction?

"And God said, 'See, I have given you every herb (*eseb*, plant) that yields (*zara*) seed (*zera*) which is on the face of all the earth, and every tree whose fruit yields seed; to you it shall be for food. Also, to every beast of the earth, to every bird of the air, and to everything that creeps on the earth, in which

> there is life, I have given every green herb (*eseb*) for food'; and it was so." (Genesis 1:29,30)

Why is a difference made here between the food of mankind and all the fauna? Elsewhere we are told that the Lord has given the animal creation not just the greenery of the pastures but the fruit trees as well (Joel 2:22). Is it significant that the man and the woman were given plants and fruit trees that yielded seeds whereas these are not mentioned as food for animals? We can only assume that this held true in the Garden of Eden whilst not afterwards.

The word "seed" (*zera*) is used ten times in Genesis 1,[5] the same frequency as the phrase "and God said". There a spiritual lesson here, linking the giving of seed bearing food for mankind with the word of God, natural with spiritual food.[6]

Animals were beasts that would perish, without any capacity to understand the word of God. The man and the woman were given natural food which differentiated them from the animal creation and in this they were to see the great spiritual privilege God had given them – they alone could understand and spiritually digest His word.

Like Job, they were to "treasure the words of his mouth more than [their] necessary food".

---

5 In verb and noun forms.

6 Note the words of the Lord Jesus, "the seed is the word of God".

5 |

Created to give God glory

IT was now the end of the sixth day, dusk was approaching and the next day began in the evening.[1] It would bring the third blessing in these opening chapters of the Bible:

"And on the seventh day God ended his work which he had done, and he rested on the seventh day from all his work which he had done. Then God blessed the seventh day and sanctified it, because in it he rested from all his work which God had created and made." (Genesis 2:2,3)

Comments made about the Sabbath at Sinai should be added to these words. It was a day on which God rested and was refreshed and the literal meaning of the word, "refreshed", is 'to take breath'. We can think of it in the modern sense, after working hard we may say 'let's pause and take breath' meaning we will stop and consider with satisfaction what we have done.

This seventh day was the first full day together in the lives of Adam and the woman. It was not spent in dressing the Garden but in rest, in worship and praise of the One who had made them. There was "joy and gladness ... thanksgiving and the voice of melody" (Isaiah 51:3). On this day the principles of the Sabbath were laid down and in the keeping of them, the Lord was refreshed.

---

1 It has been suggested (Brother W. H. Carter, *Times and Seasons*) that the sun, moon and earth were made in conjunction and therefore the first New Moon would appear two to three nights later. This would mean that the seventh day of creation was the first day of a new month and also, logically, a civil New Year's day, the first day of the first year. Therefore it was the equivalent of the first of Tishri, the seventh month (Leviticus 23:23,24).

All of God's creative work was finished, all was very good, all that was needed for the outworking of His purpose on the earth was in place. Of course, God did not need physical rest, therefore there must be a spiritual meaning to these words. The Sabbath was made for man, not man for the Sabbath and it was in the worship of the Lord by the man and woman whom He had made that He would be refreshed. This is why the day was blessed – the activities of the day were to be an essential part of the commitment of the man and the woman to the Lord God. He had made them, therefore He was worthy of honour and praise as their Creator.

> "You are worthy, O Lord, to receive glory and honour and power; for you created all things, and by your will they exist and were created." (Revelation 4:11)

The KJV of Revelation 4:11 has, "for thy pleasure they are and were created" and Eden means 'pleasure' from a root word meaning 'delight'. It was created as a place to give pleasure and delight to all concerned with it – the husband and wife together in the relationship God had given them, both of them in worship of their Creator; the Lord in His delight with what He had made and their acknowledgement and honouring of Him as their Lord God.

But, it was not just on the Sabbath that God was to be honoured in this way, it set a pattern that should have been present every day of their lives. God wanted from them that which He desires from all His children – faith that the promised reward would come and in believing this daily, they would give God pleasure:

> "Now faith is the substance of things hoped for, the evidence of things not seen ... But without faith it is impossible to please him, for he who comes to God must believe that he is, and that he is a rewarder of those who diligently seek him."
> (Hebrews 11:1,6)

Many years later the Son of God, the last Adam, would commit himself in faith to his Father's will and a voice from heaven would acknowledge the delight that this gave the Lord God: "This is my beloved Son, in whom I am well pleased."

The principles of God are changeless and He desires to see in us the faith that He asked of His first son. Adam should have believed in hope that God would reward him with the gift of immortal life, after a period of probation in which he should diligently serve the Lord. If he lived in this way, God would view him with favour and his reward would be to eat from the tree of life and live forever. The Book of Proverbs mentions this tree four times,[2] as many times as does Genesis. Perhaps Solomon had Adam in mind when he wrote these words:

> "He who earnestly seeks good finds favour, but trouble will come to him who seeks evil ... The fruit of the righteous is a tree of life, and he who wins souls is wise."
>
> (Proverbs 11:27-30)

The Bible echoes are obvious: here are good and evil, here is access to the tree of life for the righteous. If Adam glorified God in bringing forth much spiritual fruit, then he would have access to the fruit of the tree of life.

Two different Hebrew words are both translated as "seek" in these verses. They can be paraphrased like this to see the differences between them: the one who enquired after evil would find it; the one who rose early to search diligently for good would gain favour from the Lord. Isaiah says of such a man:

> "The Lord GOD ... awakens me morning by morning, he awakens my ear to hear as the learned." (Isaiah 50:4)

By piecing together such scriptures there is a picture of Adam rising day by day to listen to God's word, diligently seeking it, and growing closer to Him. As he did this he was to "win the soul" of his wife that she might share the reward with him also.

But, he should also have warned her of the consequences of disobedience for "by the law is the knowledge of sin" and so, in the giving of this first commandment and the warning of the

2 Proverbs 3:18; 11:30; 13:12; 15:4.

punishment for disobedience, Adam was taught the meaning of sin by his God.

Yet the quest for wisdom, which was to be the downfall of the woman, was not wrong: the Lord wanted His offspring to "increase in wisdom and stature, and in favour with God". But, this was to occur through diligently seeking the Lord and in acceptance of the progressive revelation of Him through His word, for it is "the holy scriptures which are able to make you wise unto salvation through faith". Day by day, in their lives together in the Garden, under the tutelage of the Angel of the Lord, Adam and the woman should have grown spiritually, as the Lord desired.

Perhaps of all scripture, Psalm 19 is the most complete commentary on Genesis 1 and 2:

- Verses 1-6 speak of the knowledge of God that comes from a study of His creation.
- Verses 7-14 switch to use the Yahweh name seven times, (just as there is a similar switch in the description of God between the first two chapters of Genesis) and these verses tell us of the way in which the knowledge of the Lord comes from meditation on His word.
- Verse 11 tells us "in keeping of them there is great reward" and uses the same word found in Genesis 2:15, to "keep the garden". Within the Garden of Eden, God's laws were to reign supreme and it was Adam's responsibility to keep it so. If they disobeyed, "dying you shall die" would become a reality; if they obeyed, then they would be rewarded with immortality.

DIGRESSION: John 17

Late in the evening before his death, Jesus rose from supper and led his disciples eastward through Jerusalem towards the Garden of Gethsemane. Almost certainly, his route led them through the temple courts and somewhere he stopped and spoke the words recorded in John 15-17.

In them is the prayer he gave, lifting up his eyes to heaven and addressing his Father. His anxiety for his disciples is paramount in the words he uttered: they were his sheep and would shortly be scattered abroad as their shepherd was taken. They were his own and he had loved them and would love them to the very end (John 13:1). They had belonged to his Father and He had given them to His Son – five times Jesus mentions this.

These last phrases take us back to Genesis 2 and 3 but indirectly for they are a direct quotation from Numbers 8:

> "Thus you shall separate the Levites from among the children of Israel, and the Levites shall be mine ... For they are wholly given to me from among the children of Israel; I have taken them for myself instead of all who open the womb, the firstborn of all the children of Israel ... I have taken the Levites instead of all the firstborn of the children of Israel. And I have given the Levites as a gift to Aaron and his sons from among the children of Israel, to do the work for the children of Israel in the tabernacle of meeting ..." (Numbers 8:14-19)

The Levites belonged to God but He gave them to the High Priest for the work of the tabernacle and they were to "keep charge of the tabernacle of the Testimony".

After the Fall, Adam had said: "the woman you gave me ..." Just as the Levites were given to the High Priest and the disciples to the Lord Jesus Christ, the woman had been given to Adam to help in the keeping of the Garden and yet, in spite of all that God had done, that relationship failed.

The Lord Jesus was anxious that this should not recur amongst those whom he wished for his bride. He shared with his Father all that he had done for them and it is a list of all that Adam should have done and perhaps did not:

- And this is eternal life, that they may know you, the only true God, and Jesus Christ whom you have sent.
- I have glorified you on the earth. I have finished the work which you have given me to do.
- I have manifested your name to the men whom you have given me out of the world. They were yours, you gave them to me, and they have kept your word.

- Now they have known that all things which you have given me are from you.
- For I have given to them the words which you have given me; and they have received them, and have known surely that I came forth from you; and they have believed that you sent me.
- I pray for them. I do not pray for the world but for those whom you have given me, for they are yours.
- Holy Father, keep through your name those whom you have given me, that they may be one as we are.
- I kept them in your name. Those whom you gave me I have kept;
- I have given them your word;
- (I pray) that you should keep them from the evil one.
- Sanctify them by your truth. Your word is truth.
- I do not pray for these alone, but also for those who will believe in me through their word; that they all may be one,
- And the glory which you gave me I have given them, that they may be one just as we are one:
- And I have declared to them your name, and will declare it, that the love with which you loved me may be in them, and I in them.

It is sobering to read these words of our Lord and realise that they are the antithesis of Adam's behaviour. This is how he should have behaved; this is the spiritual leadership he should have given to his wife. This is the finest expression of a bridegroom's love for his bride so that they can, through God's grace, share eternity together and it was lacking in Adam.

In doing these things his spiritual work would have been complete and his love for his wife shown. We do not know how much of this was attempted, but Adam's failure is laid before us in Genesis 3.

6 | The Fall

AFTER meditating on the message of the first two chapters of Genesis, and the blessing that God gave Adam and the woman, it is a shock to turn to Genesis 3. It brings a feeling of melancholy and deep sadness to read of the rejection of the Lord and the consequences that followed.

As we see the woman tempted to eat forbidden food, how ironical it is that the last instructions from the Lord to Adam and the woman concerned their diet. There were spiritual lessons to be learned from this. They could feed on the word of God, animals could not. What then was the woman doing listening to an animal, the serpent, rather than God's word through her husband?

There is also another link with the previous chapters. Adam and the woman were both naked (*arowm*) but not ashamed – a comment on their innocence and ignorance of good and evil. The serpent was crafty (*aruwm*) and there is a deliberate word play here. The woman now listened to the serpent and sought wisdom from eating the forbidden fruit: through this act her innocence would be lost and she would realise her nakedness.

The serpent

What does Genesis tell us of this animal?

1. The Lord God created all things in the heavens and earth and everything is described as "very good". The serpent was part of this, a creeping thing, made on the sixth day along with the rest of the animals. Therefore, it was made

for God's pleasure (Revelation 4:11) and had a role to play in His purpose, as did all that He had made.

2. It is found in the Garden. It was, therefore, brought to Adam along with all the other animals. He gave it a name but it was not suitable to be the help he needed for God's purpose.
3. It could both speak and understand speech. It is not known whether it was made like this, whether this ability was unique or whether all the animals could communicate in this way at this time.
4. It was a beast of the field but the most cunning of them all. The Septuagint describes it in this way:

   > "Now the serpent was the most crafty [in Hebrew, *aruwm*] of all the brutes on the earth, which the Lord God made." (Genesis 3:1)

   This is not a comment on its morality. One writer describes it in this way: "*aruwm* is a neutral word, one that was originally without special moral connotations."[1] It was a beast with animal cunning and the Lord made animals with such senses for their survival. The word is translated most often as "prudent" and when the Lord Jesus Christ told his disciples, "Behold, I send you out as sheep in the midst of wolves, therefore be wise as serpents and harmless as doves", he was warning them to be careful about the dangers they would face, to be prudent, as they went out to preach the Gospel.
5. Its Hebrew name is *nachash*, always translated as "serpent". However this name is almost identical to a word that means: to observe, learn by experience, practise divination (it means 'to foresee').

Amongst Moses' final message of warning to the second generation in the wilderness were these words:

> "When you come into the land which the LORD your God is giving you, you shall not learn to follow the abominations of those nations. There shall not be found among you anyone

1 Hamilton, volume 1, page 188.

who makes his son or his daughter pass through the fire, or one who practises witchcraft, or a soothsayer, or one who interprets omens (*nachash*), or a sorcerer, or one who conjures spells, or a medium, or a spiritist, or one who calls up the dead. For all who do these things are an abomination to the LORD ..." (Deuteronomy 18:9-12)

Moses contrasted these things with the words of the true prophet whom God would send to His people. They would learn truth, not from a *nachash* but from one who gave them the word of the Lord, as Eve should have learnt from Adam.

The following table helps to identify exactly who said what and compares the words of the Lord with those of the woman and the serpent to see how they differ.

The Lord	**The serpent**	**The woman**
And the LORD God commanded the man, saying,	Has God indeed said?	And the woman said to the serpent,
Of every tree of the garden you may freely eat;	You shall not eat of every tree of the garden?	We may eat the fruit of the trees of the garden;
	Then the serpent said to the woman,	God has said
but of the tree of the knowledge of good and evil you shall not eat, for in the day that you eat of it you shall surely die.	You will not surely die. For God knows that in the day you eat of it your eyes will be opened, and you will be like God, knowing good and evil.	of the fruit of the tree which is in the midst of the garden, You shall not eat it, nor shall you touch it, lest you die.

The serpent, made before Adam, had heard the words of God, "Let us make man in our image and after our likeness" and from this experience foresaw a time when this would happen. Later, when present in the Garden, it heard the commandment to Adam, the prohibition of eating fruit from the tree of knowledge of good and evil. It then misrepresented these words to the woman, trying to suggest that God's purpose for her and her husband could be accomplished through eating the forbidden fruit. Note that it simply described the Almighty as God instead of the Lord God; it had no comprehension at all of the covenant nature of Yahweh with His people.

The words of the woman

When considering the woman the first question to be asked is, "Where was Adam?" It appears that she had wandered from her husband and she was alone with the serpent in the Garden. This was desperately dangerous for her and, as it began to speak, all her instincts should have been to flee and return to Adam, yet she did not. She appears to try to correct the snake but her words were also flawed; her teaching by Adam was either incomplete or she had not listened to him.

- She too did not use the Yahweh name but called the Almighty, God.
- We "may eat", she said, denying the generosity of the Lord who had said "you may freely eat".
- She told the serpent "God has said" but this was incorrect. God had *commanded* Adam and He had emphasised two more times that it was not a request but a commandment.
- She modified God's words adding, "we may not touch it" and weakening the punishment to "lest we die".

It is at this point that the teaching of James came into play in her life:

> "Let no one say when he is tempted, 'I am tempted by God'; for God cannot be tempted by evil, nor does He Himself tempt anyone. But each one is tempted when he is drawn away by his own desires and enticed. Then, when desire has conceived, it gives birth to sin; and sin, when it is full-grown, brings forth death." (James 1:13-15)

It is particularly poignant that the woman, the help given to Adam so that they might have Godly children, gave birth not to a son, but to sin. Whatever the serpent had said to her, the responsibility was hers. It was the process described in James' words that took over her mind, the temptation to take and eat was within her. All the trees of the Garden were pleasant to the eyes and good for food but only the tree of the knowledge of good and evil was lusted after by her because she thought it would make her wise. Here was the lust of the eyes, the lust of the flesh and the pride of life and it is the latter that is linked to her desire for wisdom. Whatever God had promised was not enough and she had a desire to order her life according to what she wanted and to achieve this by herself. She lived in an environment that was very good but this goodness was not enough. It is as if she believed that God had held something of greater goodness back from them and she was determined to get it. Here, in the very first sin, is the fundamental reason for its wrongness: it was a denial of the position of the Lord as her God, the One who had the right to rule her life. She showed a usurping of His authority and a worshipping and serving of herself rather than Him.

Psalm 19 emphasises for us the wrongness of the woman's actions, the contrast between the true and the false.

The tree was good for food	The judgements of the LORD are true and righteous altogether ... sweeter also than honey and the honeycomb
It was pleasant to the eyes	The commandment of the LORD is pure, enlightening the eyes
It was to be desired to make one wise	The testimony of the LORD is sure, making wise the simple

For the woman the word of God was not enough and her desires overruled His commandment; equality with God was something to be grasped at (Philippians 2:6, NIV), so she saw, she took, she ate and she was lost.

The man with her

From the way the woman described the forbidden tree as being in the middle of the Garden, it appears that the dialogue between her and the serpent was not held adjacent to it. She then went to the tree, pondered over it, touched it and nothing happened. Emboldened she took the fruit and ate it. And Adam was there; she had taken him with her and he acquiesced in this. "She also gave to her husband with her and he ate." What was he doing? Why was he there? Why did he not intervene and stop her? In these words the whole relationship between husband and wife, established by the Lord, was turned on its head. Adam was the gardener, his was the responsibility to feed his wife both naturally and spiritually. Now the woman had taken on both roles.

The Apostle Paul wrote that "Adam was not deceived, but the woman being deceived, fell into transgression" and this can be read in one of two ways:

1. Adam ate knowing exactly what he was doing. He did this to support his wife, listening to her words, putting her leadership before that of God.
2. The woman was first deceived and ate; nothing happened to her and so Adam took the fruit she offered and ate after her. He knew God's commandment, but decided to ignore it; he was not deceived but was wilfully disobedient and, through his action, sin entered the world (Romans 5:12).

I suggest the second of these options is the most likely. Indeed the Hebrew behind the phrase "with her" is used elsewhere in the Bible of those who associate themselves in actions with one who leads (see, for example, the command to Noah to lead his family into the ark, Genesis 6:18).

The woman took the lead, Adam had abrogated his responsibility for leadership, and so by one man sin had entered the world and death would now follow.

How sad is all of this, especially when we remember that there were two trees in the middle of the Garden. As they took and ate of the tree of the knowledge of good and evil, nearby was the tree of life. Its proximity highlighted the choice that God had laid before them. Be obedient to the Lord and He would reward them with fruit from this tree and they would indeed become immortal like the angels. Disobey God, seeking to take their own route to becoming like the angels, and death would follow.

The tragedy of the wrong choice they made is highlighted by dwelling once more on the role of the word of God in these chapters. In Genesis 1, the word of the Lord had made the heavens and the earth, "He spoke and it was done, He commanded and it stood fast" (Psalm 33:9). Every part of His creation obeyed His command. In Genesis 3 He commanded, man and woman disobeyed Him and rejected His word.

Their eyes were opened

What a let-down! The serpent had promised the woman that if they ate, they would become as gods, knowing good and evil, but there is no record of either of these things happening immediately after they ate the forbidden fruit. The serpent was a liar and nothing it said was true. The only thing that we read happened immediately was that their eyes were opened and they knew that they were naked:

> "Then the eyes of both of them were opened,[2] and they knew that they were naked; and they sewed fig leaves together and made themselves coverings." (Genesis 3:7)

There was a sense of shock and shame as they realised what they had done. They had not become immortal like the angels. They had been misled and they now knew that God's word was indeed the truth. There was embarrassment that they were naked and a fear of the Lord from whom they hid. How ironical that they did this amongst the trees – those that were good for food, given by the Lord's generosity. They would look and realise that what God had given had been more than enough for them. Why had they been so foolish to take the one forbidden fruit?

---

2 Four thousand years later, similar language was used by Luke as he described two people, probably a husband and wife, whose hearts burned within them as the Lord Jesus Christ opened the scriptures to them. It was at the breaking of bread that followed that we read, "their eyes were opened and they knew him". If only the first husband and wife had reacted to the word of God in a similar way.

The covering they made was a loincloth, a garment similar in design to that which Jesus wore when he took upon himself the garment of a slave and washed the disciples' feet. Adam and the woman were now in bondage to sin and death but the covering they provided could not overcome this. It was made from fig leaves and apart from the two trees at the centre of the Garden, this is the first named tree in scripture. The Lord Jesus tells us that the fig tree represented a fruitless nation of Israel and the old covenant. Salvation could not come through it, just as it could not come from the covering Adam and the woman provided. It is significant that the only time the word "sew" is used in the New Testament was by the Lord Jesus Christ when he spoke of these things:

> "No one sews a piece of unshrunk cloth on an old garment; or else the new piece pulls away from the old, and the tear is made worse." (Mark 2:21)

Salvation by grace could not be tacked on to the law: a new garment, a new covenant was needed.

The tragedy now unfolds before our eyes:

> "And they heard the sound of the LORD God walking in the garden in the cool of the day, and Adam and his wife hid themselves from the presence (from the face) of the LORD God among the trees of the garden." (Genesis 3:8)

It is possible that there had been regular, perhaps daily, communion between the Lord and His people. Adam was not put into the Garden and simply left there with the woman. They had been created for God's pleasure and if, in constant contact with Him, they increased in wisdom and understanding then daily they would be His delight, rejoicing always before Him.

Many years later at Sinai, like Adam, Israel were given God's laws and commanded to keep them. If they obeyed then the promise was, "I will walk among you and be your God, and you shall be my people". No doubt this was also the Lord's desire from the beginning but it could only take place if Adam had been in spiritual harmony with his Maker for "can two walk together unless they be agreed?" God asked through His prophet.

This wonderful opportunity was now lost and in fear of the Lord, led by Adam, they hid themselves. Even in this act their lack of faith was evident for –

> "He who covers his sins will not prosper, but whoever confesses and forsakes them will have mercy."
>
> (Proverbs 28:13)

The divine inquisition

We now reach the first question in the Bible and sadly it is Almighty God asking "Where are you?" of the man He would punish for his sin.[3] Of course the omnipotent Lord God knew where Adam was; the question was asked to draw him out of hiding and to demand an explanation from him. Notice that Adam did not mention his sin but only the immediate consequence, "I was afraid because I was naked". What a contrast there is with the picture at the end of Genesis 2. Then they were both naked and, in complete innocence, not ashamed. Now they were naked and full of guilt and shame for what they have done, the natural and spiritual consequences of their actions.

It was the woman's fault, said Adam describing her as "the woman you gave to be with me" as if God was implicated in this. Yet his very words show the problem. She was indeed given to be *with him*; he should have been the one providing spiritual leadership. Yet she gave the fruit to the man who was *with her*, and in this subtle difference, once again we see his neglect of his role.

It was the serpent's fault, said the woman, it deceived me and I ate.

Note the reactions of the man and his wife. Both acknowledged that they had disobeyed God, yet both held something back; neither of them would take full responsibility for their actions – someone else was to blame. In view of this, it is difficult to see their responses as true confessions. To confess carries the meaning of to 'praise'. In confessing our sins before

3 There is a contrast with the question at the beginning of the New Testament by men seeking their saviour, "Where is he that is born the king of the Jews?"

the Lord, and acknowledging that we alone are responsible, we praise Him by showing that His word is true and right. Ultimately, sin is a denial of His omnipotence. An example of this principle in action is seen in the Parable of the Prodigal Son who returned to his father, fully acknowledging what he had done, and was instantly accepted and forgiven by him. It is also present in the behaviour of David after his sin with Bathsheba: finally after months of hiding his sin from God, he was painfully honest about it and its consequences.

> "Have mercy upon me, O God, according to your lovingkindness; according to the multitude of your tender mercies, blot out my transgressions. Wash me thoroughly from my iniquity, and cleanse me from my sin. For I acknowledge my transgressions, and my sin is always before me. Against you, you only, have I sinned, and done this evil in your sight, that you may be found just when you speak, and blameless when you judge." (Psalm 51:1-4)

Neither Adam nor his wife were yet willing to take this step.

The serpent was not given an opportunity to speak to the Lord but His speech to it introduced the first promise of salvation in scripture. What irony there is in God's opening words. Because it was cunning above all the animals, it was now cursed above all the animals. As a sign to all men that it was cursed it would be a creeping thing in the dust for ever. Later the Law of Moses laid special emphasis on the unclean nature of creeping things. They were an abomination to the Lord; His people were to have nothing to do with them, let alone eat them and, in doing this, they would be holy as He is holy (Leviticus 11:41-44). Separation from that which the serpent came to represent is essential for God's people.

7 | The first promise

AS we come to the promise of salvation in Genesis 3:15 there is comfort in the fact that it was given before the punishment that followed. The natural flow of events would be to follow the questioning with the sentence for sin but God did not do this. First of all, He told of the divine grace that would permeate the rest of His word.

Adam and the woman had done nothing to deserve this; all they could expect was the carrying out of the sentence of death for sin. Yet God gave them a picture of hope for, in due time, one would come who would overcome sin so that His purpose would prevail in the earth. Many years later, one of His prophets would record a most intimate reflection by the Lord as He mused over what he had done for His people, Israel, and how they had behaved in turning from Him. According to the covenant He had made with them, He could cast them off forever yet He would not for, said He: "I am God, and not man, the Holy One in your midst, and I will not come to destroy" (Hosea 11:9, RSV).

Every week, sharing the bread and wine we reflect on this wonderful picture of our God. His righteousness demands that the wages of sin is death, yet His mercy transcends His judgements. It is significant that every verse in the Bible that speaks of God's grace and mercy together puts these two words in this order. His mercy, the forgiveness of our sins, can only come through His grace, that favour towards us that is never merited by anything we achieve for the victory over sin was won by one man only, the seed of the woman ("which seed is Christ" wrote Paul). “He shall bruise your head, and you shall bruise his heel.”

There is intense imagery in these words. Here is a picture of our Lord Jesus Christ confronting a serpent in the way; it seeks to bite him, yet it does not for “the sting of death is sin” and our Lord is holy, unharmed by sin, undefiled by it. Instead, he stamps on its head, crushing and destroying it totally but the force and energy needed to do this, and prevent its bite, bruises his heel. He is wounded but not fatally.

Here then is the victory won by the Lord Jesus. Sharing our nature he was tempted in every way as are we. In the words of the above picture the serpent was ever there seeking to bite him. Yet every day his victory was absolute; the serpent was vanquished daily as he fought against sin. Finally came the cry on the cross, “It is finished”, and that which had the power of death was destroyed. This last complete and absolute act of obedience to his Father demanded the laying down of his life. The bruising of his heel was complete and the grave claimed him for three days and nights until he arose with the words, “You have redeemed me O LORD God of truth” on his lips (Psalm 31:5).

The seed of the serpent

One of the attributes of snakes is that they cannot hear. They do not have ears but pick up vibrations to sense their prey. Hence, they become a type of a people who will not hear and so cannot understand the word of God. The Psalmist understood this when he drew this analogy between wicked people and snakes:

> “The wicked are estranged from the womb; they go astray as soon as they are born, speaking lies. Their poison is like the poison of a serpent; they are like the deaf cobra (adder) that stops its ear.” (Psalm 58:3,4)

Throughout the Old Testament, the wicked are described in this way. Isaiah spoke of those who are separated completely from God by their sins. They poison people by the lies they speak, they “hatch adders’ eggs” (they are the seed of the serpent) and they are completely consumed by their sinful ways, without God in their lives (Isaiah 59:3-5).

However, it is Matthew who develops this theme in some detail. He begins with the preaching of John Baptist:

> "But when he saw many of the Pharisees and Sadducees coming to his baptism, he said to them, 'Brood of vipers! Who warned you to flee from the wrath to come? Therefore bear fruits worthy of repentance, and do not think to say to yourselves, "We have Abraham as our father".'"
>
> (Matthew 3:7-9)

How this must have annoyed them. They believed they were accepted by God simply because they were descendants of Abraham. No, said John, spiritually you are descendants of the serpent.

Jesus then took this up:

> "Therefore I speak to them in parables, because seeing they do not see, and hearing they do not hear, nor do they understand. And in them the prophecy of Isaiah is fulfilled, which says: 'Hearing you will hear and shall not understand, and seeing you will see and not perceive; for the hearts of this people have grown dull. Their ears are hard of hearing, and their eyes they have closed, lest they should see with their eyes and hear with their ears, lest they should understand with their hearts and turn, so that I should heal them.'" (Matthew 13:13-15)

They were, said the Lord, the serpent's seed and so were spiritually deaf; sin had spawned a great number of men who would ultimately conspire together to put him to death and Matthew completed this picture when he wrote:

> "Then assembled together the chief priests, and the scribes, and the elders of the people, unto the palace of the high priest, who was called Caiaphas, and consulted that they might take Jesus by subtilty, and kill him." (Matthew 26:3,4, KJV)

How precisely Matthew picked up the theme of the serpent's seed. Here are all the leaders of Israel; they are a whole generation of serpent's offspring, and like the serpent in Eden they use craftiness to achieve their aim.

The sentence of death

"With the froward I will be froward" wrote the Psalmist and this principle is at work as the Lord turned from the serpent to address the woman and the man. As He spoke to them, the consequences of their sin were unfolded before them.

The woman had been given to Adam as the ideal help for him in the work God had set before him. Only she could join with him to provide the Godly seed the Lord desired to fill the earth; the commandment to them both was "to be fruitful and multiply". Now this was compromised by sin and the word "multiply" is used again:

> "To the woman He said: 'I will greatly multiply your sorrow and your conception; in pain you shall bring forth children; your desire shall be for your husband, and he shall rule over you.'" (Genesis 3:16)

She and Adam could have rejoiced in the children God would have given them, bringing them up to know the Lord. Now this would be replaced by the physical pain of childbearing, a reminder at each birth of what might have been. She would feel sorrow and this word is used twice to her and then also to Adam in verse 17. It can carry one of two meanings:

1. She would feel physical pain in the labour and hardship of childbirth and would sorrow that this agonising toil was a contrast with the easy work given in the Garden where they could freely eat of all trees but one.
2. It can also mean emotional sorrow and here is a picture of how the woman would feel when she gave birth to her sons, not in the sinless world God had provided her but in one subject to sin and death – a state brought about by her foolishness.

In this picture of childbirth is seen the new relationship with her husband. He was to lead the household, to provide spiritual leadership for both her and the children they would have together and she would deeply wish that this would be so.

Then to Adam He said, "Because you have heeded the voice of your wife". It was not just that Adam had listened to his wife;

he had obeyed her. God drove home to him his folly: five times the word "eat" is used in His words to the man. Because he ate of the forbidden tree, because God's generous provision of the trees of the Garden was not enough for him, the growing of food for him and his family would now need hard labour. For Adam, as for his wife, this would be a matter of both hard toil and emotional sadness. Each day as he rose to work in the fields the memory of the fruit of the Garden would haunt him. Furthermore, his diet was changed and now he would eat of the herb of the ground, like the animals in the Garden. Without the given promise, and a response to it in faith, he would be like the beasts that perish.

In the sweat of your face

Once again though, there was a ray of hope hidden in the punishment God foretold. Adam had rejected the generosity of a God who had freely given him food from all the trees of the Garden bar one. He was now told that he would feed his family by the sweat of his face. No doubt many people through scripture toiled and perspired, we all do! Yet the word "sweat" is only used three times in the Bible:

> "In the sweat of your face you shall eat bread till you return to the ground, for out of it you were taken; for dust you are, and to dust you shall return." (Genesis 3:19)
>
> "They shall have linen turbans on their heads and linen trousers on their bodies; they shall not clothe themselves with anything that causes sweat." (Ezekiel 44:18)
>
> "And being in agony, he prayed more earnestly. Then his sweat became like great drops of blood falling down to the ground." (Luke 22:44)

Through the use of this word, the work of the first Adam and the last Adam are compared. The first Adam would toil every day of his life to provide food for himself and his family – his work would never be completed. The last Adam said: "My food is to do the will of him who sent me, and to finish his work" (John 4:34). Here is the last Adam about his Father's business, doing the work of the One who sent him. What hard toil it was and, like the first Adam, it was for his family, for the children God gave him. He too was a man of sorrow and it took all of his effort, all of his strength to overcome self, to achieve that victory on the cross, so that he could cry, "It is finished".

A covering for sin

It was only at this point that Adam's wife was given a name: she would be called Eve for all life would come from her. In this we see a measure of faith on Adam's part. God's blessing had been replaced by a curse, the sentence of death had been passed yet He had promised salvation through an offspring of a woman and Adam acknowledged this in the name given. Life would come through the woman and the special seed she would have.

God's grace was shown in the clothing He now provided:

> "Also for Adam and his wife the LORD God made tunics of skin, and clothed them." (Genesis 3:21)

The hopelessness of the covering they had made for themselves was now apparent to Adam and Eve. God had stripped away their excuses and forced them to recognise what they had done. Yet He did not leave them in this state. He now provided a covering that they would take with them out of the Garden and yet again in this act the kindness and compassion of our Lord was at work.

- They had made loincloths, the garments of slaves that were deliberately humiliating in the way they provided the minimum body covering.
- In contrast, God provided coats, and the word carries the idea of total covering. They were long sleeved, full-length coats.
- They made a covering from fig leaves.
- In contrast, God showed that sacrifice and the shedding of blood was essential for a covering of sinful people. The word "coat" is used extensively of the garments of the priests under the law. It carries a spiritual significance.[1] It

1 It is also used of Joseph's coat of many colours.

is noteworthy that when the burnt offering was offered to the Lord, all was burned on the altar except the skin which was given to the priest (Leviticus 7:8). The provision of the skin to Adam and Eve therefore pointed forward to the need for a priest to intercede for mankind. Sin had destroyed the intimacy between man, woman and God in the Garden and another way was needed through which mankind could approach God. The provision of the coats made from an animal skin pointed forward to this.

These coats would be important to them as they left the Garden. Not only was their nakedness covered and their embarrassment relieved, there was the comfort of knowing that their expulsion was not the complete end of their relationship with God. He had promised that one would come who would conquer sin. Their coats would be a daily reminder, as they put them on, of a greater covering yet to come.

Behold the man

Twice in these early chapters we read of God communing with the angels about His intentions. Firstly in Genesis 1, telling us that man would be made in His image and capable of developing spiritually to be like Him.

Now He spoke to His angels again: "Behold the man." 'Look at him and see what he has done. He has become like one of us knowing good and evil.' This was what the serpent had promised Adam and Eve as a consequence of eating the forbidden fruit. Yet we have seen the serpent was a liar; in fact nothing the serpent promised materialised.

They had known "good" from the beginning for all was very good, an ideal world for them to flourish in. They had experienced sin through the breaking of the law, now they would know evil (Hebrew, *ra*, perhaps better understood as 'trouble') through the Lord's condemnation and their punishment for sin.

What would God do? He had told Adam that he would die, return to the dust and he had to be prevented from eating from the tree of life.

However, yet again, in the midst of this tragedy, hope shines through for when Pilate had examined Jesus he was brought out before the serpent's seed and the governor announced:

> "'Behold the Man!' Therefore, when the chief priests and officers saw him, they cried out, saying, Crucify him, crucify him! Pilate said to them, You take him and crucify him, for I find no fault in him." (John 19:5,6)

What a contrast there is between the first Adam and the last Adam. The first man put out his hand, took and ate, believing that equality with God was a thing to be grasped at. The second man, even though he was the Son of God, rejected this path and took on him the role of a servant to undo Adam's work and open up the way back to God. When beholding the first we realise that our only hope is to turn from him and behold the second.

And the Lord Jesus Christ spoke of the way to achieve this. A year before his death he told his disciples:

> "This is the bread which comes down from heaven, *that one may eat of it and not die*. I am the living bread which came down from heaven. *If anyone eats of this bread, he will live forever*; and the bread that I shall give is my flesh, which I shall give for the life of the world." (John 6:50,51)

And in the Upper Room:

> "And as they were eating, Jesus took bread, blessed and broke it, and gave it to the disciples and said, '*Take, eat*; this is my body.'" (Matthew 26:26)

The links with Genesis are unmistakeable. Here is the truth, fully exposing the lies of the serpent. Here is the way; nobody will be able to make the journey back to God except through him. Here is the life and only through eating this food, freely offered through the invitation, "take, eat", can life eternal be found.

The first Adam had taken and eaten, death followed and so all who are "in Adam" die. The last Adam suffered death that all who are in Christ may take and eat and be made alive at his coming.

8 |

Expulsion from the Garden

"Therefore the LORD God sent him out of the garden of Eden to till the ground from which he was taken. So he drove out the man; and he placed cherubim at the east of the garden of Eden, and a flaming sword which turned every way, to guard the way to the tree of life." (Genesis 3:23,24)

THE sentence passed on Adam was not just of death but of a mortality[1] which would remind him daily, and with increasing intensity as he grew old, of God's righteousness. He had been found unworthy of immortality and sentenced to return to the dust. Not only that, but all his offspring would in their turn inherit mortality from him. As a consequence of his actions, "through one man sin entered the world, and death through sin, and thus death spread to all men, because all sinned" (Romans 5:12). Every parent can enter into some of the heartbreak Adam would feel at the birth of his children as he realised afresh that his disobedience had condemned them also to death.

Adam was formed from the dust of the ground outside the Garden; he was given life and then taken inside it by God. While he was sinless and in the Garden he was not reminded that he had come out of the ground. How this changed when he sinned: he was expelled from the Garden to "the ground from which he was taken". Perhaps he went to the very spot where God had

1 Cf. *The Divine Law*, page 30.

taken earth, formed him and given him life for Isaiah says, "Look to the hole of the pit from which you were dug" suggesting that the very hole in the ground had been left there by God. If this was so, what a powerful daily exhortation it would be for Adam to see this pit and to know that this was where sin would take him – back to the dust of the earth.

But this was not all: his dominion over the earth was removed and he was cast out of the Garden – possibly all the events of Genesis 3 occurred in one day. He was "sent out", dismissed or sent away, with the idea of the angels forcing him out. But, he was also "driven out" and a quite different word is used, which is translated "divorced" in Leviticus 22:13. This was the immediate punishment Adam suffered. Of course he knew of the change to his body, he was mortal but he would live another 930 years – he would hardly feel old on the first day of his expulsion. Yet it was the first day in which he could not share intimate communion with the Lord around the word of God. This is the immediate consequence of sin: it separates us from God. To most of our world, whose senses are dulled by sin, this is no longer of interest. To Adam it must have been devastating: for the first day in his life, the One who made him and sustained him was not there by his side.

What a dreadful change it was that took place within him, in some ways worse than the sentence of death. He who had been one with his Maker was now estranged from Him.

He had been made capable of moral development. He had a unique ability amongst all creation to take in spiritual teaching. In a sense he was made with a neutral mind which could either be filled with the things of God or the things of man. He was free to choose the way of the Lord and "the wisdom which is from above" or to choose the way of man and "the wisdom which is earthly, sensual, devilish". One would lead to union with his God and immortality; the other would lead to banishment and death. It was the desire of his Creator that Adam would choose the former of his own free will. Yet it needed daily communion with the Lord and an ever-watchful concentration on the word of God and the second of these had been lacking.

Once Adam had sinned, expulsion from God's presence was inevitable. Once outside the Garden the influence of the divine mind on him was lessened and the influence of the things of this world took over.

The New Testament tells us that sin is the most addictive thing on earth. "Sin became exceeding sinful" wrote Paul and went on to write of the wretched man that he was because of this. It is described in the Letter to the Hebrews as "the pleasures of sin": we do those things that please us and our egos rather than those that please God and our natural minds take great satisfaction from them.

Once Adam had sinned, this gratification of his own desires took over. Like a drug addict he was hooked, his ego, his will began to rule his life.

One Christadelphian writer wrote of the deceitfulness of sin in this way:

> "Let us think a little further about sin. I wonder if we have given sufficient attention to it. Sin leaves its mark upon the individual. If anyone of us sin, it leaves its mark upon us. A man may be guilty of a little sharp practice in his business and he experiences a sense of shame. But the second time he does it, the shame is not so keen and after repeated acts he comes at last to rationalise, as modern psychologists describe it. He rationalises the process and justifies, what, at the beginning caused him a sense of shame. Thus it is that we sometimes behold the spectacle of a man who was once upright in his dealings, gradually falling away from the standard of right until at last we read of him being in the court, having been guilty of some serious embezzlement or some other crime. But it's been by a gradual decline in many cases, through the lowering of a standard; and instead of a consciousness of sin, very often that man only manifests self pity.
>
> "Why is it? It is because sin has a peculiarly blinding effect upon us. Sin distorts the view of righteousness. Sin deceives.

> The Apostle speaks of the deceitfulness of sin and in a very striking figure he can even say: 'that Satan himself is transformed into an angel of light'; that so deceiving is sin, that he can even parade as righteousness. But here is one of the dire consequences that comes with sin, that the more a man becomes familiar with it as performing and yielding himself to it, so he becomes less aware of the *real* character of sin. It is one of the most striking of the moral laws of God, that the more a man knows of sin the less he is aware of what it is."[2]

So Adam would come to recognise that within him dwelt no good thing, that he was helpless to overcome the power of sin and death that now dominated him. Who would rescue him from his body of death? It was totally beyond him to live a sinless life. His prayers to and worship of the Lord would take on a new and urgent meaning as he sought the coming of the promised seed. He needed the one who would be sent by God; the one who would destroy the power of the serpent, who would overcome this power of sin and open the way back into the presence of God. How he would come to dwell on the promise of Genesis 3 and to repeat it over and over to his sons. The promise of the Coming One would daily fill his mind until the day of his death, as it does to all of us who await the coming of the Lord Jesus Christ.

The Cherubim

Adam had been given dominion over the rest of creation and had been told to keep the Garden. This Garden was now no longer in his keeping and authority over it had been given to other beings, the Cherubim.[3] They were placed at the entrance on its east side. As Adam and Eve left they would travel from west to east. This began a pattern in Genesis: when people travelled towards the west from the east, they were spiritually moving towards God, when in the opposite direction, they were going away from Him.

2 Brother J. Carter, *Address on the Atonement*; Melbourne, 1958.

3 The meaning of the name is obscure and may come from a root meaning to praise and honour God.

For example, when Abraham came to the Promised Land from Ur he moved westwards; when he sent all his non-believing children away they were sent to the east.

The Cherubim, as the guardians of God's holiness, now had the duty to bar man from the Garden and access to the tree of life. Yet at the same time they were put there to preserve the way, symbolising that, at some future date it would be opened for mankind.

Through the rest of Genesis, the Lord would now reveal how this would occur.

SECTION THREE:
From Eden to Ur

9 |

The way of Cain

GENESIS 4 commences a new section of the book. It begins with the development of Adam's family and is given in three parts, each telling us of a line of descent.

"Now Adam knew Eve his wife, and she conceived and bore Cain ..." (Genesis 4:1)

"And Cain knew his wife, and she conceived and bore Enoch." (verse 17)

"And Adam knew his wife again, and she bore a son and named him Seth." (verse 25)

From this time forward two ways will develop: the way of Cain, which will take him and his descendants further away from God and the way of the Lord, taken by those seeking a way back to Him. This was the way taken by the descendants of Seth.

But, these chapters also show the way in which evil dominated good. The record starts with one man who totally rejected God. Then, like a deadly plague, sin spread across the world until, just before the flood, all flesh had corrupted God's way upon the earth. There are such strong links between the behaviour of Cain and that of his father, Adam, that it appears the Apostle Paul had these chapters open in front of him when he wrote, "by one man sin entered into the world, and death by sin; and so death passed upon all men, for that all have sinned". Look at these similarities between this father and his son:

- Each misused God's gift of the fruits of the earth.
- Each hid from God after his sin.

- The Lord interrogated both men after their disobedience, forcing them to face up to what they had done.
- Both men failed in the role of being a keeper.
- For both the consequences of their actions involved a curse from God.

"A man from the Lord"

"Now Adam knew Eve his wife, and she conceived and bore Cain, and said, 'I have acquired a man from the Lord'."

(Genesis 4:1)

These are unusual words. It appears that Eve thought Cain was the promised seed of the woman and that she was the chosen mother. She called her son Cain (*Qayin*), which sounds like the Hebrew word *qanah*, meaning acquired or possessed. It appears that Adam played no part in this naming for once again Eve took charge of events and it is all about her: "I have ...", rather than the purpose of God. No doubt she believed that she would be saved through giving birth to this son (1 Timothy 2:15). She had faith in the promise that God had given them, but her understanding was incomplete and once more it appears that Adam's instruction of her was lacking.

There is a contrast with the words of Mary when she was given the news of the birth of Jesus:

"Then Mary said, 'Behold the maidservant of the Lord! Let it be to me according to your word'. And the angel departed from her." (Luke 1:38)

There was nothing in this woman of the "I have" of Eve but a humility that all would occur according to the purpose of the Lord. Was Cain brought up heeding the words of his mother rather than those of his father, believing that he was the promised one? His actions are those of an arrogant man, unwilling to listen to the words of God.

We do not know who named Abel, all we are told is: "Then she (Eve) bore again, this time his brother Abel." The emphasis is on the fact that Abel and Cain are brothers, the first pair in Genesis and in the way each reacted to the knowledge of the Lord and chose a different path in life. In this a pattern was set that would be reproduced later, Ishmael and Isaac, Jacob and Esau.

"Abel" means 'breath', taken from a Hebrew word, *hebel*, meaning vanity or transitory. Through his name we are given a glimpse into the minds of Adam and Eve outside the Garden. There must have been sadness in the irrevocability of what they had done; try as they may they could not undo the consequences of their sin. Their daily toil seemed endless, achieving nothing for them.

> "'Vanity (*hebel*) of vanities', says the Preacher; 'Vanity of vanities, all is vanity'. What profit has a man from all his labour in which he toils under the sun?" (Ecclesiastes 1:2,3)

Hebel also takes us back to the way God gave life in the beginning, breathing into the nostrils of Adam, yet because of sin, Abel's life was to be but a vapour, passing quickly away. David understood these things and the meaning of the names when he wrote:

> "LORD, what is man (*Adam*), that you take knowledge of him? Or the son of man, that you are mindful of him? Man (*Adam*) is like a breath (*hebel*); his days are like a passing shadow."
> (Psalm 144:3,4)

Consider the relationship between Adam and his sons a little further. Throughout Genesis we read of sons who took different paths in life: Ishmael and Isaac, Esau and Jacob. In each pair, one chose the way of the Lord, the other the way of Cain. Yet each was brought up in a Godly household and given the same opportunities. The Lord knew that Abraham would command his children (all of them, not just Isaac) to keep the way of the Lord and it grieved Abraham intensely when Ishmael rejected the teaching of his father. This is seen in our families today: one child may grow up to accept the Lord, another to reject Him. Each is given the same opportunity, each makes a personal choice and I suggest that this principle was present in the lives of Cain and Abel. Adam would teach his sons of his failure and exhort them to learn from it. The words of Solomon to his son, Rehoboam, as he saw him growing up in a wayward fashion, are quite remarkable when read them with Adam and his sons in mind:

> "The wise shall inherit glory, but shame shall be the legacy of fools. Hear, my children, the instruction of a father, and give attention to know understanding; for I give you good doctrine: do not forsake my law ... Let your heart retain my words; keep my commands, and live." (Proverbs 3:35-4:4)

Cain and Abel would both learn from Adam about what happened in Eden and would understand the implications of what had been said. They would know of the need for animal sacrifice, yet only one of them responded to this teaching.

In the process of time

How often would Adam go back to the entrance to the Garden to see if it was open? Perhaps daily to start with, after all he wanted this more than anything else. However, Genesis 4 suggests that by the time Cain and Abel were grown men a specific pattern had emerged:

> "And in the process of time it came to pass that Cain brought an offering of the fruit of the ground to the LORD."
> (Genesis 4:3)

"In the process of time" literally means "at the end of days", hinting that once a year a journey was made back to the entrance of the Garden to come before the Lord as represented by the Cherubim. If this was indeed an annual event then it may have been on the anniversary of the expulsion and an offering[1] was made to see if the way back could be opened. This looked forward to the Law and the Day of Atonement, the one day a year when the High Priest could enter the Holy of Holies.

It was Cain's responsibility, as the eldest son, to lead this worship (the beginning of the principle of the role of the first born as priest). The offering should have been an animal and its skin retained for Cain following the pattern established at the

---

1 The word *minchah*, "offering", is never used of a sin offering but mainly of a meal offering and sometimes of the evening burnt sacrifice (e.g., 1 Kings 18:29,36) given as a present to God and burned on the altar.

end of Genesis 3. Yet, it was Abel who was obedient and who took on this role.

Cain was not wrong to bring the fruits of the ground; his error was that he did not accept the need for such offerings to be made after the sacrifice of an animal. Like his mother before him, his understanding was inadequate.

What a contrast there was between the offerings of Cain and Abel. Cain apparently made no effort to bring the best of his firstfruits but Abel also brought an offering[2] and his was "the firstborn of his flock and of their fat". Mankind had not yet been allowed by God to eat flesh and so Abel had chosen to work as a herdsman to breed animals solely for sacrifice.

What care went into this: he did it in obedience to the word of God and in faith. He brought to the Lord the very best he could, coming to seek out and honour Him, believing that He would indeed fulfil His promise. In contrast, Cain had chosen to follow the occupation of his father, given after the Fall.

> "By faith Abel offered to God a more excellent sacrifice than Cain, through which he obtained witness that he was righteous, God testifying of his gifts; and through it he being dead still speaks ... But without faith it is impossible to please Him, for he who comes to God must believe that He is, and that He is a rewarder of those who diligently seek Him."
>
> (Hebrews 11:4,6)

The Lord accepted Abel's sacrifice but not Cain's and perhaps it was the Cherubim, with the sword of fire that consumed his animal, so that the smoke rose as a sweet savour to the Lord.

This was the first acceptable offering made to God in scripture and there is a pattern in it for all who approach Him:

1. Abel sought out the way of the Lord and came to Him in worship;

---

2 Cassuto, volume 1, page 204: 'The Hebrew does not imply that Abel also brought fruits of the ground, simply that he also brought an offering and his was ..."

2. Having known His way, he did all according to the pattern given to him;
3. He willingly gave of his very best;
4. He did it in faith, believing in the promised reward of salvation;
5. Through his faith and works, God accounted him righteous.

Why are you angry?

Cain was inflamed with anger, consumed by it. Yet the Lord still sought to show him the right way and to encourage him in it. 'If you do what is right, you will have the excellency' (the position of priest to the family).

The alternative, that 'sin was crouching at the door' is difficult to understand but there are two New Testament passages that help us:

> "God will render to each one according to his deeds: eternal life to those who by patient continuance in doing good seek for glory, honour, and immortality; but to those who are self-seeking and do not obey the truth, but obey unrighteousness – indignation and wrath, tribulation and anguish, on every soul of man who does evil ..." (Romans 2:5-9)
>
> "Therefore humble yourselves under the mighty hand of God, that he may exalt you in due time, casting all your care upon him, for he cares for you. Be sober, be vigilant; because your adversary the devil walks about like a roaring lion, seeking whom he may devour. Resist him, steadfast in the faith ..."
> (1 Peter 5:6-9)

These passages give us an apt description of Abel and Cain. Abel searched for immortality through access to the tree of life and patiently waited for the coming of the Lord. Self-seeking Cain would not humble himself when chastised by God and so the power of sin was like a beast, crouched there waiting to devour him.

What he did next is the exact opposite of what he should have done. He needed faith; faith comes by hearing and hearing by the word of God, yet Cain would not listen. *He spoke* to Abel, he was in no mood to listen to anything his brother said. This is a picture of an angry, jealous man, out of control and murder followed. "My punishment is greater than I can bear", he said. Yes, he was full of remorse but, unlike the prodigal son, did not have sufficient faith to humble himself and ask for forgiveness.

He was the first man to be cursed by God and this sentence links him with the serpent, the very first being to be cursed. The word is an antonym of "bless" and its meaning is difficult to describe. Perhaps the best definition is "to be rendered powerless" or "unable to resist".[3]

Cain was a man who turned his back on God and who, consequently, was helpless in the face of temptation. Within just one generation man had become completely Godless. We see a physical and spiritual wanderer moving ever further away from God. He is first met outside the entrance to the Garden. He moved away from it to talk to his brother and then further still as he went away from the presence of God to the land of Nod. "Banished and homeless" describes him well.

Adam was put in a garden full of fertility; God made every tree that was good for food to grow out of the ground. When this generosity was denied by Eve, the ground was cursed: men would henceforth have to toil and sweat to produce a harvest. Now, following Cain's further rejection of God, the ground was cursed further: "When you till the ground, it shall no longer yield its strength to you. A fugitive and a vagabond you shall be on the earth."

Cain's reaction to this was one of breathtaking defiance. He was to be a vagabond (*nood*), a wanderer, and so he went to Nod (*nowd*), the land of vagabonds, and drew men together into a city, calling it Enoch (his name means dedicated[4]) after his son. Cain, as the son of Adam, had rejected his father's teaching and the way of the Lord and now he threw down a challenge. He would ensure that his descendants would not be wanderers

---

3 *Theological Wordbook of the Old Testament* (TWOT); #168.

4 Generally, in this book the meaning of names is taken from Jones, *Dictionary of Old Testament Proper Names*, published in 1856.

but would be knit together in cities, dedicated to resisting the curse that God had placed on him. No doubt his mindset was that described by the Psalmist:

> "... Likewise the fool and the senseless person perish, and leave their wealth to others. Their inner thought is that their houses will last forever, their dwelling places to all generations; they call their lands after their own names. Nevertheless man, though in honour, does not remain; he is like the beasts that perish. This is the way of those who are foolish, and of their posterity who approve their sayings." (Psalm 49:10-13)

The way of Cain is taken by those men and women who go away from God, those who lack faith in the promises and God's ability to provide salvation. The further they go, the more they are totally in the grip of sin, unable to resist it. So Cain became the first of the serpent's seed and the following chapter describes the growth of his natural and spiritual family.

10 | The sons of God and daughters of men

IN Genesis 4 and 5 two genealogies unfold (see opposite). "And Cain knew his wife, and she conceived and bore Enoch. And he built a city, and called the name of the city after the name of his son – Enoch." (Genesis 4:17)

This city is thought to be Eridu, which was probably the very first city in the world. Its remains have been excavated and can be seen just eight miles from Ur in Mesopotamia.

It was here that the Cain family settled and grew. It became a centre of polygamy, musical instruments used in worship, and metal working. Lamech specialised in sharpening brass and iron instruments and, as a man who threatened murder, it is possible he was a weapons manufacturer, as were the Philistines many years later. He worked in brass and iron, metals mentioned here for the first time. They become synonymous later in the Bible with weaponry used by those in opposition to the people of the Lord – Goliath against David, Greece and Rome in the image of Daniel 2.

Throughout the book of Genesis, cities were built by those who opposed God and His ways. In contrast, those who believed in the promises were tent dwellers "having no continuing city" but looking for that which God would provide. Their construction work was confined to altars, built for the worship of the Lord.

Cain's genealogy is cut short at Naamah and this name is seen only once more in the Bible. The Ammonitess mother of Rehoboam, whom Solomon unwisely married as a young man before he became king, was also called Naamah. It means

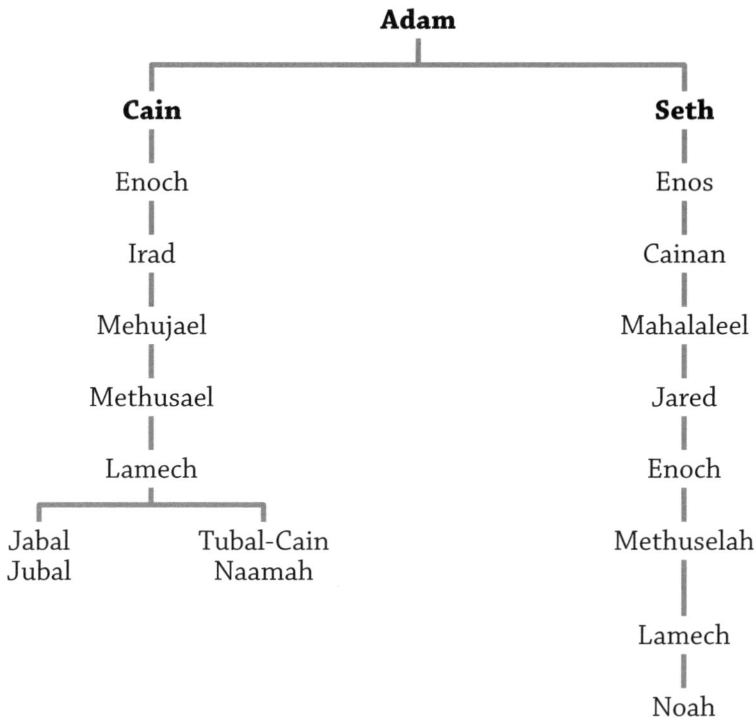

pleasantness or loveliness. She is the first woman identified as a daughter in scripture and is the first of the daughters of men whom we shall meet in Genesis 6.

The boast of Lamech

> "Then Lamech said to his wives: 'Adah and Zillah, hear my voice; wives of Lamech, listen to my speech! For I have killed a man for wounding me, even a young man for hurting me. If Cain shall be avenged sevenfold, then Lamech seventy-sevenfold.'" (Genesis 4:23,24)

Here is the climax of the way of Cain. In anger Cain had slain his brother and the same word is now used by his great-great-great-grandson who boasted that he could murder anyone who opposed him, presumably with the weapons he made. Had he already done this or was it a threat? It is perhaps best paraphrased as, 'I have already killed a man who wounded me and I will kill even a young man if necessary'.[1]

The sons of God

> "And Adam knew his wife again, and she bore a son and named him Seth, 'For God has appointed (*shiyth*) another seed for me instead of Abel, whom Cain killed'. And as for Seth, to him also a son was born; and he named him Enosh. Then men began to call on the name of the LORD."
>
> (Genesis 4:25,26)

Seth was born after the murder of Abel and we do not know what other children were born to Adam and Eve in the preceding period of many years. However, initially there must have been a great increase in population and it is possible that Cain either took his wife with him when he left or found her in Nod when he arrived.

These other children of Adam and Eve are not named and we assume that none of them were children who would call upon the name of the Lord. For this to occur the attitude of both parents was essential, working together to bring up their offspring.[2]

There must have been, therefore, a change in Eve when Seth was born. She did not presume to address the Lord by His name but she acknowledged that this birth was God's doing, using the words "He has appointed", in marked contrast to "I have got ..." when Cain was born. Here also is her acceptance that her chosen one, Cain, had been a murderer, totally unworthy of what she had expected of him. Only the Lord could choose the one through whose line salvation would come and now He had done this through the birth of Seth.

---

1 Cf. Hamilton, volume 1, page 241.

2 This was also the situation at the birth of Solomon. We know from 1 Chronicles that he was the fourth living, named son of David and Bathsheba. Yet the first three are not mentioned in 1 Samuel 12. It may that the trauma of their initial relationship was not healed until Solomon was conceived and that God waited for this.

This humility extends to the birth of Enos, whose name means 'mortal man'. Death had entered the world and this is emphasised in the genealogical record in Genesis 5. The descendants of Adam and Eve had inherited mortality from their parents and it was acknowledged in the name of their grandson.

In this situation what was the only thing that mortal men, believing in the promise, could do? *Then* began men to call upon the name of the Lord. An alternative to this in the KJV margin is "call themselves by the name of the LORD". These are the Lord's men, the sons of God, and with these words comes the beginning of a principle of worship that runs through the whole of scripture.

Both Abraham and Isaac called upon the name of the Lord.[3] Each of them did this at a time of stress in their lives when they looked for guidance and the Lord provided it. At these times, each built an altar and called upon the name of the Lord. There was a pattern in their actions for all who come to the Lord in faith:

- Each faced problems in life.
- Each prepared a place at which they could worship God through offering acceptable sacrifices.
- Each sought God's help through prayer – they "called".
- Each invoked the name of the Lord. Although this was not fully revealed to the patriarchs they knew it was linked to the promises made to them. Their worship and prayers were towards their God who would guide them in their lives and fulfil His word to them.

Many years later the prophet Joel picked up this theme of the Lord fulfilling His word to people who called upon His name: "I am the LORD your God", He said, and 'whoever calls on my name shall be delivered.' It was this message that was at the heart of Peter's preaching at Pentecost as he reached out with the Gospel message to the people of Jerusalem.

3 Genesis 12:8; 13:4; 21:33; 26:25.

Yet the most profound use of this phrase is seen in Psalm 116 where three times the Psalmist tells us of one calling upon the name of the Lord. These words were spoken in this Passover Hallel by our Lord on the night before his death. They were uttered in "prayers, supplications, strong crying and tears", in his three prayers in Gethsemane just hours later. It is the most moving picture of the Lord Jesus Christ: he faced such stress in his life that he sweat great drops of blood striving against sin. As the patriarchs built altars and offered sacrifices and called upon the Lord, so the one who was both altar and offering said, "I will offer to you the sacrifice of thanksgiving, and will call upon the name of the LORD".

Genesis 5 then tells of the ten generations that run from Adam to Noah. The chronology in Appendix 2 shows the interaction of such long lives. For example, Noah could have spoken to someone who knew Adam.

The detail given for each generation is similar in each case. From Seth onwards we read of a firstborn son, his age when his first son was born, the fact that he had further children, the length of his life and the fact that he died. Because of this last point, it has been described as a list of death and this is certainly true. Yet it is also a list of hope. This is the list of those who led the worship of the Lord – the responsibility given to the firstborn in each generation. Through it runs that thin blue line of faith in the promise, passed on from father to son. Progressing down the list, the attack of the world increases until faith depends on just one man, Noah.

Enoch walked with God

In the middle of this genealogy is the record of Enoch. He shared the same name as the son of Cain. He too was dedicated, but to the Lord not to the way of Cain. In him was the beginning of a spiritual fight-back against the forces of evil. When he was born, both Adam and Seth were still alive and perhaps it was from them that he learned the way of the Lord. He was contemporary with Lamech and saw the growth of violence that sadly would fill the earth in the years to come.

The description of him is different from those of his forbears and New Testament references about him add further details of his life.

> "Enoch lived sixty-five years, and begot Methuselah. After he begot Methuselah, Enoch walked with God three hundred years, and had sons and daughters. So all the days of Enoch were three hundred and sixty-five years. And Enoch walked with God; and he was not, for God took him."
>
> (Genesis 5:21-24)

> "By faith Enoch was translated that he should not see death; and was not found, because God had translated him: for before his translation he had this testimony, that he pleased God." (Hebrews 11:5, KJV)

> "And Enoch also, the seventh from Adam, prophesied of these, saying, Behold, the Lord cometh with ten thousands of his saints, to execute judgment upon all, and to convince all that are ungodly among them of all their ungodly deeds which they have ungodly committed, and of all their hard speeches which ungodly sinners have spoken against him."
>
> (Jude 14,15, KJV)

Enoch and Lamech were contemporary and Lamech was a murderer who threatened anyone who opposed him.

Here is a suggested sequence of events:

- The descendants of Cain increased and became ever more Godless and violent. Adam had died and the promise of salvation through a chosen seed seemed an empty one. They said, "Where is the promise of his coming? For since the fathers fell asleep, all things continue as they were from the beginning of creation".
- Enoch was a man of faith who pleased God, believing that He would indeed reward those who sought Him. He walked with God, a phrase that tells us of a mind and direction of life that was in harmony with his Maker.

- He was also a prophet, warning that the Lord would come. Even though thousands of faithful people had died, they would be raised and come with the Lord in judgement against the ungodly including those such as Lamech, who had spoken harshly against the saints.
- Because of Enoch's prophecy of judgement, Lamech sought him to kill him but could not find him. The Lord had taken him away to protect him – a righteous man had been taken away from the evil to come (Isaiah 57:1).

These words from Isaiah 57 are preceded by the statement that "the righteous perish". Enoch was removed from trouble but he died as do all mortal men and women. Indeed the writer to the Hebrews confirms this for he wrote of Enoch, and the other faithful of that chapter, that "these all died in faith, not having received the promises". Enoch's was a sudden death, his life taken away by the Lord in such a way that he did not perceive his decease. By the lifespans of his time, he was a young man – his age was the equivalent of about thirty to forty years today.

How much did God reveal to Enoch? He was a prophet and God revealed to him the judgement to come. He called his son Methuselah, 'when he is dead it shall be sent', and in this name we see both the certainty of God's judgements and also His longsuffering for Methuselah lived longer than any other person mentioned in the Bible.

Lamech, the father of Noah, died five years before his father. He also knew the events of Genesis 3 yet his reaction to the curse on the earth was to look to his son to provide comfort for him, a mindset which saw the toil of his hands because of the curse on the earth by God as nothing more than a nuisance to be alleviated by his son.

11

Noah and the Flood

MANY times in the Bible we read of a particular cycle of events. People worship the Lord, they turn away from Him; as a Father He chastises them to turn them back to Him and reformation occurs. Truth rarely succumbed to violent opposition. Lamech did not succeed; the Samaritans did not prevent Nehemiah from rebuilding the walls of Jerusalem; Saul's pogrom in Jerusalem did not quash the ecclesias. What did overcome was the insidious pressure of the world and, in particular in Old Testament times, sexual relations with those who did not share the faith of God's people. In the words of Paul, they were unequally yoked with unbelievers.

Here, at the beginning of Genesis 6, is the first occurrence of this:

> "Now it came to pass, when men began to multiply on the face of the earth, and daughters were born to them, that the sons of God saw the daughters of men, that they were beautiful; and they took wives for themselves of all whom they chose." (Genesis 6:1,2)

The phrase "sons of God" occurs eleven times in the Bible. Six of them are in the New Testament where they refer to disciples in a new relationship with the Father through His Son. Three times it is met in Job: once in chapter 38 it refers to the angels at creation, twice in chapters 1 and 2 its meaning is less certain – men or angels?

The remaining two occasions are found in Genesis 6, describing the marriages of the sons of God to the daughters of men and we know that these cannot involve angels for they neither marry nor are given in marriage (Matthew 22:30). The Lord uses this language to show the differences between the peoples descended from the two, named sons of Adam and Eve.

The genealogy of Cain's family ends with the first named daughter, Naamah. Lamech's violent opposition had failed to quench the faith of those, descended from Seth, the sons of God who called upon the name of the Lord. Yet his female descendants almost accomplished it by intermarriage with Seth's family. These women were chosen because of their physical attractiveness, not because they were suitable partners for the work of the Almighty. The principles of God-given marriage, laid down from the beginning, were cast aside.

So we see that the descendants of Seth, saw, chose, took – exactly the same process followed by Eve when she satisfied her own desires and ate the forbidden fruit.

Disaster then followed.

A corrupted earth

The events in chapters 6 to 9 are structured in a way that focuses our minds on the central point, the judgement of God on a wicked world.[1]

The generations of Noah (6:9,10);
  God sees that the earth is corrupt, *shacath* (6:11,12);
    God's instructions to Noah about the forthcoming destruction of the earth (6:13-22);
      The family enters the ark (7:1-9);
        The flood begins, the ark is closed (7:10-16);
          The waters rise (7:17-20);
            All life on land dies (7:21-24).
          The waters recede (8:1-5);
        The flood ends, the ark is opened (8:6-14);
      The family leaves the ark (8:15-22);

1 Taken from D. Dorsey, *The Literary Structure of the Old Testament*, page 52.

God's instructions to Noah about the renewal of the earth (9:1-7);

God promises never again to destroy, *shacath*, the earth (9:8-17);

The generations of Noah (9:18,19).

The early verses of Genesis 6 are a terrible comment on the impact of sin. A world made very good had so changed in about 1,500 years that, "the LORD was sorry that he had made man on the earth, and he was grieved in his heart". We get a sense of the sadness and loss the Lord felt at the state of the world. It grieved Him: not only was He displeased with that which had been made for His pleasure, He felt hurt and pain that mankind had so turned away from Him.[2]

In the beginning, He had blessed Adam and Eve after their marriage by Him – they were "to be fruitful and multiply and fill the earth" (with Godly descendants). God saw everything He had made and it was very good.

Now He looked again at His creation, for the next time after Genesis 1 that the phrase "God saw" is used is in verse 5 of chapter 6: "God saw that the wickedness of man was great in the earth". Men had indeed fulfilled part of His purpose: they had taken wives and multiplied but had not filled the earth with a Godly seed for, "the earth also was corrupt before God, and the earth was filled with violence".

What a contrast there is between these two statements: a world filled with violence rather than with Godly people. This is a picture of a world in real, spiritual danger:

> "And the LORD said, 'My Spirit shall not strive with man forever, for he is indeed flesh; yet his days shall be one hundred and twenty years'." (Genesis 6:3)

How did God "strive" with the world? Once again, it is the New Testament that interprets the old, this time through the words of the Apostle Peter:

---

2 The Hebrew word translated "grieved" carries all these meanings.

> "For Christ also suffered once for sins, the just for the unjust, that he might bring us to God, being put to death in the flesh but made alive by the Spirit, by whom also he went and preached to the spirits in prison, who formerly were disobedient, when once the divine longsuffering waited in the days of Noah, while the ark was being prepared, in which a few, that is, eight souls, were saved through water."
>
> (1 Peter 3:18-20)

Noah was a preacher of righteousness, a prophet like Enoch foretelling that God would indeed bring judgement on the ungodly. As such, he had the spirit of Christ (1 Peter 1:11) within him urging men and women in bondage to sin and death to repent and receive the salvation of their souls through the special seed whom God had promised. And they mocked saying, "Where is the promise of his coming?" They were the serpent's seed and their ears were closed to the message of the prophets.

When we consider such a world, we marvel at the longsuffering of the Lord.

Enoch had given the world a sign about the coming judgement and named his son Methuselah – 'When he is dead it shall be sent'. The sign of the coming judgement would be the death of this son and it did not happen for 969 years, the longest lifespan in the history of the world. Here is the patience of God, a prolonged period in which He strived with mankind through His prophets even though what He saw grieved Him in His heart.

This is the picture of that world:

- They were mighty men, men of renown (*shem*, name), strong, capable men who had "made a name" for themselves and did not need the Lord. Some versions have "heroes" instead of "mighty men" which gives another perspective on what they did. They were honoured for their stand against the Gospel, society leaders who had achieved fame in so doing.
- Every thought and intent of their hearts was evil every day. There was no room left for God in their lives.

- They had corrupted the earth and corrupted His way. The word is more often translated "destroyed" and this brings home the enormity of what they had done. They had destroyed all that God had made. The beauty of the earth and of His relationship with man and woman had gone.
- They had done this "before God". There was still a parody of worship, corrupt and apostate though it was.
- The earth was filled with violence.
- They were flesh and for the first time the word is used to describe not just the physical nature of the human race but its spiritually Godless state. God's pleading through the prophets would not work because the people were flesh (Genesis 6:3). All flesh had corrupted God's way (verse 12).

How fitting was God's punishment:

> "So God looked upon the earth, and indeed it was corrupt (Hebrew, *shachath*); for all flesh had corrupted (*shachath*) their way on the earth. And God said to Noah, 'The end of all flesh has come before me, for the earth is filled with violence through them; and behold, I will destroy (*shachath*) them with the earth'." (verses 12,13)

Like a shining beacon in a dark world, one man stood firm. In contrast to the list above, we read of four attributes of Noah:

1. He found grace in the eyes of the Lord. This is the first time grace is mentioned in scripture. It is the undeserved favour that God gives; it has to be searched for and prayed for, before it is found. And the Lord saw him for:

   > "The eyes of the LORD are on the righteous, and his ears are open to their cry." (Psalm 34:15)

2. He was a righteous man – achieving this through God's grace and faith in His promises. This is the first mention of the Hebrew word *tsaddiyq* – just, righteous, in the Bible. Noah became an "heir of the righteousness which is by faith" and because of this was invited into the ark by the Lord (Genesis 7:1).
3. He was perfect in his generation. This is the first of two uses of this Hebrew word, *tamiym*, in Genesis. We meet

the second use in chapter 17 where the Lord commanded Abraham to walk before Him and be perfect. The word caries the idea of completeness and is used later in the Law to describe animals fit for offering to the Lord. They had to be perfect, without blemish. Of course Noah was not sinless, but his trust that the grace of God could make him righteous brought such complete reconciliation with the Lord that he is described in this way.

4. He walked with God, as did Enoch. Noah could have talked with Enoch's son, Methuselah, who would have told him of his father and his prophecies.

There is a progression in these four points which applies to disciples in every age. It is God's grace that we first seek, conscious of our need of salvation. Through grace we become righteous with an unassailable faith in the promises. Being fully persuaded of them, every day we try to walk in the way of the Lord.

Preparing for the Flood

Throughout these chapters in Genesis, Noah's three sons are listed as Shem, Ham and Japheth. Yet this was not their birth order. Noah was warned by God of the flood to come when he was 480 years old. He immediately began to build the ark to save his family but no sons were born to him for another twenty years. The order of events was as follows:

Noah's age	Event
480	God speaks about the judgement of the earth in 120 years time.
500	Japheth born as eldest son (5:32; 10:21).
502	Shem born (11:10).
?	Ham, the youngest son (9:24) born fairly soon after Shem. All the sons were married by the time of the Flood.
600	The Flood.

We do not know if the construction of the ark took all 120 years; indeed there is a hint at the end of Genesis 6 that the ark was finished, the animals assembled together with their food but no call came immediately. It would be at that time that the scorn of his neighbours was greatest.

Yet God had prepared Noah for the day with the promise of an unbreakable covenant if his faith stood firm:

> "I will establish my covenant with you; and you shall go into the ark – you, your sons, your wife, and your sons' wives with you." (Genesis 6:18)

Four times Noah did "according to all that God commanded him", so that when the day came and the Lord said "Come" he was ready and they all went in "the very same day".

The command was 'Come inside': the Lord was there waiting for them and once they were safely inside the ark the door was shut – only then did the Flood commence.

This pattern of Noah's faith and works, of his readiness for the Day of the Lord whenever it would come, was used by the Lord Jesus Christ. He used just two examples of Old Testament life, those of Noah and Lot, in his exhortation about his return. Luke wrote of the day Noah entered the ark, the day Lot left Sodom and of the day when the call will come to go and be with our Lord (Luke 17:22-37). It is clear from his words that this one call will come in one literal, twenty-four hour day and afterwards the door will be shut for those who are not prepared for their Lord's return. There will be "wailing and gnashing of teeth", a pleading to be accepted as there must have been when the rains began. People would have hammered on the door of the ark, but to no avail for the Lord had shut it and it could not be opened by any man.

A record of twelve parts

The record of the Flood from Genesis 6:9 to 9:17 is set out in twelve paragraphs leading us through events stage by stage, the purpose of God being unfolded step by step. The twelve fall naturally into two groups of six as follows.

Paragraph 1: the state of the world, the reason why God would judge it leading on to ... **paragraph 6:** the covering of the earth by the waters.

Paragraph 7: the end of the Flood as the ark rested on Ararat leading on to ... **paragraph 12:** the rainbow sign of the covenant that God would never again destroy the world by water.

One writer gives the following poetic picture of these events:

> "The series of paragraphs is composed of two groups, each comprising six paragraphs: the numerical symmetry should be noted. The first group depicts for us, step by step, the acts of divine justice that bring destruction upon the earth, which had become filled with violence; and scenes that pass before us grow increasingly gloomier until in the darkness of death portrayed in the sixth paragraph there remains only one tiny, faint point of light, to wit, the ark, which floats on the fearful waters that have covered everything, and which guards between its walls the hope of future life.
>
> "The second group shows us consecutively the various stages of divine compassion that renews life upon the earth. The light that waned until it became a minute point in the midst of the dark world, begins to grow bigger and brighter till it illumines again the entire scene before us, and shows us a calm and peaceful world, crowned with the rainbow that irradiates the cloud with its colours – a sign and pledge of life and peace for the coming generations."[3]

It is difficult to be certain about how long each stage of the Flood lasted but we are given two absolute dates of the beginning and end:

> "In the six hundredth year of Noah's life, in the second month, the seventeenth day of the month, on that day all the fountains of the great deep were broken up, and the windows of heaven were opened." (Genesis 7:11)

3 U. Cassuto, volume 2, pages 30,31.

> "And it came to pass in the six hundred and first year ... in the second month, on the twenty-seventh day of the month, the earth was dried." (8:13,14)

The Flood therefore lasted one year and eleven days. If these were lunar months (just over twenty-nine days long), then the Flood lasted exactly 365 days by our calendar.

DIGRESSION: Psalm 29

Psalm 29 was written by David, yet it speaks in detail of the Flood – it was either revealed directly to David or passed down to him through the ages.

The Hebrew word for flood, *mabbuwl*, is found only in the Genesis record and Psalm 29:10. Seven times in Genesis God spoke to Noah. Seven times the Psalmist tells of "the voice of the LORD" as David described the waters flooding over the earth like a tsunami, trees crashed over, snapped off by the deluge. Animals aborted their young, earthquakes shook the world, fires raged, perhaps from volcanic action. Not only did the heavens open, the great underground springs of the earth burst out onto the earth above (Genesis 7:11). This was no gentle rising of waters but a cataclysmic event that destroyed all living beings.

Yet, in the ark the mighty ones (*ben El*, 'sons of God') spoke of His strength and glory, honouring His name, worshipping Him in the beauty of holiness. It was the God of glory who spoke and this phrase is only used once more in the Bible, in Acts 7 where Stephen spoke of God's revelation of Himself to Abraham.

The Psalm ends with the promise of a blessing that God would give to Noah after the Flood:

> "Give unto the LORD, O you mighty ones, give unto the LORD glory and strength. Give unto the LORD the glory due to his name; worship the LORD in the beauty of holiness. The voice of the LORD is over the waters; the God of glory thunders; the LORD is over many waters. The voice of the LORD is powerful; the voice of the LORD is full of majesty. The voice of the LORD breaks the cedars, yes, the LORD splinters the cedars of Lebanon. He makes them also skip like a calf, Lebanon and

Sirion like a young wild ox. The voice of the LORD divides the flames of fire. The voice of the LORD shakes the wilderness; the LORD shakes the Wilderness of Kadesh. The voice of the LORD makes the deer give birth, and strips the forests bare; and in his temple everyone says, 'Glory!' The LORD sat enthroned at the Flood, and the LORD sits as King forever. The LORD will give strength to his people; the LORD will bless his people with peace."

12

A new heavens and a new earth

THE first heavens and earth had been destroyed by water, and were now replaced by a new heavens and earth (2 Peter 3:5).

Genesis 8 and 9 describe this new beginning and the language used has many similarities with that of the opening chapters of the book:

- As the dry land appeared out of the waters at creation, so now the waters were dried up from off the earth.
- God commanded that the empty earth should be filled first with animals, as in the beginning.
- Noah and his family were sent out of the ark, and the presence of God, into the earth; as Adam and Eve were sent out of the Garden.
- Abel offered a burnt offering before the entrance to the Garden; Noah offered a burnt offering (before the ark?).

The parallels between the events of Adam's life and that of Noah are clear, emphasising that the same spiritual cycle of events occurred to both men.

Adam	**Noah**
Given dominion over the earth (1:28)	The fear and dread of every creature was upon Noah (9:2)
Blessed by God, "be fruitful and multiply" (1:28)	Blessed by God, "be fruitful and multiply" (9:1)

Adam	Noah
Put in a garden to tend and keep it (2:15)	Became a husbandman (9:20)
Sin brought awareness of nakedness (3:7)	Was aware of nakedness brought about by his behaviour (9:24)
Sin brought a curse on his son (4:11)	His behaviour brought a curse on a grandson (9:25)
Three named sons, through one comes Messiah	Three named sons, through one comes Messiah
Through Seth men began to call upon the name of the Lord.	The Lord was the God of Shem ("name") and his descendants.

The new beginning

> "So God blessed Noah and his sons, and said to them: 'Be fruitful and multiply, and fill the earth.'" (Genesis 9:1)

There was, however, one important difference between the blessing given to Adam and Eve and that now given to Noah. This one was shared, not with his wife but with his sons. Noah would live for many more years after the Flood but there is no record of him having any more children. The fulfilment of the blessing depended on his sons, Japheth, Shem and Ham. They had seen the wickedness of the world destroyed by water; they had also seen God's glory in the ark and experienced the presence of the Angel of the Lord. God's judgements and His salvation would have had a powerful impact on them and prepared them for their new responsibilities. They had been men of faith who had instructed their wives in the spiritual truths of the promises so that, when the command was given, "Come in to the ark, you and all your household", all had instantly obeyed and had gone to be with the Angel.

Like Abraham after him, Noah had instructed his household to keep the way of the Lord. They had listened and now the responsibility to fill the earth with a Godly seed passed to them.

The events of chapters 8 and 9 after the Flood are woven together, one part leading to the next until we come to Noah's blessing of his sons. It is useful to list the main points to see the links between them:

- God commanded Noah to leave the ark taking his family and the animals with him.
- He obeyed and then immediately, in response to God's commandment, he built an altar and offered a burnt offering.
- This was accepted by God, it was a sweet savour to Him.
- In response to Noah's actions God lifted part of the Edenic curse. The ground would never again be cursed, the seasons, seedtime and harvest would continue and He would never destroy every living thing again. He would do this even though the basic problem was still present in mankind; the intentions of men and women to do evil were deeply embedded in their hearts from childhood.
- Because of Noah's obedience, God blessed him with the same words used by the Lord when blessing Adam and Eve, "be fruitful and multiply and fill the earth".
- God's promise that He would never again destroy mankind by a Flood was then supported by a new covenant that He made with Noah and his sons.
- Yet, in spite of the commitment shown by both the Lord and Noah plus his sons, his children begin to drift away from God. Noah became drunk; the handling of the situation by Ham showed a lack of honour for his father.
- Not only did Noah not pass on the patriarchal blessing to his sons, he cursed Canaan. The evil imagination of the hearts of men began to direct their lives.

We now have a complete picture of Noah and his desire for himself and his sons. "Moved with godly fear" he had prepared an ark for the saving of himself and his family. That same reverential awe of the Lord was still with him as he began a new life with his family. He had received a renewal of God's blessing – to fill the earth with a Godly seed, and his willing dedication of his family to God through the burnt offering was the beginning of this. He would instruct his sons in the way of the Lord that it might be well with them and their lives prolonged on the earth. Yet this would not be sufficient.

Altar building

> "Then Noah built an altar to the LORD, and took of every clean animal and of every clean bird, and offered burnt offerings on the altar. And the LORD smelled a soothing aroma. Then the LORD said in his heart, 'I will never again curse the ground for man's sake, although the imagination of man's heart is evil from his youth; nor will I again destroy every living thing as I have done. While the earth remains, seedtime and harvest, cold and heat, winter and summer, and day and night shall not cease'." (Genesis 8:20-22)

This is the first mention of an altar in the Bible. It is also the first time that we read that a burnt offering produced a sweet savour that rose and was accepted by God, representing the faith that delighted Him and there is a play on words in these verses. The name Noah means 'rest', *nuwach*. The same word is the root of the word "soothing", Noah's offering to God rose as a soothing aroma, a savour of rest to Him.

In this, there is an echo back to the seventh day of creation, the day of rest for the Lord when He received worship and honour from the first man and woman. Was Noah's offering a Sabbath day one?

Later, Moses was instructed that the burnt offering had to be cut into four component parts before being placed on the altar and the words of Jesus tell us the full significance of this.

> "Jesus answered him, 'The first of all the commandments is: Hear, O Israel, the Lord our God, the Lord is one. And you shall love the Lord your God with all your heart, with all your soul, with all your mind, and with all your strength'."
>
> (Mark 12:29,30)

Heart, soul, mind, strength: this was a total dedication of one's life represented by the four parts of the burnt offering. It was this commitment that Noah gave as he came out of the ark and his sons began to refill the earth. It was a similar commitment that the Lord asked of Israel as they prepared to leave the wilderness and enter the land He had promised them.

> "Now this is the commandment, and these are the statutes and judgments which the LORD your God has commanded to teach you, that you may observe them in the land which you are crossing over to possess, that you may fear the LORD your God, to keep all his statutes and his commandments which I command you, you and your son and your grandson, all the days of your life, and that your days may be prolonged. Therefore hear, O Israel, and be careful to observe it, that it may be well with you, and that you may multiply greatly as the LORD God of your fathers has promised you."
>
> (Deuteronomy 6:1-3)

This example of recommitment to the Lord, shown in a burnt offering, is repeated six more times in Genesis for seven times in total men built an altar.

Chapter	**Builder**	**Journey**	**Command**
8:20	Noah	Leaves the ark	"Be fruitful and multiply and fill the earth."
12:7	Abraham	Moves to Shechem	"Unto your seed will I give this land."
12:8	Abraham	Moves to Bethel	
13:18	Abraham	Moves back to Bethel	"I will give the land to you and to your seed forever."
22:9	Abraham	Journeys to Moriah	"Your seed will possess the gate of his enemies."
26:25	Isaac	Moves to Rehoboth	"I am with you and will multiply your seed."

Chapter	Builder	Journey	Command
35:7	Jacob	Returns to Bethel	"Be fruitful and multiply, I give the land to you and your seed."

There is a pattern connecting each of these events. Faithful people journeyed; when they settled at a new destination they built an altar, and made a burnt offering as a sign to the Lord that they were fully committed to Him in their new location. From Abraham onwards, it would also be a sign to the inhabitants of the land that the incomers were men and women of the Lord. He, in turn, responded to His people who worshipped Him in this way, confessing their belief in His promises. They were sojourners, strangers and pilgrims who sought a country of their own. So, on each occasion the Lord reassured them: the household of faith would grow, they would have the land of promise; yet more than this, the earth would be filled with a Godly seed, the Lord's purpose would triumph.

The Noachic covenant

> "And as for me, behold, I establish my covenant with you and with your descendants after you, and with every living creature that is with you: the birds, the cattle, and every beast of the earth with you, of all that go out of the ark, every beast of the earth. Thus I establish my covenant with you: never again shall all flesh be cut off by the waters of the flood; never again shall there be a flood to destroy the earth. And God said: 'This is the sign of the covenant which I make between me and you, and every living creature that is with you, for perpetual generations: I set my rainbow in the cloud, and it shall be for the sign of the covenant between me and the earth.'"
>
> (Genesis 9:9-13)

Seven times in total God spoke directly to Noah. Initially God told him of the impending judgements, then He commanded him to enter the ark and, after the Flood was over, told him to leave it.

Noah obeyed these three commands and so the Lord now spoke to him four more times, commanding him to be fruitful and multiply and then telling him of the covenant He would make with him.

The word "covenant" is also mentioned seven times as part of the blessing God gave him. Noah was saved by a faith that was shown in his works; the covenant was made with him and he became an "heir of righteousness through faith" as the Letter to the Hebrews tells us.

Part of the tragedy of the Flood was that the whole of the animal creation, which had been put in subjection to mankind, was destroyed because of his sin, except for those taken into the ark. They too now needed to replenish the earth and the Lord spoke of this first. The relationship between mankind and the animals would change. For the first time they were given for food; dominion over them was removed and the fear of mankind by them replaced it.

They became part of the covenant God made with Noah that the earth and its inhabitants would never again face destruction by water and this promise was emphasised five times.

God said, "This is the sign of the covenant which I make":

- Between me and you, and every living creature that is with you.
- Between me and the earth.
- Between me and you and every living creature of all flesh.
- Between God and every living creature of all flesh that is on the earth.
- Between me and all flesh that is on the earth.

But the Lord expanded this further. The covenant was with Noah and his descendants, "the birds, the cattle, and every beast of the earth" and this is a Bible echo that takes us to the beginning of Ezekiel's prophecy where we read of representatives of each of these four groups.

- Noah and his offspring = Man;
- Birds = Eagle;
- Cattle = Ox;

- Beasts of the earth = Lion.

Here are the four faces of the Cherubim and, following Ezekiel's wonderful picture of these guardians of God's glory and of the Lord Jesus Christ, we read:

> "Like the appearance of a rainbow in a cloud on a rainy day, so was the appearance of the brightness all around it. This was the appearance of the likeness of the glory of the LORD. So when I saw it, I fell on my face, and I heard a voice of one speaking." (Ezekiel 1:28)

The sign of the covenant is the rainbow, sunlight reflected off water droplets in clouds at a time when the sun emerges after rain. Not only is it a sign to us that never again will rain perpetuate into a global flood; it is also a sign to God for He said that when He looks upon it He will remember the words He spoke and the rain will cease. But it is also a sign of the Lord's everlasting covenant: His people will be fruitful, multiply and fill the earth, His glory will prevail and each time we see the rainbow we are reminded of this.

13 |

Noah drunk and naked

A NEW beginning had taken place, sin had been washed away out of the world and the one faithful family had worshipped the Lord in the ark whilst devastation occurred outside. This had been a special time, Noah's family knit together by these things, preparing for the new world that awaited them. The command had been to multiply and fill the earth and the records of the Flood and of the way this command was fulfilled are connected by the events at the end of Genesis 9. These are introduced in this way:

> "The sons of Noah who went forth from the ark were Shem, Ham, and Japheth. (Ham was the father of Canaan.) These three were the sons of Noah, and from these the people of the whole earth were dispersed." (Genesis 9:18,19, ESV)

Two points emerge from these verses:

1. Ham and his son Canaan receive special emphasis; they will play a significant part in what follows.
2. The descendants of Noah "were dispersed" (the word literally means to be broken up, scattered) suggesting that they would not willingly choose to fill the earth but that they would be forced to do so.

Noah the husbandman

The incident of Noah's drunkenness must have occurred some years after the Flood. His youngest son, Ham, now had a son, Canaan, who was old enough to be involved in his grandfather's displeasure.

The Bible makes no comment on Noah's intoxication. Wine is a gift from God (Psalm 104:15) but abstinence was demanded of priests coming to worship before Him (Leviticus 10:9). The whole emphasis of this event is on Noah's sons and grandson.

> "And Ham, the father of Canaan, saw the nakedness of his father, and told his two brothers outside." (Genesis 9:22)

The language suggests that this was not a quick, shocked glance at his naked father before he hurriedly left his tent but rather that he dwelt on the sight.

He went and told his brothers and perhaps his son also. This was not a quiet word, asking for help to cover up their father's embarrassment. Ham made the matter conspicuous before his brothers. Had he been complicit in Noah's drunkenness? Habakkuk suggests that this may have been the case in words that echo back to Noah:

> "Woe to him who gives drink to his neighbour, pressing him to your bottle, even to make him drunk, that you may look on his nakedness." (Habakkuk 2:15)

In contrast, his brothers then quietly covered up their father without looking at him. The Hebrew suggests that they took *the* garment and a number of writers identify this as Noah's robe of authority that Ham had taken out of his father's tent and shown to them. It was laid on their shoulders as they went backwards into Noah's tent, shouldering the responsibility to alleviate their father's shame at being exposed. Ham went and told his *two* brothers, yet Shem and Japheth took (singular verb) the garment implying that Shem took the leadership in this action.[1]

How did Noah know what had happened? Was it gossiped in their tents? Was this the work of Canaan? When Noah awoke he blamed his youngest son and the description can also mean his smallest or least significant. There is a link back to the words of the Lord to Noah after the Flood: "the imagination of man's heart is evil from his youth" clearly applied to Ham at this time.

---

1 E. Hengstenberg, *Christology of the Old Testament*, volume 1, page 17.

This incident leads us into one of the great prophecies of the Old Testament, one that begins to define the relationships between the nations:

> "So Noah awoke from his wine, and knew what his younger son had done to him. Then he said: 'Cursed be Canaan; a servant of servants he shall be to his brethren.' And he said: 'Blessed be the LORD, the God of Shem, and may Canaan be his servant. May God enlarge Japheth, and may he dwell in the tents of Shem; and may Canaan be his servant.' And Noah lived after the flood three hundred and fifty years. So all the days of Noah were nine hundred and fifty years; and he died." (Genesis 9:24-29)

For the first time man blessed God,[2] giving praise to the Lord who would fulfil all He had promised. Noah now knew that these things would come through Shem and his descendants and the words "God of" are linked to a specific man for the first time.

The Lord is the God of Shem. He alone of Noah's sons had some understanding of Yahweh as his God, linked back to the promise of Genesis 3. He alone appears to be a worshipper of Him using His name. From him will come Abraham and God's chosen people. Descendants of Shem, coming to know and accept fully the name of the Lord, will then ascribe back to Him, in their worship, the blessings He had promised His people from the beginning.

Japheth's understanding of God was based on Him as the Elohim; he had a general concept of the divine being but no further interest than that. He will have more sons than Shem or Ham and his descendants will spread out further in the earth, across seas to the isles. Salvation, and a full understanding of the name of the Lord, will be offered to his descendants for the Gospel will go out to the uttermost part of the earth. The nations that are saved will dwell in the tents of Shem, going up to Jerusalem year by year to worship the King, the Lord of Hosts and keep the feast of tabernacles (Zechariah 14:16).

---

2 See Appendix 1 (page 402).

One of Noah's sons, Ham, had shamed his father and now one of Ham's sons, Canaan, was cursed by Noah in return. No relationship of Canaan with God is recorded; His name or titles do not appear linked to this man in any way. Canaan's name means the submissive or humiliated one and Noah's words came true as Israel later took and subdued the land:

> "So on that day God subdued (*kana*) Jabin king of Canaan in the presence of the children of Israel." (Judges 4:23)

His descendants, the Canaanites, will have no part in God's blessings. They will be cursed by Him and become the lowest of servants, just as the serpent was made the lowest of all animals, going on its belly. Their descendants will be part of the confederation that, as the enemies of God, will seek to destroy Israel. Yet through their defeat they will ultimately come to understand what they have done, and to seek the name of the Lord.

This prophecy therefore is ultimately about the nations of the earth and their understanding of the name of the Lord for His whole purpose is that –

> "Men may know that you, whose name alone is the LORD, are the Most High over all the earth." (Psalm 83:18)

14 |

All the nations of the earth

IN Genesis chapters 10 and 11 we read of the naming of the nations, the confusion of tongues and the scattering of people throughout the earth.

Noah's descendants and their lands are all listed in chapter 10 and a similar phrase is used about each of the offspring of the three sons; they settled according to their tongues, families and nations. For example:

> "These were the sons of Shem, according to their families, according to their languages, in their lands, according to their nations." (Genesis 10:31)

This expansion did not happen immediately after the Flood. Noah and his sons came out of the ark as one family with one language and they all stayed together. They became dominated by one man, Nimrod, who sought to establish a kingdom, uniting all men in defiance of the Lord's command to fill the earth.

It was at this time that God intervened, in the days of Peleg (his name means 'division') within one to three hundred years after the Flood. A universal language was replaced by a confusion of tongues and so people were scattered through the earth, as God had commanded.

It is sad to see the shortness of this timescale. It was nearly 1,700 years after creation before God intervened and flooded the earth. It took less than three hundred years before He intervened again because of the wickedness of the earth. When we reach

Genesis 12 we shall see that it was even less time than this before the Lord intervened again.

The bounds of the nations

These chapters pose two questions. What is the importance of these events in God's promises? Why did He place the nations in the territories allocated to them?

The answers are found in Deuteronomy and in the words of Paul in Acts:

> "When the Most High divided their inheritance to the nations, when he separated the sons of Adam, he set the boundaries of the peoples according to the number of the children of Israel. For the LORD's portion is his people; Jacob is the place of his inheritance." (Deuteronomy 32:8,9)

> "The God who made the world and everything in it is the Lord of heaven and earth and does not live in temples built by hands. And he is not served by human hands, as if he needed anything, because he himself gives all men life and breath and everything else. From one man he made every nation of men, that they should inhabit the whole earth; and he determined the times set for them and the exact places where they should live. God did this so that men would seek him and perhaps reach out for him and find him, though he is not far from each one of us. For in him we live and move and have our being. As some of your own poets have said, 'We are his offspring'." (Acts 17:24-28, NIV)

We know precisely what this number, mentioned in Deuteronomy, is. The number of the children of Israel that went down into Egypt was seventy and the number of descendants of Shem, Ham and Japheth listed in Genesis 10 is also seventy.

Israel is God's chosen land, Jerusalem His dwelling place and this was determined from the very beginning for it was the place of the Garden of Eden. Now, in the scattering at Babel, all the Gentile nations of the earth were put in their territories in a way that was somehow connected with God's purpose with His people and His land. Throughout the pages of scripture this principle is at work: for example, the nations of Nebuchadnezzar's image existed because God raised them up as part of His dealings with His chosen people.

The scattering of the nations was a judgement on a wicked people, yet in it the mercy and forbearance of the Lord is seen. As Paul tells us, this scattering provided an environment in which nations might come to know the Lord in their own lands, firstly through Israel as a kingdom of priests. When this failed because of Israel's apostasy, it was through the preaching of the Gospel by the new Israel as seen in the Lord Jesus' last words to his disciples before his ascension:

> "But you shall receive power when the Holy Spirit has come upon you; and you shall be witnesses to me in Jerusalem, and in all Judea and Samaria, and to the end of the earth."
>
> (Acts 1:8)

Yet this too would ultimately fail to bring the whole earth back to God and so the Day of the Lord must come as Paul went on to say:

> "Truly, these times of ignorance God overlooked, but now commands all men everywhere to repent, because he has appointed a day on which he will judge the world in righteousness by the man whom he has ordained. He has given assurance of this to all by raising him from the dead."
>
> (Acts 17:30,31)

Nimrod

> "Cush begot Nimrod; he began to be a mighty one on the earth. He was a mighty hunter before the LORD; therefore it is said, 'Like Nimrod the mighty hunter before the LORD'. And the beginning of his kingdom was Babel, Erech, Accad, and Calneh, in the land of Shinar. From that land he went to Assyria and built Nineveh, Rehoboth, Ir, Calah ..."
>
> (Genesis 10:8-11)

In Nimrod, and the detail of the rebellion against God that led to the tower of Babel, spiritual warfare is evident once more. It was not between the descendants of Cain and Seth this time but now between those of Shem and Ham.

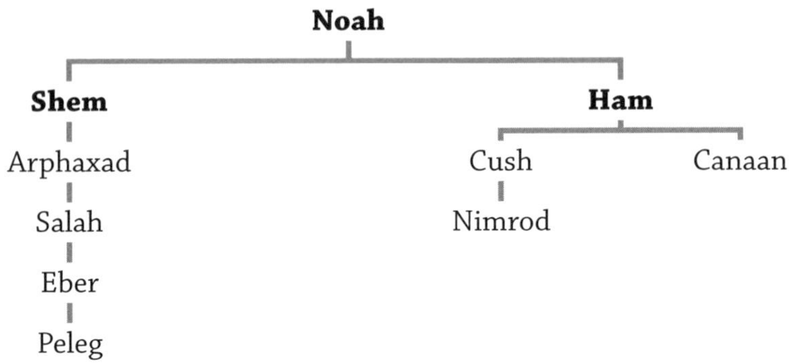

Ham was involved in the viewing of Noah's nakedness, his son was cursed by Noah and condemned to servitude. No doubt a sense of resentment permeated his family leading to a time of rebellion against God.

There is also a sense of déjà vu – a similar society has existed previously.

In the days of Noah there were "mighty (*gibbowr*) men, men of renown" (*shem*, name) who filled the earth with violence. Now a rebellion against God occurred, led by "a mighty (*gibbowr*) one in the earth" who also practised violence for he was a great hunter and his followers sought to "make a name" for themselves. The name, Nimrod, comes from *marad*, to rebel, and means 'come let us rebel'. It is linked to Merodach or Marduk (Jeremiah 50:2), 'your rebellion'. Bel Merodach was the city god of Babylon who 'lived' in a palace, Esagalia, the house that raised high its head. Adjacent to this was a large ziggurat, Etemenanki, ninety metres high, which was one of the wonders of the world.

Two quotations from non-scriptural works about Nimrod and the gods of Babylon give further detail.

The Jerusalem Targum of 1 Chronicles 1:10 says this of him:

"He was powerful in hunting and in wickedness before the Lord, for he was a hunter of the sons of men, and he said to them, 'Depart from the judgment of the Lord, and adhere to the judgment of Nimrod!' Therefore is it said: 'As Nimrod [is] the strong one, strong in hunting, and in wickedness before the Lord.'"

Josephus wrote:

"Now it was Nimrod who excited them to such an affront and contempt of God. He was the grandson of Ham, the son of Noah, – a bold man, and of great strength of hand. He persuaded them not to ascribe it to God, as if it was through his means they were happy, but to believe that it was their own courage which procured that happiness. He also gradually changed the government into tyranny, – seeing no other way of turning men from the fear of God, but to bring them into a constant dependence upon his power. He also said he would be revenged on God, if he should have a mind to drown the world again; for that he would build a tower too high for the waters to be able to reach. and that he would avenge himself on God for destroying their forefathers."[1]

Yet, as always, it is the Bible that gives us the clearest picture for it tells us:

"And the beginning of his kingdom was Babel."

(Genesis 10:10)

This is the second time in the Bible we meet the word "beginning" and the first time we read of a kingdom.

It was "in the beginning" that the Lord began His work of creation of the earth and the people upon it. To the man He gave dominion, he was to rule over it as a king, yet sin destroyed this and his dominion was taken away and given to the angels.

Now there was another beginning, led by a man who sought dominion over all the earth. Not content with Babel he went out into Asshur and built the city complex of Nineveh. Yet Asshur was a son of Shem, this was not a territory allocated to

---

1 Josephus, *Antiquities of the Jews*, chapter 4, paragraph 2.

the sons of Ham by God. Here is the beginning of the kingdom of men.

The tower of Babel

Nimrod's work therefore was a refutation of all that the Lord stood for and this is expanded in Genesis 11:

> "Now the whole earth had one language and one speech. And it came to pass, as they journeyed from the east, that they found a plain in the land of Shinar, and they dwelt there. Then they said to one another, 'Come, let us make bricks and bake them thoroughly'. They had brick for stone, and they had asphalt for mortar. And they said, 'Come, let us build ourselves a city, and a tower whose top is in the heavens; let us make a name for ourselves, lest we be scattered abroad over the face of the whole earth'. But the LORD came down to see the city and the tower which the sons of men had built. And the LORD said, 'Indeed the people are one and they all have one language, and this is what they begin to do; now nothing that they propose to do will be withheld from them. Come, let us go down and there confuse their language, that they may not understand one another's speech'. So the LORD scattered them abroad from there over the face of all the earth, and they ceased building the city. Therefore its name is called Babel, because there the LORD confused the language of all the earth; and from there the LORD scattered them abroad over the face of all the earth." (verses 1-9)

After the Flood, as men left Ararat, they moved eastward into the Tigris-Euphrates basin (Shinar means 'country of two rivers'). Once again the movement of people towards the east[2] carried a spiritual meaning of moving away from God.

Although different families were developing from each of the three sons, and Noah was still alive, Nimrod had his hold on them all and they moved as one group, bound together by one language. The word "language" carries the idea of 'edge' or

2 KJV margin, eastward, as chapter 13:11.

The gate of the god

This is the first mention of Babel or Babylon in scripture. The Bible gives the meaning of its name as "confusion" because there the Lord confounded (*balal*) the language of the whole earth.

However, the original Akkadian name was *Bab-Ilu*, meaning 'the gate of the god'. The entrance to the Garden of Eden, guarded by winged cherubim with faces of man, lion, eagle and ox had long gone (perhaps destroyed in the Flood). Yet the memory of it must have persisted. Now continued the great battle between the true and the false, typified in the contrast between Jerusalem and Babylon, that will permeate right through scripture.

In the Pergamon museum in Berlin is a reconstruction of the famous Ishtar gate of Babylon, the gate of the god, guarded by embossed tiles of lions and aurochs (oxen). Ishtar was the goddess worshipped there, the mythological wife of the god-man Nimrod.

'border'; the common language was a glue that bound the people together.

There, in the land of Shinar, they settled and built both a city and a tower using burnt brick and bitumen. This was an extremely expensive building process needing a great deal of timber to fire the bricks. Most buildings, including ziggurats, were built of sun dried bricks and hence this tower was special indeed.

Three times men said, "Let us" and there was an urgency and an imperative to this: they were determined to work out the evil intents of their hearts. The previous time we read, "Let us" is Genesis 1:26. We see Nimrod seeking to usurp God. Rather than establishing a place for the worship of the Lord he built a tower and city as the place which glorified his own achievements.

The third time they used this phrase, "Let us make us a name (*shem*) lest we be scattered abroad upon the face of the whole earth", they use words found on the lips of the Lord when He said, "Let us make man in our image". Presumably, Shem was there at Babel, the son for whom the Lord was his God. He would be the one carrying the truth of God's command to refill the earth to the subsequent generations. We can imagine him saying that this had been the divine command from the beginning, this was why the Lord made man. Their response – 'We don't need your teaching about the Lord, we'll make a name for ourselves and we are staying here'.

So they built a city and a tower, as high as they could. Were they doing this so that, if there was another flood, they would be safe? If so they had no trust at all in the mercy of God who had given them a sign that He would never again destroy the world by water. They were indeed the spiritual heirs of Cain, faithless as was he and depending on the works of their hands as did Cain's descendants. Their first father and mother had eaten forbidden fruit, wishing to be equal with God. Now their progeny built a tower up to heaven, the realm of the Lord, and desired to make their own name, discarding His. Yet in the Lord's sight they were "children of men", *ben-adam*, with a play on words. They were literally descendants of Adam and also, as was he, mortal creatures of the earth, earthy. Who were they that they dared to build to heaven?

However there is another, more sinister, reason for the ziggurat. These buildings were often called houses and they were built to house their gods. One writer described this as follows:

> "The ziggurat was not only a staged tower. It was a gigantic plinth whose true purpose was to support a sanctuary, the habitation of the god. Further, the god could leave this dwelling, and descend to the lower level of the city – to men. Using the stairways of the tower, the deity could come down to the lower temple at the base of the tower, and there manifest himself."[3]

What folly this was, for "the LORD came down".

---

3 A. Parrot, *The Tower of Babel*, page 61.

This section of scripture has a structure that is often used in the Bible. It uses inverted parallel phrases, a chiasmus, to draw our attention to the key phrase (this is much easier to see in writing than to explain). Here it is:

The whole earth had one language (Genesis 11:1);
  They journeyed there (verse 2);
    Go to, let us make ... (verse 3);
      Let us build for ourselves (verse 4);
        A city and a tower (verse 4);
          The LORD came down ... (verse 5).
        The city and the tower (verse 5);
      Which men had built (verse 5);
    Go to, let us confound ... (verse 7);
  Scattered from there (verse 8);
The language of the whole earth (verse 9).

How wonderful this is. They had made the highest structure men could build and God had come down to see it. In Deuteronomy 32 (quoted above) the Lord is described as the Most High. Whatever kingdom Nimrod sought to make, it was El Elyon, the Most High God, who reigned.

> "For the LORD Most High is awesome; He is a great King over all the earth." (Psalm 47:2)

DIGRESSION: "One people with one language"

There are links between Genesis 11 and the book of Daniel. The next time, after Genesis, that "the land of Shinar" is mentioned is in Daniel 1, setting the location for the rest of the book and linking it with the events at Babel. The Genesis record tells us of the building of the tower of Babel and also that God's intervention determined that the city was not completed – they left off building it. Many years later, another man was determined to finish off this building project and boasted of it:

> "The king (Nebuchadnezzar) spoke, saying, 'Is not this great Babylon, that I have built for a royal dwelling by my mighty power and for the honour of my majesty?'" (Daniel 4:30)

The historian Herodotus wrote about this building of the city of Babylon in the days of Nebuchadnezzar, made from baked bricks cemented together with bitumen, like Babel. He went on to describe a great tower built in the centre of the city, like that built by Nimrod:

> "The centre of each division of the town was occupied by a fortress. In the one stood the palace of the kings, surrounded by a wall of great strength and size: in the other was the sacred precinct of Jupiter Belus, a square enclosure two furlongs each way, with gates of solid brass; which was also remaining in my time. In the middle of the precinct there was a tower of solid masonry, a furlong in length and breadth, upon which was raised a second tower, and on that a third, and so on up to eight. The ascent to the top is on the outside, by a path which winds round all the towers. When one is about half-way up, one finds a resting-place and seats, where persons are wont to sit some time on their way to the summit. On the topmost tower there is a spacious temple ..."[4]

These things were built in the plain of Dura (dwelling), picking up the words in Genesis 11:2, "they journeyed eastward and found a plain in the land of Shinar and dwelt there".

In Daniel 2, we find Nebuchadnezzar acting as did Nimrod. His actions were in direct opposition to what God had revealed. He had been told that he was the head of gold of an image; he would be superseded by another power and, eventually, all these kingdoms of men would be swept away. God would then *set up* a kingdom that would never be destroyed.

In response to this Nebuchadnezzar *set up* a golden image. Not content with being a head of gold he made a golden image, thirty metres high, at which people were to worship both him and his gods (Daniel 3:12). Very probably it was his likeness that topped the pedestal.

This was done to unite all the peoples of his empire into one, with him as their head:

---

4 Herodotus: Book 1, paragraph 181.

"The Tower of Babel" by Bruegel the Elder (1563). The winding stairs in the picture link to Herodotus' view of stairs down which the god came.

> "Then a herald cried aloud: 'To you it is commanded, O peoples, nations, and languages, that at the time you hear the sound of the horn, flute, harp, lyre, and psaltery, in symphony with all kinds of music, you shall fall down and worship the gold image that King Nebuchadnezzar has set up; and whoever does not fall down and worship shall be cast immediately into the midst of a burning fiery furnace.'" (Daniel 3:4-6)

This was clearly an attempt to undo the scattering at Babel through the confusion of tongues by uniting the nations of his empire through worship of the golden idol. This phrase "peoples, nations and languages" is used seven times in Daniel. The first six are about the struggles of the kingdoms of men against the power of God, but the seventh is quite different:

> "I was watching in the night visions, and behold, one like the Son of Man, coming with the clouds of heaven! He came to the Ancient of Days, and they brought him near before him. Then to him was given dominion and glory and a kingdom,

> that all peoples, nations, and languages should serve him. His dominion is an everlasting dominion, which shall not pass away, and his kingdom the one which shall not be destroyed."
> (Daniel 7:13,14)

What reassurance there is in these words. Daniel, as does John in Revelation, makes it clear that the apostate worship and violence that began in Nimrod's day would continue until the time of the end. Yet whatever opposition true disciples face, the Lord will come, as Enoch prophesied, and only then will all nations be united together as one. Then will come the time foretold by the prophet, "I will change the speech of the peoples to a pure speech, that all of them may call upon the name of the LORD and serve him with one accord" (Zephaniah 3:9, ESV).

15

The generations of Shem

THE remaining verses of Genesis 11 are another genealogy, leading from Shem to Abraham. It appears that Shem's descendants stayed in Mesopotamia after the events of Babel and, like the patriarchs before the Flood, they faced a continuing attack on and erosion of their faith.

Because of the great length of life experienced in those days Noah died just two years before the birth of Abraham, but all those listed as Shem's descendants were alive at that time.

Although Abraham is mentioned first in the list of Terah's sons, he was not the firstborn. Abraham was seventy when he left Ur, seventy-five when he left Haran after the death of his father aged 205. Once again scripture puts the most important son, the one through whom the Lord will work, first in the family list.

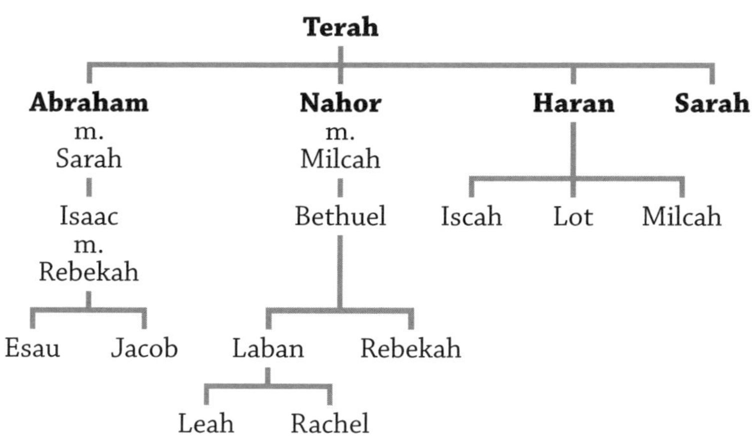

From Ur to Haran

Abraham's journey from Ur to Canaan took place in two stages and it was his father, Terah, who led the family north six hundred miles along the Euphrates valley until they reached Haran. Terah's son, Haran (not the same word as the name of the city) had died in Ur and his other son, Nahor, did not accompany them at this time. Lot travelled with them and Josephus wrote that Abraham had made him his heir. Sarah was barren and this was the case for all her married life until the birth of Isaac. In a society in which the birth of a son was so important, it is a mark of Abraham's character that, aged seventy, he had not taken another wife.

The text presents a problem about Terah. On one hand we are told he worshipped other gods in Ur:

> "And if it seems evil to you to serve the LORD, choose for yourselves this day whom you will serve, whether the gods which your fathers served that were on the other side of the River, or the gods of the Amorites, in whose land you dwell. But as for me and my house, we will serve the LORD."
>
> (Joshua 24:15)

It has been suggested that the names Terah, Sarai, Milcah, Laban were all related to moon worship[1] whilst Abram means 'exalted father' or 'father of heights', a name perhaps given to one who was brought up to be a priest in the ziggurat.

On the other hand, Genesis suggests that Terah also worshipped the Lord:

> "Then Laban said ... 'The God of Abraham, the God of Nahor, and the God of their father judge between us'. And Jacob swore by the Fear of his father Isaac." (Genesis 31:51-53)

These two passages can be reconciled by seeing Terah as a man who listened to his son's preaching about this new God, Yahweh, and accepted it, but not wholly for his old gods were not put away. He led his family as far as Haran but no further; they "dwelt" there and the language tells us of them settling down, yet

1 G. Wenham, *Genesis 1-15*, page 252.

this was not the land to which the Lord was leading them. It was a centre of moon worship, as in Ur which they had left.

At some later stage, Nahor led his family from Ur to Haran, for it is later called the city of Nahor (Genesis 24:10). Later still the area was called Padan Aram (25:20); this was the place where Abraham's steward went to find a bride for Rebekah and where Jacob fled when Esau threatened to kill him.

Five years elapsed before Terah died, during which time Abraham and Lot grew rich amassing wealth and slaves before they finally left for Canaan. God removed Abraham (Acts 7:4): although He had been patient, waiting until Terah died, His purpose demanded Abraham's journey to Canaan and now the time had come for him to make it.

SECTION FOUR:
Abraham, the friend of God

16 | People of the promise

A NEW section of the Genesis record begins in chapter 12. We are just a fifth of the way through the book yet almost two thousand years have passed since Adam, about half the period of the entire Old Testament.

The early chapters of Genesis are some of the most concentrated scripture we have: events, principles, teaching pour out of the pages – at times almost too much information to digest. Yet in a way these chapters are merely a prologue for what follows, for a new way, a completely different approach, was needed in man's relationship with God as the first eleven chapters are a record of failure.

- In the beginning God blessed Adam; the command was to fill the earth with a Godly seed. Mankind failed because of sin.
- After the Flood, in a new beginning, God blessed Noah; the command was to fill the earth with a covenant people. Mankind failed because of sin.
- At Babel, in a new beginning, God scattered people throughout the earth. They were put in their territories so that they might seek after God and find Him. However, they took with them the pagan worship of Babel. Mankind failed because of sin.

All that the Lord had done through both His goodness and His severity had not touched the hearts of men and women; flesh had triumphed. The name of God which was to be known and honoured throughout the earth had been discarded and replaced by men who said, "Let us make us a name" and "Let us build a city", following the way of Cain, the city builder.

It is a picture of humanity without hope for, by the beginning of Genesis 12, even the descendants of Shem had turned to other gods. Ten generations had passed from Adam to Noah and the new start after the Flood; a further ten generations passed from Noah to Abraham. What would the Lord do next? How would His purpose to fill the earth with His glory be fulfilled?

The household of faith

The Lord began with one man and one family showing how, through them, all the families of the earth could be blessed. Through this family the promise of the special seed, seen initially in Genesis 3:15 but not explained, would be developed so that finally Abraham would see the day of the Lord Jesus Christ and would rejoice. Men had sought to make a name and the Lord's response will be to magnify and make great the name of one man in a special way. Men had sought to build a city for themselves; now this chosen family would leave behind the city of their origins and become altar builders, concentrating on the worship of the Lord, looking for the city whose builder and maker would be the Lord.

The Lord directed these men in many ways.[1] Providing they believed in Him, He gave them abiding support and compassion throughout their struggles with their human nature. He communicated with them in many ways:

- He addressed them directly and His words carried the authority of His name; for the first time the phrase "the word of the LORD" is used.
- He manifested Himself to them in His glory. He appeared (literally, 'let Himself be seen') to His chosen family and this lent extra authority to His word.

1 The following points draw on W. Kaiser, *Toward an Old Testament Theology*.

- For the first time the Angel of the LORD appeared in scripture, reinforcing the authority of God's message.
- Men were given detailed promises showing what the Lord would accomplish and these were accompanied by His blessings to those who chose to be a part of His purpose.

These things speak of a theophany, an outpouring of God's intentions with the earth and its inhabitants. The rest of the book of Genesis tells us of the reactions of the men and women who received it and the triumph of faith in their lives.

17 | Abraham the father of the faithful

THE next eleven chapters in Genesis occupy just thirty years and focus on one man, Abraham.[1] It is as if the progress of history has slowed almost to a stop as God reveals His purpose in detail to him.

In these chapters the same figure of speech, a *chiasmus*, is used as when describing the Flood. Once again this pattern focuses on a key, central point.

Abraham leaves Ur, commencement of his physical and spiritual journey (12:1-9).

> Abraham lies about Sarah, God protects her in a foreign king's court (12:10-20).
>
> > Lot settles in Sodom, Abraham looks to God (13:1-18).
> >
> > > Abraham intercedes with his trained people to save Lot (14:1-24).
> > >
> > > > **THE COVENANT**
> > > >
> > > > **Abraham is blessed by Melchizedek, the promise of an heir is confirmed by the covenant** (14:18–15:20).
> > > >
> > > > **Isaac is promised, their names are changed. The covenant is confirmed by the rite of circumcision, a work of faith** (17:1-21).
> > >
> > > Abraham intercedes as a priest for Lot and his family (18:1-33).

---

1 I have used Abraham and Sarah throughout rather than Abram and Sarai although their names were not changed until some time after his calling.

Lot flees Sodom (19:1-38).

Abraham lies about Sarah, God protects her in a foreign king's court (20:1-18).

The birth of Isaac and his sacrifice, the end of Abraham's physical and spiritual journey. He dwells at Beersheba (21:1–22:19).[2]

Life in Ur of the Chaldees

In 2000 BC, Ur was a large city of perhaps 300,000 people, one of the great trading cities of its day. It lay on a bend of the Euphrates about 150 miles (241 km) south-east of Babylon at a time of peace and prosperity in the fertile basin of two rivers. Interestingly, Ur lay in exactly the opposite direction from the one Nimrod took when he left Babylon and went north-west to Nineveh. Perhaps this was deliberate, a reaction of its settlers against the violence of that man. Both Bethuel and Laban, descendants of Nahor, are described as Syrians or Arameans. Aram was a son of Shem and at least some of the Shemites moved south to Ur after the confusion of tongues at Babel.

The city was a centre of moon worship through the god, Nanna, and there was a ziggurat for this religion, 150 × 200 × 80 feet high at its centre (46 × 61 × 24 m). One of its symbols was a horned bull, the horns representing the shape of a waxing moon, a crescent shape met in the scriptures and linked to Canaanite idolatry.[3]

Ur is mentioned four times in scripture and on each occasion it is "Ur of the Chaldees", defining the key point about the city – it was a city where the Chaldean sect dominated. Later they were priests of the god of Babylon[4] and magicians at Nebuchadnezzar's court. It was they who led this pagan worship of the moon in Abraham's home city.

How then did Abraham fit into all of this? Was he initially a pagan priest or was he a lone figure like Enoch or Noah seeking

2 This pattern is based on one described in B. Waltke, page 20.

3 For example, Judges 8:21; Isaiah 3:18.

4 Herodotus, Book 1, paragraph 181.

to tell the people of his day about the Most High God? This question has puzzled Jewish writers through the ages, some even suggesting that his calling was "an act of discrimination and unfair privilege".[5]

The scriptures, old and new together, give us the answer and tell us of a remarkable man and why God called him.

The role of a prophet

It is Moses who tells of the role of a prophet in the words of Deuteronomy 18. This chapter speaks of our Lord Jesus Christ as the prophet like Moses, the one whom God would raise up and to whom ultimately Israel will listen. But these words do not speak solely of Christ, they give some important principles about the role of God's prophets in general.

The Canaanite prophets in the land were an abomination to God. They consulted spirits, claimed to speak to the dead and were soothsayers (Hebrew, *nachash*). Those who did this were like the serpent (*nachash*) of Genesis 3, they were the serpent's seed.

In contrast to these, the true prophet speaks in the name of the Lord; God puts His words into his mouth and he foretells all that God commands him.

Amos adds that, "Surely the Lord GOD does nothing, unless He reveals His secret to His servants the prophets" while Solomon also tells us that, "His (God's) secret is with the righteous".

What men the prophets were: trusted with the whole purpose of the Lord; righteous men through faith in the things revealed to them. They, like God's kings and priests, were anointed ones,[6] all of them types of The Anointed One, the Messiah to come, who would be prophet, priest and king.

But what motivated them, why were they chosen and why did they respond as they did, often at great personal cost to themselves?

Consider these two passages.

---

5 N. Leibowitz, *New studies in Bereshit Genesis*, page 116.

6 See Numbers 11:23; 1 Kings 9:16.

> "Blessed be the God and Father of our Lord Jesus Christ, who according to his abundant mercy has begotten us again to a living hope through the resurrection of Jesus Christ from the dead, to an inheritance incorruptible and undefiled and that does not fade away, reserved in heaven for you, who are kept by the power of God through faith for salvation ready to be revealed in the last time ... Of this salvation the prophets have inquired and searched carefully, who prophesied of the grace that would come to you, searching what, or what manner of time, the Spirit of Christ who was in them was indicating when He testified beforehand the sufferings of Christ and the glories that would follow. To them it was revealed that, not to themselves, but to us they were ministering the things which now have been reported to you through those who have preached the gospel to you by the Holy Spirit sent from heaven – things which angels desire to look into."
>
> (1 Peter 1:3-12)
>
> "For the testimony of Jesus is the spirit of prophecy."
>
> (Revelation 19:10)

This was the great privilege of God's prophets. They were men who had some understanding of the promise of the seed of the woman and desired to learn more. Their anointing was with the spirit of prophecy that they might testify the secret things revealed to them about the Lord Jesus Christ.

And Abraham was one of them, the first man in scripture to be directly named as a prophet, the first one to whom the sufferings of Christ and the glory that would follow would be revealed. These are the things he shared with Isaac and Jacob after him; they became a family of prophets, men who were witnesses to the Lord in a dark and pagan world. From these prophets came the Children of Israel, who were exhorted to remember the things revealed to their fathers and to share in their faith.

It was the wonder of these things that brought forth the paean of praise to the Lord that is Psalm 105. Here is the call to the seed of Abraham to remember their fathers, God's anointed prophets who were protected by Him. They were to pay heed to the covenant that had come to them through Abraham, Isaac and Jacob and rejoice in God's wonderful works.

We too take part in this for, as Abraham's seed and heirs according to the promise, these things are written for our learning as well as his:

> "Oh, give thanks to the LORD! Call upon his name; make known his deeds among the peoples! Sing to him, sing psalms to him; talk of all his wondrous works! Glory in his holy name; let the hearts of those rejoice who seek the LORD! Seek the LORD and his strength; seek his face evermore! Remember his marvellous works which he has done, his wonders, and the judgments of his mouth, O seed of Abraham his servant, you children of Jacob, his chosen ones! He is the LORD our God; his judgments are in all the earth. He remembers his covenant forever, the word which he commanded, for a thousand generations, the covenant which he made with Abraham, and his oath to Isaac, and confirmed it to Jacob for a statute, to Israel as an everlasting covenant, saying, 'To you I will give the land of Canaan as the allotment of your inheritance', when they were few in number, indeed very few, and strangers in it. When they went from one nation to another, from one kingdom to another people, he permitted no one to do them wrong; yes, he rebuked kings for their sakes, saying, 'Do not touch my anointed ones, and do my prophets no harm'."
>
> (Psalm 105:1-15)

18 | The calling of Abraham

"Now the LORD had said to Abram:
Get out of your country,
From your family
And from your father's house,
To a land that I will show you.
I will make you a great nation;
I will bless you
And make your name great;
You shall be a blessing.
I will bless those who bless you,
And I will curse him who curses you;
And in you all the families of the earth shall be blessed.
So Abram departed as the LORD had spoken to him ..."
(Genesis 12:1-4)

THERE was an imperative urgency to Abraham's call, 'get out now', and it was a command to leave everything of his old life behind. If he did this then he would be blessed, but these blessings were conditional on his obedience. Like book ends of the record of God's dealing with Abraham, we meet the same language in Genesis 22 when Abraham was called to sacrifice Isaac.

- **Chapter 12:** The Lord had said to Abram: "Get out (*laqach*) ... to a land that I will show you." So Abram departed as the Lord had spoken to him.
- **Chapter 22:** God tested Abraham, and said to him, "Take now (*laqach*) your son, your only son Isaac, whom you love

into the land of Moriah". So Abraham rose early in the morning ... and went to the place of which God had told him.

These two passages provide a framework for our consideration of Abraham. They tell at the beginning, and remind at the end, that he was man of both faith and works and that each was essential for the blessing of the Lord to be worked out in his life.

The calling of Abraham is such a seminal one in the Bible record that we would expect to find many references to it elsewhere. The following have been selected to try and build a picture of this man, who was so important to God's purpose, and of his life in Ur.

1. "The God of glory appeared to our father Abraham." It was Stephen who opened his defence speech in the temple with these words (Acts 7:2). This was the scripture he chose to commence his reasoning about the Messianic hope to the Jews who would kill him.

   God did not just speak to Abraham; there was also a divine manifestation, the first of a number that He would make to him.[1] He was one of those prophets described by Peter, seeking to understand the sufferings of Christ and the glory that would follow; now that glory was revealed to him.

   The phrase, "God of glory" occurs only one other time in the Bible, in Psalm 29. The God of glory, in the being of the Angel of the Lord had been with Noah in the Ark, preparing him for a new beginning. Now He appeared to Abraham, preparing this man for the new covenant that He would make with him.
2. Exodus tells us exactly when Abraham left Ur:

   "Now the sojourn of the children of Israel who lived in Egypt was four hundred and thirty years. And it came to pass at the end of the four hundred and thirty years

1 Genesis 12:7; 15:1; 17:1; 18:1.

– on that very same day – it came to pass that all the armies of the LORD went out from the land of Egypt."
(Exodus 12:40,41)

The border of the land of Egypt was the Red Sea and Israel crossed this on the 17th Nisan. Their sojourning began on the same day that Abraham left Ur, exactly 430 years later. Immediately after the Red Sea crossing, as Israel became travellers on their journey to the Promised Land, they sang the song of praise recorded in Exodus 15. It records their worship of Yahweh. He was their God, their salvation and they exulted, "Who is like you O LORD amongst the gods, glorious in holiness?" Later in the song came the declaration of their trust that the Lord, their God would lead them to the land He had promised them and, in particular, to the special place He had chosen for His inheritance.

The links with Abraham are obvious. He too came out of a country dominated by the religion of pagan gods. His family had worshipped them, as Israel had worshipped the gods of Egypt (Ezekiel 20:5-10). Yet Abraham had refused these gods, instead he believed that the Lord was the one true God. Abraham, as Israel, would be led by God to the land that He would show him and eventually, like them, he would come the special place that the Lord had chosen for His inheritance. But the date that links the exodus of Abraham with that of Israel is also the date when the ark came to rest on Ararat (Genesis 8:4). Was Abraham called at a time when he was meditating on the salvation of Noah and his family from a wicked world and on the covenant God made with him? Did he know of the glory of God manifest to Noah in the ark?

3. "Look to Abraham your father, and to Sarah who bore you; for I called him alone (*echad*, one)[2] and blessed him and increased him" (Isaiah 51:2).

---

2 "Called him alone" is used by the KJV, NKJV, Rotherham and the LXX.

Other versions put a different slant on this, saying "he was but one"[3] when called. Just as Noah was the one man who found grace in God's sight, so Abraham was the only faithful man God found in Ur[4] and therefore the only one He called. He was a prophet, a lone voice speaking truth in Ur of the Chaldees and he was not listened to by his own people, as was the Lord Jesus Christ. So he was given a threefold commandment to leave.

> "He (Jesus) began to teach in the synagogue. And many hearing him were astonished, saying, 'Where did this man get these things? And what wisdom is this which is given to him, that such mighty works are performed by his hands' ... But Jesus said to them, 'A prophet is not without honour except in his own country, among his own relatives, and in his own house'. Now he could do no mighty work there, except that he laid his hands on a few sick people and healed them. And he marvelled because of their unbelief. Then he went about the villages in a circuit, teaching." (Mark 6:2-6)

There is no suggestion that Abraham performed miracles like Christ, but we can imagine the response to his words: 'Isn't this Terah's son? Who does he think he is?' Abraham left his home town never to return to it.

The first promise

The promise made to Abraham in Ur was the first of seven that God would give to him and that number, representing completeness, is emphasised in the seven statements of this promise[5] in Genesis 12 – beginning with one man, "I will make you" and ending with "all the families of the earth will be blessed".

3 "He was but one" is used by the RV, ESV, NIV.

4 Although Terah and Nahor accepted some of Abraham's teaching about the Lord (Genesis 31:53) it did not develop into faith in the promises. They travelled with Abraham to Haran but not into the Promised Land.

5 We shall come across this pattern later for God made seven statements in the promise-blessings to Isaac (26:3,4) and Jacob (27:28,29).

In the chapters before Genesis 12, we read five times of God cursing part of His creation. Now, in chapter 12, we find that the Lord promised Abraham what He would do using the phrase "I will" five times; the word "bless" is used five times also, the fivefold structure emphasising that this was the outworking of the grace of God in his life. Here, in just seven verses are the promise-blessings, the great theme of Genesis showing the whole purpose of God.

It begins with the commandment for Abraham to leave all – country, family, father's house and travel to a land that God would show him. This was essential; the land was inextricably linked to the promises that followed. This one began with three personal commitments from God to Abraham.

1. I will make you a great nation:

   How Abraham would wonder at the first statement God made. He was already a man of many years and Sarah was barren. They appear to have given up all hope of a child. Lot had become his heir,[6] yet now the Lord promised him many offspring.

2. I will bless you:

   As God had blessed Adam and Noah, linking Abraham with the divine purpose from the beginning.

3. And make your name (*shem*) great:

   In this promise, the Lord reminded Abraham that He had been the Lord, the God of Shem as He was now his God. Abraham's name would be honoured and esteemed by his descendants, that great nation that would look to "Abraham our father". Yet, apart from David to whom God said, "I have made you a great name", such a promise was unique. Elsewhere, only the name of the Lord is described as great. There is therefore also a spiritual greatness which is associated with the change of Abram to Abraham as we shall see when we reach Genesis 17.

4. So that you shall be a blessing:

6 Josephus, Book 1, chapter 7.

These three personal commitments were made for a reason; through them Abraham would become a blessing. But to whom? This question is then answered in the group of three statements that follow.

5. I will bless those who bless you:

   Those who associate themselves with Abraham will become part of this purpose: "if you are Christ's then are you Abraham's seed and heirs according to the promise."

6. And I will curse (*arar*, curse bitterly) him who curses (*qalal*, despises or curses[7]) you:

   God's total rejection will fall on those who despise and belittle the promise of salvation offered through Abraham. In this is seen the forerunner of the sin unto death, the denial of the Lord's power to save through His Son.

7. So that in you all the families of the earth shall be blessed:

   The call of the Gospel to become part of the Israel of God will go out to all the nations of the earth. Those who respond will share the promise-blessings; those who despise it will be judged and totally rejected by the Lord.

Amongst the riches of this promise it is easy to overlook the fact that each of the seven statements makes direct reference to Abraham personally: "I will make you ..."; "I will bless you ..." It is Abraham who is at the centre of them. He is the one through whom the Lord will work. It is his faith and works that will be essential for the fulfilment of God's purpose.

No doubt, as he meditated on these words, Abraham's mind went back to the Tower of Babel. There God had confounded the tongues of the people, nations had formed and were still spreading out through the world. Now God had promised him that, through him, all these nations would share the blessing.

Into the land of Canaan

Abraham left Haran as God had commanded him. In so doing he had obeyed two of the Lord's commands. He had left his

7 The use of *qalal* as a curse is seen in Leviticus 24.

country, never to return. He had left his father's house, leaving it behind in Haran when Terah died. But he had not yet left his wider family for we read that Lot went with him. The language is important: Abraham was the spiritual leader, Lot followed him, with all the wealth brought from Ur and accumulated in Haran. One suggestion made about "the people they had acquired" who went with them is that these were people converted to belief in the Lord by Abraham's preaching there.[8]

"And the Canaanite was in the land." What a shock this must have been to Abraham. He had left idolatry behind in Ur and Haran but here was something much worse. Here were the descendants of Canaan, relatives of Nimrod and they had been cursed by God through the words of Noah. Yet they were there as part of God's purpose, He had set their boundaries as He had done for all nations and specific mention is made of the borders of Canaan:

> "And the border of the Canaanites was from Sidon as you go toward Gerar, as far as Gaza; then as you go toward Sodom, Gomorrah, Admah, and Zeboiim, as far as Lasha."
>
> (Genesis 10:19)

These wicked people had brought the worship of the moon god with them from Babel and their lifestyles were totally corrupt and dissolute, abominable to God; Sodom and Gomorrah would shortly be destroyed by Him.

From the beginning of the occupation of the land by God's people, He set them a test: they had to dwell there but keep themselves separate from the Canaanites. They were to be in the world but not part of it; "children of God without fault in the midst of a crooked and perverse generation, among whom you shine as lights". Our lives should be similar for the words just quoted were written by Paul for all readers throughout the ages. It is a constant struggle to set the boundaries, to discern what is a danger to our spiritual health and must be avoided, what we may take from the world and what we must shun. So it was for

8 Cassuto, volume 2, page 306.

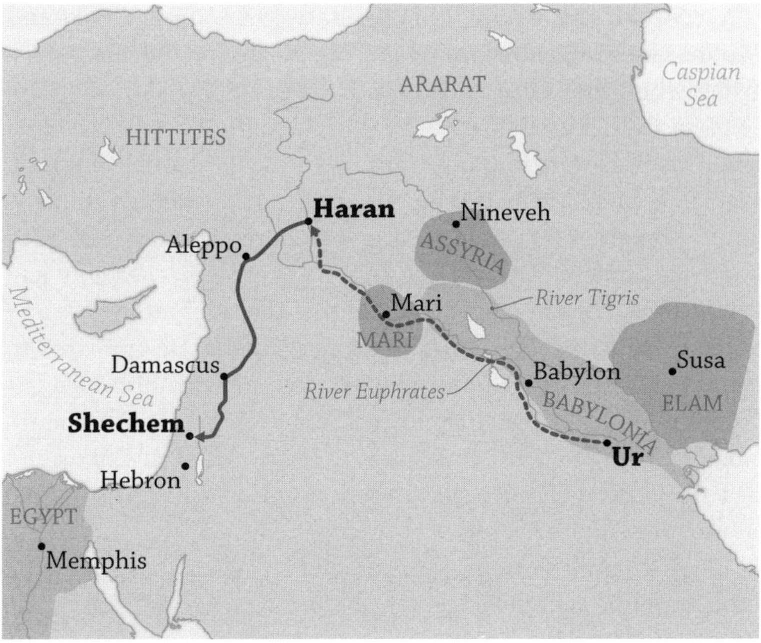

Map of Abraham's journey into Canaan.

Abraham and his descendants and it is a theme met a number of times in the following chapters.

> "Abram passed through the land to the place of Shechem, as far as the terebinth tree of Moreh. And the Canaanites were then in the land. Then the LORD appeared to Abram and said, 'To your descendants I will give this land'. And there he built an altar to the LORD, who had appeared to him. And he moved from there to the mountain east of Bethel, and he pitched his tent with Bethel on the west and Ai on the east; there he built an altar to the LORD and called on the name of the LORD. So Abram journeyed, going on still toward the South."
>
> (Genesis 12:6-9)

How wonderfully well Abraham met this challenge as he travelled through the land from north to south, still guided by the Angel of the Lord. Each stopping place tells us something of his faith.

Shechem: This is a ridge between Mount Gebal and Mount Gerizim, the place where the Lord directed the twelve tribes when they entered the land. Six tribes stood on Gerizim to bless and six on Ebal to curse. Shechem therefore was a place where choices were made: be faithful to the Lord and be blessed, turn from Him and be cursed. Abraham now makes his choice.

Moreh: The name means 'teacher' and may well have been the personal name given to a Canaanite teacher who had established a pagan place of worship at the terebinth there and given it his name. Note God's encouragement. He appeared to Abraham again, the God of glory had come with him into the land and now, for the first time, it was promised to Abraham's seed. This is the third time[9] that "seed" is used in Genesis to describe special offspring who are part of God's purpose, linking Abraham with the promises to Adam and Noah.

Abraham's response was to build an altar and worship the Lord, a public acknowledgement before Him of his faith in the promise just made.

This was a great witness: the first thing he did as he arrived in Canaan was to declare the difference between him and its inhabitants. We can imagine them coming to greet him and enquire about him. Who was he? Where had he come from? What were his gods? There was no equivocation on his part, indeed the directness of the language tells of the man of faith who was also a man whose actions demonstrated his faith: he entered the land and built an altar; he moved again and built another altar. What an example this is for our lives. We may move house, change jobs and the key things we need to do first are to seek out the ecclesia and explain to our new neighbours or colleagues who we are and what we believe.

Bethel: Abraham pitched his tent with Bethel ('the House of God') in front of him and Ai ('a heap of ruins') behind him, to the east, the direction from which he had travelled from Ur. He has now declared his choice. In leaving his country and his

---

9 Genesis 3:15; 9:9; 12:7.

father's house he had left behind all that was temporary and that would decay away. Before him was the House of God and those things which were eternal. There he called upon the name of the Lord, the first of the three occasions he would so do.[10]

There is a parallelism between events at Shechem and those at Bethel. At the former the Lord made His will known to Abraham and at the latter Abraham showed his devotion to the name of the Lord who had made such a promise.

Was his behaviour and devotion to Yahweh so remarkable in the eyes of the Canaanite inhabitants that later, when he sought to buy the cave of Machpelah for a burial place, they called him "a prince of God"[11] even though he presented himself as a sojourner and a stranger?

Going down into Egypt

When we dwell on the faith in action of Abraham's life, it comes as a surprise to read that he left the Promised Land and went down to Egypt.

We know from chapter 10 about the origin of the people of Egypt (*Mizraim*) – see illustration below.

The journey into Egypt set the pattern for all interactions between God's people and this land. It was a place of refuge in time of trouble or difficulty yet no spiritual good ever came from going there.

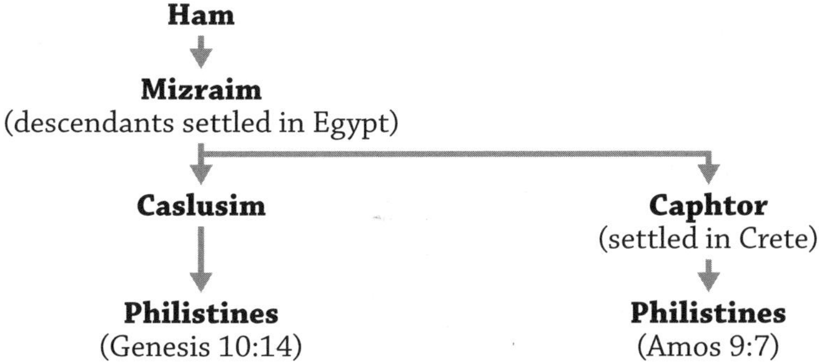

10 We considered "calling upon the name of the Lord" in detail on page 80.

11 Genesis 23:6, margin.

And in this journey is seen Abraham's main weakness. He was a man of driving energy, able to accumulate and manage a huge enclave – a camp that must have grown to over a thousand people. He was used to working out the issues of his life himself and now he was faced with a test, a severe famine in the land to which God had brought him. Did he seek God's guidance? There is no mention of prayer, of seeking God's help; he went down to Egypt and he attempted to sort out the problem for himself.

Sarah must have been a stunningly beautiful woman. She was, at this time, well over sixty years old yet Abraham knew that there was something so attractive about her that she would be desired, and she was. She was also his half-sister and so his deception was not an outright lie (Genesis 12:13). As her husband, he feared that he may be killed so that another might have her. As her brother, in the absence of her father, he was the one who could legally deny her to any who asked for her ... except Pharaoh.

In all that followed Abraham did not tell Pharaoh of the true relationship between Sarah and himself, even when he was given many gifts by the king, probably as the bride price. Just as Abraham was silent, so the Lord did not speak to him through these events, yet Pharaoh became aware that a great power was at work. The God-given blessing was at risk by Abraham's behaviour, yet Sarah's integrity was intact: 'take your wife and get out' said the king; his men escorted Abraham to the boundary of the land and expelled him. How humiliated Abraham must have been by all of this. He must have lost respect in Sarah's eyes, he lost God's voice, built no altars, put the blessing at risk, brought the contempt of Pharaoh on himself and was thrown out of the land.

Yet there was more, he came out with "sheep, oxen, male donkeys, male and female servants, female donkeys, and camels". These things would cause him much trouble in the years ahead, Lot would leave him after an argument over their flocks, his taking of Hagar the Egyptian would prove to be a family disaster. The Lord is a gracious God, willing to forgive those who seek Him but Abraham, and all of us, have to live with the consequences of our actions.

19 |

Separation from Lot

LOT is a conundrum.

Three times the Apostle Peter wrote that he was a righteous man (2 Peter 2:7,8); he also described him as Godly, a man vexed daily by the wickedness of Sodom, and the Lord delivered him.

Yet we read in Genesis 13 that he parted from Abraham and there is no doubt that this was in accord with the will of God; in separating from Lot, Abraham had now completely left his family, fulfilling the third of God's commands about separation (Genesis 12:1).

How are these two views reconciled?

Compare the two men's reactions to their departures from Haran and Egypt:

> "Then Abram took Sarai his wife and Lot his brother's son, and all their possessions that they had gathered, and the people whom they had acquired in Haran, and they departed to go to the land of Canaan. So they came to the land of Canaan."
>
> (Genesis 12:5)
>
> "Then Abram went up from Egypt, he and his wife and all that he had, and Lot with him, to the South." (Genesis 13:1)

The departure from Haran is a picture of harmony and unity of purpose between Abraham and Lot. The family members are together, mentioned first, then their possessions and servants. We read that "they departed ...", "they came ..."

Yet when Abraham left Egypt, He and Sarah led the way, taking all that he had with them, and Lot is mentioned last, merely accompanying him. There is a hint here that Lot was unwilling to go. Although they had been expelled he too had grown rich in Egypt and perhaps left it under protest. Lot was a man for whom the riches of this life were important.

All of Abraham's actions as he left Egypt were those of a changed man. He had learned a hard and humiliating lesson and was now determined to return to the land and the Lord:

> "And he went on his journey from the South as far as Bethel, to the place where his tent had been at the beginning, between Bethel and Ai, to the place of the altar which he had made there at first. And there Abram called on the name of the LORD." (Genesis 13:3,4)

This was a journey of about 200 miles (322 km). We can imagine him rising early day by day and setting his face towards the land. In fact the "land" (of Canaan) is mentioned six times in this chapter; the whole focus of events is about it and what it meant to Abraham. He returned to it and he would never leave it again.

As he called upon the name of the Lord for the second time we can imagine his prayer for forgiveness and acceptance by Yahweh. He was now faced with the problem of increasing estrangement from Lot and throughout all of their interactions Abraham's loving concern for his nephew shone through.

His journey was one of both physical and spiritual ascent. He came *up* out of Egypt finally ending up at Hebron, the highest city in Israel, yet Lot is not mentioned as a participant in this spiritual renewal.

The language used to describe Abraham's sojourn in Egypt and that of the Children of Israel is very similar. This comparison can be extended when thinking of Abraham's return and the beginning of the Exodus. It gives a clue about the underlying issue that caused strife between Abraham and Lot.

Genesis 13	**The Exodus**
Abraham went up out of Egypt (verse 1)	The Children of Israel went up ... out of the land of Egypt (Exodus 13:18)

Genesis 13	**The Exodus**
He was very rich in silver and gold (verse 2)	They took of the Egyptians jewels of silver and jewels of gold (Exodus 12:35)
Let there be no strife (*meriybah*) between me and you (verse 8)	The Children of Israel strove with Moses because there was no water ... He called the name of the place Massah and Meribah because of their striving (Exodus 17:2,7)

Unlike Egypt, which had the constant flow of the Nile to water the land, Israel depended on the former and latter rains. If these failed, as they had done, drought and famine followed. It is likely that, as Abraham returned, after a short time in Egypt, the land was still recovering. Even in the best of times access to cisterns and their stored rainwater was jealously guarded and disputed.[1] The problem between the herdsmen of Abraham and Lot was about a scarcity of water resources for their increased flocks and this was a cause of strife. Centuries later Israel would strive with Moses over a lack of water and now we see Abraham show the same meekness and quietness of spirit in his dealing with Lot as did Moses with Israel.

There is no doubt that Abraham was aware of the spiritual danger in a split. The Canaanite and the Perizzite[2] were in the land (Genesis 13:7) and this is a spiritual danger flag like that in verse six of chapter twelve. "We are men – brethren",[3] said Abraham as he pleaded for unity, and the *whole* land is before us, big enough for us both. When he offered Lot the right hand or the left hand, it has been suggested that this was an offer to go either north or south. Either direction would keep Lot safely in the Promised Land yet he journeyed east, away from God and back in the direction of Ur. He ended up on the very edge of the

1 Cf. Isaac and Abimelech, Genesis 26.
2 Perizzites were rural Canaanites, village dwellers.
3 Young's Literal Translation.

land for economic reasons, a mistake that would later be followed by the tribes of Reuben, Gad and Manasseh.

> "And Lot lifted his eyes and saw all the plain of Jordan, that it was well watered everywhere (before the LORD destroyed Sodom and Gomorrah) like the garden of the LORD, like the land of Egypt as you go toward Zoar. Then Lot chose for himself all the plain of Jordan, and Lot journeyed east. And they separated from each other." (Genesis 13:10,11)

It was just like Egypt from which he had come. It was also fertile as had been the Garden of Eden and, as Eve saw, chose and took the forbidden fruit, so Lot followed the same process. His name means 'covered' or 'veiled'; he saw what he wanted but was blind to the spiritual consequences of his actions.

Blessings in this life

There is an important lesson for us from Lot's life. In following Abraham he had become rich. His initial decision was to live *near* Sodom and we can imagine his self-justification: the land was not big enough for him and Abraham, here was good grazing ground, Sodom was evil but he would remain separate from it. His decision was made to preserve his wealth; it was an economic one. He was the first disciple to go into isolation for material reasons and it did him no good. Lot was a faithful man but he was a man who believed that faith should bring its rewards in this life and in some ways this is true. Those who follow Christ's example are honest and diligent at work, treating others with respect and integrity and may benefit from this. They show love and kindness at home trying to generate a stable family life in which to raise children. They seek to manage their material lives being content with what they have and recognising that Godliness with contentment is great gain.

None of us is perfect in these things, but this is how we try to behave and often it does bring rewards in this life if we are seen to be good and faithful servants.[4]

---

4 I acknowledge that this is a general principle and that Ecclesiastes tells us trouble can come upon the righteous and unrighteous alike. Sometimes we have no answer

This was certainly true of the life of the nation of Israel. They were blessed by God by being His covenant people but He did not routinely reward them in miraculous ways if they kept His laws. It was rather that His laws were designed to benefit, in this life, those who followed them.

> "Surely I have taught you statutes and judgments, just as the LORD my God commanded me, that you should act according to them in the land which you go to possess. Therefore be careful to observe them; for this is your wisdom and your understanding in the sight of the peoples who will hear all these statutes, and say, 'Surely this great nation is a wise and understanding people'. For what great nation is there that has God so near to it, as the LORD our God is to us, for whatever reason we may call upon him? And what great nation is there that has such statutes and righteous judgments as are in all this law which I set before you this day?"
>
> (Deuteronomy 4:5-8)

> "Now this is the commandment, and these are the statutes and judgments which the LORD your God has commanded to teach you, *that* you may observe them in the land which you are crossing over to possess, *that* you may fear the LORD your God, to keep all his statutes and his commandments which I command you, you and your son and your grandson, all the days of your life, and *that* your days may be prolonged. Therefore hear, O Israel, and be careful to observe it, *that* it may be well with you, and *that* you may multiply greatly as the LORD God of your fathers has promised you." (6:1-3)

The phrase "that it might be well with you" is a key one in Deuteronomy. If Israel kept the moral, social and hygiene laws that were uniquely given to them then they would flourish as a nation and in this way be blessed by God.

But what happens when God's people come to expect this as a right and lose sight of the promise of the kingdom to come?

---

to this and have to accept that the Lord alone knows.

This was Lot's fundamental problem and the reason why Abraham was commanded to separate from him. He was indeed a man of faith but the promise of a perfect, future life had become clouded by the material blessings he had achieved in his life.

The choice we make is summed up by the Apostle Paul in this way:

> "... we do not look at the things which are seen, but at the things which are not seen. For the things which are seen are temporary, but the things which are not seen are eternal."
>
> (2 Corinthians 4:18)

Seeing afar off

It was in "seeing" that the contrast between Lot and Abraham is shown to be very great. Lot "lifted up his eyes" but with his veiled sight had eyes only for Sodom; this was his desire, his choice. Abraham only lifted up his eyes when God told him to do so; he was content with whatever the Lord offered. In all of this he was an example of patient waiting for God's instructions – a lesson learned indeed from his descent into Egypt.

The Lord now gave him the second promise.

> "And the LORD said to Abram, after Lot had separated from him: 'Lift your eyes now and look from the place where you are – northward, southward, eastward, and westward; for all the land which you see I give to you and your descendants forever. And I will make your descendants as the dust of the earth; so that if a man could number the dust of the earth, then your descendants also could be numbered. Arise, walk in the land through its length and its width, for I give it to you.'"
>
> (Genesis 13:14-17)

The blessing given in Ur was now expanded further.

- 12:1 – Go to a land that I will show you;
- 12:7 – Unto your seed will I give this land;
- 13:15 – To you will I give it and to your seed forever.

For the first time he was given the promise of resurrection and immortality, an inheritance forever. Even though Sarah was still barren, he would have descendants, a special seed who would inherit it with him.

When he now looked around at the whole land promised him, he did it in an unusual fashion – looking north, south, east and west. He did not turn in a circle but ended with his back facing east, from where he had come and his face looking west, into the land. Once again, symbolically as well as physically, he turned his back on his past as the Lord commanded him. His future now lay completely in the Promised Land.

Abraham and Lot at this point are as far apart spiritually as they can be. Lot was in Sodom, the lowest city in the land. Abraham was in Hebron (it means fellowship), the highest city in the land, which would become his home. Perhaps the geographical distance between them points to a spiritual distance, a difference in the way each saw the blessings of the Lord.

20 | Victory for God's people

CHAPTER 14 is unique in this section of Genesis. From chapter 12 to chapter 22 we read of the Lord's dealings with Abraham and in every chapter except this one He spoke directly, either to the prophet or those associated with him. We do not find God's spoken words here, instead He spoke through Melchizedek. This provides a type of that which was to come; throughout the Old Testament the Lord will speak to His people through the prophets but in the New Covenant through His Son (Hebrews 1:1,2), the king-priest of the order of Melchizedek.

In this chapter, once again, there is a battle between the true and the false. It is easy to concentrate on the war in the land and the kings involved, yet this is merely an introduction to Abraham's interaction with two men, two kings – the king of Sodom and the king of Salem. Both offer him rewards; which will he choose? The future hangs on his decision.

The invasion of the land

Very little is known about the kings that came from Mesopotamia. Their initial invasion had been fourteen years previously and therefore when Lot settled in Sodom he dwelt in an area in subjection to an invading power. Sodom would have had to pay tribute to it, perhaps not what he expected when he made his choice.

The initial, invading army was made up of four kings.

- Amraphael was king of Shinar (Babylon), he is mentioned first in the list. It seems that he was the motivator, the ruler of Babylon to whom kings of the earth gave their power for a season for an invasion of the Promised Land. Those who went with him were:

- Arioch, king of Ellasar, location unknown.
- Chedorlaomer, king of Elam, the region at the head of the Persian Gulf.
- Tidal, king of nations (Gentiles).

These are descendants from all three of Noah's sons, representing all the kingdoms of the earth coming against God's land, travelling down the king's highway on the east of the Jordan to the northern tip of the Dead Sea and taking the five cities there.

After twelve years the kings of the land rebelled; Chedorlaomer and the kings with him returned to take a spoil, defeating the Canaanite inhabitants and stripping the land bare:

> "Then they took all the goods of Sodom and Gomorrah, and all their provisions, and went their way. They also took Lot, Abram's brother's son who dwelt in Sodom, and his goods, and departed. Then one who had escaped came and told Abram the Hebrew, for he dwelt by the terebinth trees of Mamre the Amorite, brother of Eshcol and brother of Aner; and they were allies with Abram. Now when Abram heard that his brother was taken captive, he armed his three hundred and eighteen trained servants who were born in his own house, and went in pursuit as far as Dan. He divided his forces against them by night, and he and his servants attacked them and pursued them as far as Hobah, which is north of Damascus. So he brought back all the goods, and also brought back his brother Lot and his goods, as well as the women and the people."
>
> (Genesis 14:11-16)

And Lot dwelt in Sodom. He had originally pitched his tent near the city, no doubt with good intentions of keeping separate from it, now he was no longer a sojourner in the land but a settled inhabitant of a Canaanite establishment. The dangers of such a move are poetically given to us in the opening words of the Psalms: "Blessed is the man who walks not in the counsel of

The battle at the Vale of Siddim, the route of the kings and Abraham's pursuit.

the ungodly, nor stands in the path of sinners, nor sits in the seat of the scornful". Later we read that Lot "sat in the gate of Sodom" (Genesis 19:1).

Lot was a man who decided to make his own choice about where to live, based on his desire for wealth. Now he had no choice, he was captured, taken away and everything he had worked for was lost.

It would probably have been one of Lot's servants, one who had gone with him to Sodom, who sought out Abraham at Hebron. Did Lot send him? Once again, one of Abraham's defining characteristics came into play. He was essentially a man of action, quick to get on with the task before him and looking to use his considerable talents to achieve his aims. As a man of faith, committed to obeying the Lord, this was admirable – an exhortation for each of us.

Abraham is called "the Hebrew", the first time we meet this patronymic in the Bible. It means 'one from beyond' (the Euphrates) and comes from the name Eber, 'he who passed over'. Abraham's descent from Eber, and through him from Shem, is emphasised in this name.

His witness to his beliefs had also impressed some of the Canaanites amongst whom he lived for Mamre, Eshcol and Aner were allies with him.

But more people were involved for Abraham took with him 318 trained men born in his own house. It is not until Genesis 18 that this emphasis on the house is seen as important. He was a man who insisted that all who lived with him knew and accepted the way of the Lord. With this number of trained men, he must have had a camp of one to two thousand people and he had taught all of them the promises and the blessings associated with them. It was indeed the household of faith, the example for the ecclesia that Paul had in mind when he wrote to the Galatians.[1]

This picture of the faith of Abraham's people is shown in two more details given to us in the text:

---

1 Cf. Genesis 18:19 with Galatians 3 and 6:10.

- They were trained – not in warfare for the word used means instructed or dedicated and refers to the spiritual education given them; they were men dedicated to the Lord. The same word is behind the modern Hebrew name Hanukkah, the Feast of Dedication (John 10:22), still kept by Jews today at which they rededicate themselves annually to God.
- There were 318 of them, an unusual number which is not found in other scriptures. However this number is the gematria (numerical equivalent) of the name Eliezer, the man introduced to us in Genesis 15 as Abraham's steward. He was a man of faith, dedicated to his master's purpose and sharing his belief. He is set before us in the Genesis record as an example of faithfulness within Abraham's house, a gentile convert belonging to the Lord through his master.

What a dramatic picture there is of the following battle. For nearly 150 miles (241 km) Abraham chased the enemy north from Hebron, finally catching them in the far north of the country at Dan and ambushing them at night. Although beaten they were not destroyed, nor were captives rescued, and they managed to flee another 40 miles (64 km) to Hobah ('hiding place') near Damascus. Here they were routed completely, the kings slaughtered and everything rescued by Abraham – not one person was lost.

It would be a triumphant and relieved people that slowly made their way south. Presumably messengers had been sent on ahead to Sodom and arrangements made to meet at Salem (why was this venue chosen?).

What would Abraham think about on the journey? There is not a hint of any criticism of Lot in his actions. He thought of Lot as his brother and, even though he had left Abraham and gone into isolation, Abraham never rejected him. He was a model of brotherly concern and compassion in his actions, reaching out to Lot, risking a great deal to rescue him. We can imagine the conversation between them and his urging of Lot to come back into fellowship with him.

But Abraham would also have had other thoughts. He had been told by God to walk through the land for God would give it to him. He had now done this from the Negev to Dan and in these journeys he had been led by God (Joshua 24:3). He had brought peace to a land that had been oppressed for fourteen years. He had a growing household of believers and neighbours who were beginning to accept his God (the word "allies" used in verse 13 is the Hebrew *beriyth*, covenant, and any covenant Abraham made would surely involve acceptance of his beliefs). With his men he could, if he wished, begin to establish rule over the country – he was, after all, the conqueror of its enemies. Many years later his greatest descendant faced a similar test. His mother had brought him up to know Gabriel's words: he would be a great king, sitting on the throne of his father David and now he had been given unlimited power by his Father at his baptism. He could, if he wished, take all the kingdoms of the world – would this fulfil the angel's words? Yet he refused to take this route for it was not his Father's will; the kingdom would not come in this way.

And Abraham faced a similar test for, as he approached Shaveh, at the northern end of the Kidron valley, two kings came out to meet him in the king's valley (cf. 2 Samuel 18:18), the king of Sodom and the king of Salem.

Melchizedek

Just three verses are given to Abraham's meeting with Melchizedek, yet its impact permeates the rest of scripture. It deliberately interrupts the continuity of the Abraham / king of Sodom interaction and helps him make up his mind about what he should do.

> "Then Melchizedek king of Salem brought out bread and wine; he was the priest of God Most High. And he blessed him and said: 'Blessed be Abram of God Most High, possessor of heaven and earth; and blessed be God Most High, who has

delivered your enemies into your hand.' And he gave him a tithe of all." (Genesis 14:18-20)

Consider these verses in more detail.

1. We know nothing of the family or background of Melchizedek; it is deliberately hidden from us (Hebrews 7:3) and, in his uniqueness, we see him as a type of the Lord Jesus Christ.
2. He was by interpretation king of righteousness and then *after that* king of Salem (peace). This was the essential point for Abraham: God's promises would indeed bring peace to His land, but what Abraham had accomplished could not fulfil this. Righteousness was necessary first; reconciliation with the Lord and the conquest of sin were essential before true, everlasting peace could reign in the land.
3. Melchizedek was a priest. This is the first mention of a priest in scripture, a priesthood that both preceded that of Levi and was pre-eminent to it. He was first of many for there was to be an order, a priesthood, of Melchizedek and this body is developed through the pages of the Bible fulfilled in the priesthood of Christ and those who belong to him. So the very last mention of a priest is found towards the end of Revelation where the members of this order are finally complete:

   > "Blessed and holy is he who has part in the first resurrection. Over such the second death has no power, but they shall be priests of God and of Christ, and shall reign with him a thousand years." (Revelation 20:6)

4. The Lord is described as The Most High God, *El Elyon*, possessor of heaven and earth. A contrast is drawn with Abraham's natural name, Abram, meaning 'father of heights', linked to worship in the ziggurat. The Lord who is above the highest heavens had come down at Babel to confuse the works of men. He is the One who had given Abraham the victory. He is the possessor of all creation and therefore He is the One who will give possession of the

land to Abraham in due time, according to His purpose. He will do it.

How beautifully the Psalmist captured these thoughts as he thought back to Abraham and the promises made to him by the Most High God:

> "Oh, clap your hands, all you peoples! Shout to God with the voice of triumph! For the LORD Most High is awesome; he is a great King over all the earth. He will subdue the peoples under us, and the nations under our feet. He will choose our inheritance for us, the excellence of Jacob whom He loves. God has gone up with a shout, the LORD with the sound of a trumpet. Sing praises to God, sing praises! Sing praises to our King, sing praises! For God is the King of all the earth; sing praises with understanding. God reigns over the nations; God sits on His holy throne. The princes of the people have gathered together, the people of the God of Abraham. For the shields of the earth belong to God; he is greatly exalted." (Psalm 47:1-9)

5. There was a fellowship meal of bread and wine in which both the Lord God and Abraham shared a blessing. In this a principle of the breaking of bread service is established. It is worship linked to the Melchisedek priesthood; it brings the Lord and His people together to share in the blessing that speaks of His purpose to fill the earth with His glory. So David, acting as a Melchizedek king-priest, when he brought the ark to Jerusalem, blessed his people and shared bread and wine with them in the place where Melchizedek blessed Abraham. Each week disciples of the Lord Jesus Christ enter into these things when they share bread and wine in memory of him. As they do this they acknowledge that this is the way in which men and women will be made righteous, looking forward with Abraham to the fulfilment of all the promises.
6. Abraham paid tithes to him. Hebrews tells us that this was an acknowledgement of Melchizedek's greatness.

We are not told in this chapter any more detail of the blessing given but there are hints elsewhere about what took place, particularly in Psalm 133:

> "Behold, how good and how pleasant it is for brethren to dwell together in unity! It is like the precious oil upon the head, running down on the beard, the beard of Aaron, running down on the edge of his garments. It is like the dew of Hermon, descending upon the mountains of Zion; for there the LORD commanded the blessing – life for evermore."
>
> (Psalm 133:1-3)

How Abraham had sought unity with Lot, his brother. He had gone far north to the foothills of Hermon to rescue him. He had brought him back as far as Zion. Probably Lot was there as Melchizedek blessed Abraham and revealed the promise of eternal life. It had been mentioned obliquely in the events of Genesis 13 but now God commanded it. It would happen. Abraham would be there when both righteousness and peace came finally to Zion, the joy of the earth.

Amongst the wonder of these things there is sadness. Lot is not mentioned in connection with them. He returned to Sodom, perhaps seduced by the words of its king.

If this was the case then once again Abraham and Lot are contrasted for Abraham would have nothing at all to do with the king of Sodom. It was a clever request he made to him: 'Give me the people, you take the spoils.' He was prepared to let Abraham have the material wealth gained in the victory but wanted the captives, for ownership of the people meant ownership of their territories; he could be king of the land.

No doubt Abraham remembered the trouble that Pharaoh's gifts had brought him. Strengthened by his worship with Melchizedek he made a solemn vow to accept nothing for himself and in return God would now promise him everything.

21 |

Exceeding great and precious promises

WE saw previously that the structure of these chapters about Abraham is written in a way that focuses our attention on the giving of the covenant in Genesis 14-17 as the central part of God's message to him.

The opening words of Genesis 15 show how this event is linked to those recorded in the previous chapter. Abraham had turned his back on any material reward from his victory and God now promised him something infinitely greater. He had delivered (*magan*) his enemies into his hands and the Lord assured him that He would continue to be his deliverer, his shield (*magen*), throughout his life.

For the first time there is a dialogue between the Lord and Abraham. He was fearful about something; God reassured him and, with infinite patience, answered his fears. I suggest that his worry arose from the departure of Lot. As Abraham and Sarah were childless, Lot had been Abraham's heir and it tells us much about him that he had rejected this position to return to Sodom. In his place Eliezer had become an 'acquired son' (this is the meaning of the word "steward" in the KJV).

Although Abraham was concerned about this lack of a true heir, he was about to learn that God would indeed deliver what He had promised; Abraham would have offspring but they would suffer persecution before they inherited the Promised Land. The covenant promise therefore taught him about these two things, the seed and the land, and God presented it in a way that demanded a response from him.

The Lord makes a promise to Abraham beginning with the words "I am".

Abraham questions God using His name, Lord GOD, Adonai Yahweh.

The Lord reassures him, shows him the stars.

He is promised the seed.

Abraham believes God and it is counted to him for righteousness.

The Lord makes a promise to Abraham beginning with the words "I am".

Abraham questions God using His name, Lord GOD, Adonai Yahweh.

The Lord reassures him showing him a vision.

He is promised the land.[1]

The exceeding great reward

> "After these things the word of the LORD came to Abram in a vision, saying, 'Do not be afraid, Abram. I am your shield, your exceedingly great reward'." (Genesis 15:1)

This is the first mention of "the word of the LORD" in the Bible and it is given through a vision. Once again the Lord revealed His glory to Abraham, perhaps in angelic form, and in this manifestation He revealed an awe-inspiring truth to Abraham and to all who follow him in faith.

God did not say that He would shield Abraham, neither did He say that He would provide a reward. Rather Abraham was told that God *was* these things and the Apostle Peter began his second letter with an explanation of the Lord's words.

> "Grace and peace be multiplied to you in the knowledge of God and of Jesus our Lord, as his divine power has given to us all things that pertain to life and godliness, through the knowledge of him who called us by glory and virtue, by which have been given to us exceedingly great and precious promises, that through these you may be partakers of the

1 This structure is taken from Waltke, page 239.

divine nature, having escaped the corruption that is in the world through lust." (2 Peter 1:2-4)

"I am your exceeding great reward" said God and it was the most exceeding great and precious thing that He could promise Abraham. Not only would he be resurrected to inherit the land for ever, in the life to come he would share the glory of the Lord – sharing, in a way that can scarcely be imagined, not just immortality but His divine nature.

Abraham's response showed his puzzlement. He had been promised children, how could such a wonderful future occur through an adopted heir?

An acquired heir

Becoming an heir in this way was a recognised Middle East custom. A childless man could choose someone to join his household as an adopted son. He would take care of his new parents and their livelihood as they grew older. In return he would inherit their estate.

If the parents later had a son, they could not totally reject the one adopted. He had to receive an inheritance alongside the natural born son. In this Eliezer became a type of the Gentiles who would become heirs with the Lord Jesus Christ through faith.

This was not a response of faithlessness, indeed Abraham called God "Adonai Yahweh", "Sovereign LORD", the first time we meet this title in scripture and the only use of it in Genesis. It was an acknowledgement that, although he could not see how God was going to fulfil His promise, he really believed that He had the power to do it.

This faith is seen on the next occasion we meet this title in scripture. It was on the lips of Moses who broke out in an impromptu prayer to the power of the God who would indeed fulfil His word and take His people into the Promised Land:

> "O Lord GOD, you have begun to show your servant your greatness and your mighty hand, for what god is there in heaven or on earth who can do anything like your works and your mighty deeds?" (Deuteronomy 3:24)

For the first time God now promised Abraham a son, a direct descendant through whom the promises would be fulfilled. Furthermore Abraham's descendants would be a great people, like the stars in the heavens. Previously the promise had been of those who would be like the dust of the earth, but now he is promised a spiritual seed who will shine like the stars for ever and ever (Daniel 12:3).

And he believed (*aman*) *in* the Lord. Of course Abraham believed what God had told him, but he also believed *in* Yahweh, in the Sovereign Lord who had shown him His glory and promised him that he would share in it. The text does not do full justice to the strength of Abraham's commitment to the Lord. One writer describes it as "Abraham was steadfast in the Lord", another that perhaps he spoke a response saying "Amen" as we do at the end of our prayers using a transliterated Hebrew word based on *aman*, to confess our trust that what we have prayed for in faith the Lord will perform.

This is the first time in the Bible that we meet the words "faith" and "righteousness" and they are deliberately introduced together. But why did God wait until this moment to declare Abraham righteous? After all, it was by faith that he left Ur, why did God not declare him righteous at that time? The answer must be that the promise of an heir was an anticipation of the promised seed, the Genesis 3:15 promise fulfilled ultimately in the birth of the Lord Jesus Christ. It is through him that Abraham would be made righteous.

The covenant of promise

It was sometime during the night that God appeared to Abraham and the covenant that followed was not completed until sunset the next day. It was a day in which God spoke frequently to him; indeed it is difficult to think of another day in the Old Testament in which such intense communication from God to man occurs. He spoke four times (verses 7,9,13,18).

The covenant that was made (verse 18, *karath*, literally 'cut') was typical of an agreement enacted between two parties in those days. Animals were sacrificed, divided into two parts and both participants passed between the two. So the presence of the Lord was there, represented in the smoking furnace and the burning lamp as they passed through the two lines of carcasses.

In this covenant God promised Abraham eternal life and inheritance of the land; Abraham promised God steadfast belief in those things and the agreement depended on both being true to their words.

Events reached a climax towards the end of the day between the time "when the sun was going down" and "when the sun went down and it was dark". This was the time of day that became known as "between the two evenings", from the time the sun began to set to sunset. It was the time of day when Passover lambs were killed, the time of the death of the Lord on the cross. It was a time when a deep sleep and a horror of darkness came upon Abraham, a type of death.

He was then told a fascinating prophecy about the trials his descendants would face.

Then God said to Abraham:

Your descendants will be strangers (*ger*, sojourners) in a land that is not theirs.	Jacob and family went down into Egypt to sojourn (*guwr*) there (Genesis 46:6; 47:4).
And will serve them.	The Egyptians made them serve with rigour (Exodus 1:13).
And they will afflict them four hundred years.	Commencing at the birth of Isaac who was afflicted by the son of Hagar the Egyptian.
And also the nation whom they serve I will judge.	I will smite all the firstborn ... I will execute judgment, I am the LORD (Exodus 12:12).

Afterward they shall come out with great possessions.	They took from the Egyptians jewels of silver and gold and spoiled them (Exodus 12:35,36).
But in the fourth generation they shall return here.	The Book of Chronicles shows families coming out in the fifth and sixth generations. Only one family appears to have returned in its fourth generation, that of Kohath (see Exodus 6). His descendants, Moses, Aaron and Miriam were the fourth generation as was Korah. This prophecy was very family specific pointing to Moses, the man who would lead out the Children of Israel from Egypt, and also to Korah who would seek to usurp him believing that he had just as much right to the leadership position.

How remarkably accurate these prophecies were, inspired by the Lord and hence exact in every detail.

They shall come back here

There is a further point to consider. In verse 16 God said that Abraham's descendants would 'come here again': "They shall come back here in the fourth generation" (ESV).

Where was this place and why did God make such a promise? It is Stephen who gives us the answer as he quotes from Genesis 15 in his speech in Acts 7:

> "And the nation to whom they will be in bondage I will judge, said God, and after that they shall come out and serve me in this place." (verse 7)

The place where Stephen stood, "this place", was "this holy place" (Acts 6:13), the temple courtyard on Mount Moriah. This was where Abraham believed God and was accounted righteous. This was the place that was despised and rejected by the Canaanite settlers yet when God passed by He loved it.

> "'When I passed by you again and looked upon you, indeed your time was the time of love; so I spread my wing over you and covered your nakedness. Yes, I swore an oath to you and entered into a covenant with you, and you became mine', says the Lord GOD." (Ezekiel 16:8)

This is the place where God made the covenant with Abraham, in the place He loved. It became the place He chose to put His name; it will become the city of the great King, the joy of the earth. But all that we read about the city of Jerusalem, its unique, privileged position in God's purpose, is because it was the place where a man first believed in Yahweh and was accounted righteous because of his steadfast faith.

I have given

The final statement of the Lord in the cutting of the covenant was a formal statement about ownership of the land. The time would come when it would no longer be possessed by the Canaanite tribes named here but by Abraham's descendants. Look at the difference between the words spoken here and those in chapter 13:

> "For all the land that you see *I will give* to you and to your offspring forever." (Genesis 13:15, ESV)
>
> "To your descendants *I have given* this land, from the river of Egypt to the great river, the River Euphrates." (15:18)

"I will give" is now replaced by "I have given". Abraham inherited nothing before his death but God had now made a solemn, binding covenant and, in the purpose of the Lord, the land was Abraham's even though he has yet to receive it, for God's gifts and calling are without repentance.

In these words about the extent of the kingdom are glimpses of the reign of Christ. It was not until Solomon's time (1 Kings 5:21) that a king ruled from the Wadi-el-Arish (the river of Egypt), on the border of Egypt, to the Euphrates. It was "the royal majesty" of the kingdom of God on earth, the partial fulfilment of the promises to Abraham, for Israel was as "the sand of the sea shore" in number. But it did not last, for Solomon's wisdom was an earthly wisdom (a wisdom also described as "the sand on the sea shore"), and the kingdom was split in two after his death. The boundaries promised to Abraham will not be restored until the Lord comes, with the wisdom from above, and makes it all his own.

> "... the Kenites, the Kenezzites, the Kadmonites, the Hittites, the Perizzites, the Rephaim, the Amorites, the Canaanites, the Girgashites, and the Jebusites." (Genesis 15:19-21)

This is the first list of the tribes of the land of Canaan, those whom Israel would have to dispossess, and it splits into two groups:

1. Kenites – linked to Heber the Kenite, a descendant of Midian and hence from Abraham.
   Kenezzites – descendants of Kenaz who was a grandson of Esau.
2. Kadmonites – origins unknown.
   Hittites – descendants of Heth and hence from Canaan, intermarried with Esau and his family.
   Perizzites – origins unknown.
   Rephaims – giants.
   Amorites – descendants of Canaan: the name is used as a patronymic to describe Canaan's offspring in a general way (Genesis 15:16), perhaps because the name means 'speaker' and relates to a position of authority in the worship of Canaanite gods.
   Canaanites.
   Girgashites – descendants of Canaan.
   Jebusites – descendants of Canaan.

Those dispossessed were either descendants of Abraham, those who chose not to listen to the Gospel and hence were not of the household of faith, or were those who migrated into the land with the descendants of Canaan before Abraham arrived.

It is important to remember that God is not willing that any should perish. Abraham's descendants could learn from him, Isaac or Jacob. The Canaanites had Melchizedek, priest of the Most High God and king of Salem, in their midst and could have listened to him or to Abraham as he witnessed throughout the land,[2] but they did not.

---

2 This was one of the reasons for the commandment to him to walk through the land, just as the Lord Jesus Christ traversed the country preaching the Gospel.

But this list has a greater importance. When the Lord began to reveal His name to Moses in Exodus 3 He introduced Himself as the God of your father, of Abraham, Isaac and Jacob. He was the God who knew the sorrow of His people in Egypt and, just as He had promised Abraham in Genesis 15, He had come to deliver them and to take them to –

> "... a good and large land, to a land flowing with milk and honey, to the place of the Canaanites and the Hittites and the Amorites and the Perizzites and the Hivites and the Jebusites." (Exodus 3:8)

Three times in this chapter the Lord described Himself in this way: the reassurance to Israel that He would indeed take them out of Egypt into Canaan and give them the land was absolutely trustworthy because He had made an unbreakable covenant with Abraham.

Moses quoted these things a number of times to strengthen the faith of the Children of Israel,[3] yet their lack of faith in the promises and the covenant with Abraham was such that they died in the wilderness.

There is a powerful message for us in all of this. Abraham's faith is our faith, an unshakeable belief that the Lord is taking us on a journey through life to His kingdom. The covenant made with Abraham is not just his guarantee but ours also, for the promise by faith in Jesus Christ is given to all those who believe.

---

3 For example: Exodus 3:8; 13:5; 33:2; Deuteronomy 7:1; 20:17.

22 | Hagar and a testing of faith

TIME rolled by: ten years had passed since Abraham and Sarah entered the land, and they still had no children. After the wonderful manifestation of the Lord, and the promise of the seed in Genesis 15, they would have hoped that a son would soon be given to them.

Sarah's words, "the LORD has restrained me from bearing" may have a deeper meaning than a reference to her perpetual barrenness for she was now about seventy-six years old and past the age of childbearing. God's promise was for Abraham to have a son and it appeared that she would not be the mother. Yet from the beginning, the promise had been that God's purpose would be fulfilled through a man and his wife. Adam and Eve had been blessed together; when Abraham left Ur he took "Sarah his wife" and time and again she is described in this way, including here in Genesis 16. Both of them were needed, together, as a vital part of God's purpose.

Is it significant that, in all that follows, we are not told of any prayer for guidance. They had seen the Lord's patience, and willingness to be questioned about His purpose, in the events of Genesis 15. However, it appears that memories of this were set aside by Sarah; she was consumed by the desire for a son by any means.

There is a link back to similar behaviour seen when they went down into Egypt. Both events showed a desire to work out God's purpose themselves rather than wait in faith for His solution.

- **Chapter 12:** Abraham had been blessed and promised *the land*. Yet after he arrived there it was barren, cursed with a famine. They went down to Egypt and brought back handmaidens, including Hagar.
- **Chapter 16:** Abraham had been blessed and promised *a seed*. Yet Sarah was barren and gave Hagar, her handmaiden to Abraham. In doing this she became despised (*qalal*) in her handmaiden's eyes.

Through the events that unfold in Genesis 16-17 we see both Abraham and Sarah completely humbled, brought to a realisation that there was nothing more that they could do but trust absolutely in the One who would reveal Himself to them as El Shaddai, the Almighty God.

Sarah and Hagar

> "Now Sarai, Abram's wife, had borne him no children. And she had an Egyptian maidservant whose name was Hagar. So Sarai said to Abram, 'See now, the LORD has restrained me from bearing children. Please, go in to my maid; perhaps I shall obtain children by her'. And Abram heeded the voice of Sarai. Then Sarai, Abram's wife, took Hagar her maid, the Egyptian, and gave her to her husband Abram to be his wife, after Abram had dwelt ten years in the land of Canaan. So he went in to Hagar, and she conceived. And when she saw that she had conceived, her mistress became despised in her eyes."
>
> (Genesis 16:1-4)

Throughout this chapter the way people are described is significant. Sarah is Abraham's wife, emphasising her position in God's purpose. Neither she nor her husband refer to Hagar by name; she is merely called a handmaid, telling us of her subservient position. Hagar is "Hagar the Egyptian", an appellation that stays with her to the very last mention of her in Genesis.[1] She came out of Egypt and spiritually never left it;

1 The importance of such labels is seen elsewhere in the Bible. For example, on every occasion but one, Michal is described as the daughter of Saul, rather than as the wife of David – her allegiance was to her father not to her husband.

although part of the household of faith, she never fully embraced it.

Sarah's words to Abraham expressed her desire, "perhaps I can build a family through her" (NIV). It was her own position that consumed her, a frame of mind seen later in the wives of her grandson. Although she gave Hagar to Abraham as a wife, it appears that she was never accepted in this role. In Abraham's mind he only ever had one wife, Sarah, and later we see him sending away all his concubines (Genesis 25:6). Throughout, Hagar remained Sarah's property.

It was like Eden all over again: Adam had listened to his wife and now Abraham was swayed by Sarah. The decision made brought not a blessing but a curse and the trouble that occurred had consequences for the generations that followed.

Sarah deserves our sympathy though and wives will understand her anguish better than husbands! Barrenness is called a reproach by childless women in scripture; the word was used by Rachel and Elizabeth (Genesis 30:23; Luke 1:35) and Rachel also used the word, *cherpah*, meaning scorn. Not only did childlessness bring despair that a wife was not providing the next generation for the family, it sometimes brought harsh and scornful treatment from other women who despised them. Perhaps Hannah is the prime example of this.

> **When childless:** "To Hannah he (Elkanah) would give a double portion, for he loved Hannah, although the LORD had closed her womb. And her rival also provoked her severely, to make her miserable, because the LORD had closed her womb."
>
> (1 Samuel 1:5,6)
>
> **After Samuel had been born:** "Hannah prayed and said: 'My heart rejoices in the LORD; my horn is exalted in the LORD. I smile at my enemies, because I rejoice in your salvation. No one is holy like the LORD, for there is none besides you, nor is there any rock like our God. Talk no more so very proudly; let no arrogance come from your mouth, for the LORD is the God of knowledge; and by him actions are weighed ... Even

the barren has borne seven, and she who has many children has become feeble.'" (2:1-5)

When Hagar knew that she was pregnant, Sarah was seen by her as despised (*qalal*, despised, cursed). The lack of a son was now clearly understood as Sarah's problem, not Abraham's. Nothing but strife now occurred and the family was torn by quarrels. Abraham was accused of favouring Hagar because she was pregnant, Hagar despised her mistress, Sarah treated her maidservant harshly and told Abraham to sort it out. Abraham left it all in Sarah's hands. The book of Proverbs sums up such folly:

"For three things the earth is perturbed, yes, for four it cannot bear up ... a maidservant who succeeds her mistress."
(Proverbs 30:21-23)

For the first time in scripture we now meet the Angel of the Lord and in his words we see the compassion and patience of God shown to oppressed Hagar as she made her way back towards Egypt. He said to her:

"Return to your mistress, and submit yourself under her hand."

Hagar had left the household of faith. If she was to be part of God's promises she must return even though it meant accepting Sarah's severe treatment.

"I will multiply your descendants exceedingly, so that they shall not be counted for multitude."

She too would have many descendants – note that God did not promise her a great nation but a miscellany of peoples.

"Behold, you are with child, and you shall bear a son. You shall call his name Ishmael, because the LORD has heard your affliction." (Genesis 16:11)

What words of reassurance these were. Sarah had made it clear that any son born would be hers, one she would take to build her family. Not so! indicated the Angel. *You* are pregnant, *you* will have a son, *you* will choose his name and these things will occur because of *your* ill-treatment. The Lord had heard – was it Hagar's prayers that had come up before Him?

> "He shall be a wild man (Hebrew, 'a wild ass of a man'); his hand shall be against every man, and every man's hand against him. And he shall dwell in the presence of all his brethren." (verse 12)

A wild ass – it was the most stubborn and untameable of animals, the animal written about in the Old Testament as typifying human nature (Job 11:12; Jeremiah 2:24). What a contrast there is when we take this figure into the New Testament for we read of our Lord entering Jerusalem riding a colt, the foal of an ass, which had never been ridden by a man. Nobody had yet tried to tame this animal so that it could be safely ridden; no man had ever tamed and overcome his own human nature. Yet the Lord sat astride this ass, which was subject to him, as he meekly entered the city where he would give up his life in absolute subjection to his Father.

In today's world we see the accuracy of the Angel's words about Ishmael's descendants. They are the Arab peoples, living in hostility to Abraham's true seed in the land of Israel and in the surrounding nations.

Hagar and the LORD God

Hagar had been a member of Abraham's household during the events of Genesis 15. She would have known that the Lord had appeared to Abraham once again. He must have told his family the promise made, that in some wonderful way He would share His nature with those who shared Abraham's faith in Him.

As we have seen, she was urged by the Angel of the Lord to return that she might be part of these things. Yet her son would be called Ishmael, 'El hears' not Ishmaiah, 'Yah hears'; "she called the name of the *LORD* who spoke to her, 'You are a *God* (El) of seeing'" (Genesis 16:13).

Hagar was like many people today. The word of the *Lord* had been shared with her but she had accepted it only as a message about *God*. The greatness of His being, the promises from the Adonai Yahweh of Abraham, had not touched her heart and would not touch that of her son. Everyone who lived with Abraham was taught the Gospel, commanded by him to keep the way of the Lord, but not everyone accepted it fully and, ultimately, those who did not were sent away. Hagar never understood that the purpose of the Lord was that the world might know and acknowledge that He whose name alone was Yahweh is the Most High God over all the earth.

Thirteen silent years

> "Abram was eighty-six years old when Hagar bore Ishmael to Abram. When Abram was ninety-nine years old, the LORD appeared to Abram ..." (Genesis 16:16–17:1)

A further thirteen years now passed and they are presented to us as silent years. Did the Lord not speak to Abraham during them, for no interaction with him is mentioned?

What was God waiting for that was not yet present in Abraham's life?

Genesis 25 tells us of other relationships that Abraham made. He took Keturah and she bore six sons to him.

> "And Abraham gave all that he had to Isaac. But Abraham gave gifts to the sons of the concubines which Abraham had; and while he was still living he sent them eastward, away from Isaac his son, to the country of the east." (Genesis 25:5,6)

He gave gifts to his concubines; there was therefore at least one other woman and they were not fully his wives, as was Sarah, but his concubines. Although they are mentioned at this time in his life, when Isaac was a fully mature man, they must have been taken by him much earlier.

The Chronicles record puts the birth order of Abraham's children as this:

> "The sons of Abraham were Isaac and Ishmael. These are their genealogies: the firstborn of Ishmael was ... these were the sons of Ishmael. Now the sons born to Keturah, Abraham's concubine, were ... all these were the children of Keturah. And Abraham begot Isaac." (1 Chronicles 1:28-34)

Isaac would be born by the miraculous intervention of the Lord in the lives of both Abraham and Sarah. He was one born out of due time, the last son of his father. It is unlikely that Abraham would use his God-given, renewed powers to father more children. When then were they born? The most probable time was during these thirteen years; they were conceived in acts, not of faith, but of the flesh and the Lord was quiet whilst all these things took place.

23

Be still and know that I am God

WE know from the Letter to the Romans that Abraham had reached a crisis in his life. He was now ninety-nine years old; Sarah was ninety. She was past the age of childbearing (cf. chapter 18:11) and he was now impotent: naturally speaking his days of fathering children were over and the children of his concubines would be his last ones. It was over fourteen years since the covenant had been made with him and as yet there was no sign that he and Sarah would have a son.

One of Abraham's strengths was his willingness to turn faith into works; he was a man of action. But his willingness for instant action also led him into trouble – going down into Egypt, taking Hagar, both had brought nothing but distress to him and his family.

And now he was completely humbled, he could do absolutely nothing to ensure the fulfilment of God's promises through a son born to Sarah.

What would we expect to see in him in this situation – despair, a wavering of faith? In fact his behaviour was exactly the opposite for Paul wrote:

> "For the promise that he would be the heir of the world was not to Abraham or to his seed through the law, but through the righteousness of faith. For if those who are of the law are heirs, faith is made void and the promise made of no effect, because the law brings about wrath; for where there is no law there is no transgression. Therefore it is of faith that it might be according to grace, so that the promise might be sure to all

> the seed, not only to those who are of the law, but also to those who are of the faith of Abraham ... who, contrary to hope, in hope believed, so that he became the father of many nations, according to what was spoken, 'So shall your descendants be'. And not being weak in faith, he did not consider his own body, already dead (since he was about a hundred years old), and the deadness of Sarah's womb. He did not waver at the promise of God through unbelief, but was strengthened in faith, giving glory to God, and being fully convinced that what he had promised he was also able to perform. And therefore 'it was accounted to him for righteousness'." (Romans 4:13-22)

With the exception of the faith of the Lord Jesus Christ, this is possibly the most wonderful confession of faith in the Bible. Abraham had been completely humbled by the changes to his body, and the effect of them on his mind was to bring him to a state of total trust in the Lord. He could not see how God would fulfil the promise about a seed, yet the Lord had made a covenant with him and he had an unshakeable conviction that what God had promised He would certainly perform. He had finally learned to be still and let the Lord take control, and God now did just that.

This sequence of events is important. It was not that a humbled Abraham listened eagerly to God and believed what He said. Rather a humbled Abraham still believed in hope that God would do what He had covenanted, even though he did not know how. Because of this faith, the Lord then appeared to him and spoke as He did. Faith came first and once again he was seen as righteous in God's sight.[1]

I am Almighty God

Once again the Lord appeared to Abraham in a vision:

> "The LORD appeared to Abram and said to him, 'I am Almighty God; walk before me and be blameless. And I will make

1 The New Testament quotes Genesis 15:6 three times and on each occasion it applies the quotation to a different period of Abraham's life. Galatians 3 to Genesis 15; Romans 4 to Genesis 17; James 2 to Genesis 22. From these we see that it was the *ongoing* faith in action that brought God's righteousness upon Abraham.

my covenant between me and you, and will multiply you exceedingly'. Then Abram fell on his face, and God talked with him, saying: 'As for me, behold, my covenant is with you, and you shall be a father of many nations. No longer shall your name be called Abram, but your name shall be Abraham; for I have made you a father of many nations.'" (Genesis 17:1-5)

For the first time the Lord spoke as Almighty God, El Shaddai, the title that was also known and understood by Isaac and Jacob[2] through Abraham's teaching. Each of them saw the Lord as the God who had the power to enact what He had promised[3] and each associated the ideas of blessing, being fruitful and multiplying their seed, with El Shaddai.

This power and determination of God was shown in the way He spoke to Abraham. Fourteen times in the chapter we see Him expressing His intent and it was a resolve to fulfil the covenant already made (see Genesis 15).

He began:

"I will make my covenant between me and you (Abraham)."

And ended:

"My covenant I will establish with Isaac."

What a wonderful picture this is, a contrast between the total inability of Abraham to achieve what he had been promised and the infinite power of the one true God, the Almighty, who would give life to the dead bodies of Abraham and Sarah that Isaac may be born. In acknowledgement of this Abraham was commanded to do two things.

He was to walk before God and Micah explains the meaning of this. It involves a rejection of self and a complete acceptance of God's ways, for how can two walk together unless they be agreed?

"He has shown you, O man, what is good; and what does the LORD require of you but to do justly, to love mercy, and to walk humbly with your God?" (Micah 6:8)

---

2 Genesis 28:3; 35:11; 43:14; 48:3; 49:25.

3 Paul portrays the Almighty God in this way in Romans 4; "What he had promised he was able to perform".

He was to be blameless (*tamiym*) and the word is translated elsewhere as complete, without blemish, perfect. God's call to Abraham was for his commitment to the covenant to be whole-hearted, the bedrock of his life. James had the example of Abraham in his mind when he wrote:

> "My brethren, count it all joy when you fall into various trials, knowing that the testing of your faith produces patience. But let patience have its perfect work, that you may be perfect and complete, lacking nothing." (James 1:2-4)

If Abraham behaved like this then God would put into action the things He had promised when He made the covenant with him. We saw that this was an agreement between two parties; each had to commit to it for it to be effective. God now called on Abraham to deliver his part of the agreement.

And once more, what He asked of him was faith, a complete and rounded faith. Perhaps Abraham's mind went back to the words written of Noah who was "perfect in his generation and walked with God". Just as God then worked through one man, Noah, now He would work through the one man He had called, Abraham, and he had to show his faith in the way he lived, walking before God and so giving honour to Him.

Abraham's complete acceptance of this was shown in his response. He twice fell on his face before the Lord in complete subjection to His will. Many years later the promised seed, the night before his death, began his hours of prayer on his knees and then fell on his face before his Father as he showed the perfection of his faith, "Not my will, but yours, be done".

I will make your name great

From the beginning, the commandment of the Lord had been to be fruitful, multiply and fill the earth (with a Godly seed) that His glory might fill the earth in His chosen people. The God of glory then appeared to Abraham, when the Lord called him from Ur, with the first in a series of promises that progressively showed him how this purpose would be accomplished.

Later a covenant had been made on the occasion of another appearance of the Lord to Abraham (Genesis 15). At that time God promised him an exceeding great reward, described by the Apostle Peter as exceeding great and precious promises to share the divine nature. Now his change of name was linked to that calling and covenantal promise.

Abram ('father of heights') became Abraham ('father of a multitude'), the father of those who would share the same covenantal promise of the divine nature, made like their Lord. "I will make your name great" God had said to Abraham and the meaning of this was now clear. He would become the spiritual father of a multitude who would stand before the Lamb at the time of his return (Revelation 7:9), sharing the glory of God (Revelation 21:11), the divine nature, as foretold in these promises.

Yet perhaps we see something more in this name change. Abram became Abraham, אַבְרָם became אַבְרָהָם and just one letter was added to make this change, the fifth letter of the Hebrew alphabet, ה.

This is the shape of the blood painted on the doorposts and lintels of the Israelite houses in Egypt on Passover night, a reminder that the shedding of blood of the Lamb was essential that these wonderful promises made to Abraham might be fulfilled.

The everlasting covenant

> "I have made you a father of many nations ... and I will make nations of you."

This is the first time that "nations" are mentioned in the promises to Abraham. Although there would be a natural fulfilment through the children of his concubines, Paul makes it clear in Galatians 3 that it was written of the Gentiles who could become part of spiritual Israel through faith.

> "I will make you exceedingly fruitful."

Abraham and Sarah would have just one son, one seed, yet through this seed Abraham would become fruitful for "if you are Christ's then are you Abraham's seed and heirs according to the promise". Both Adam and Noah had been commanded "to be fruitful and multiply" as part of God's purpose, yet ultimately both of them had failed for the world was filled with people but not with a Godly seed. Now Abraham was told that God would make him exceedingly fruitful. The Lord's purpose, that men should be fruitful, multiply, fill the earth and have dominion over it, would only be achieved through His miraculous intervention in providing a seed, initially as Abraham and Sarah's only son but ultimately the Lord Jesus Christ, His only begotten one.

"Kings shall come from you."

The rulers who were natural descendants of Abraham's concubines are described in Genesis as dukes or princes. Far greater are those who are his spiritual descendants and who will receive the many crowns that the Lord Jesus Christ will bring with him. They will live and reign with him for a thousand years in his kingdom (Revelation 20:4).

> "And I will establish my covenant between me and you and your descendants after you in their generations, for an everlasting covenant, to be God to you and your descendants after you." (Genesis 17:7)

It is these words that call forth throughout the scriptures the description of the Lord God as "the God of Abraham, Isaac, and Jacob, the God of our fathers". Whenever we read of Him in these words we can rejoice that we too are part of this covenant, given by El Shaddai, for:

> "Abraham's God is our God
> And Isaac's God is ours
> Ours is the God of Jacob
> With His almighty powers." (Hymn 238)

> "Also I give to you and your descendants after you the land in which you are a stranger, all the land of Canaan, as an everlasting possession." (Genesis 17:8)

For the first time the land of inheritance is named. God has progressively revealed details of it to Abraham as their relationship has developed through faith.

- A land I will show you (12:1).
- Unto your seed will I give this land (12:7).
- All the land you can see, to you will I give it (13:15).
- Unto your seed have I given this land, from the river of Egypt to the river Euphrates (15:19).
- The whole land of Canaan (17:8).

Circumcision of the heart

Abraham had to be circumcised. Every male member of his household and of his descendants had also to undergo this operation. It was an act of complete humiliation before the Lord, acknowledging that he was no longer capable of procreation and that only God could bring about the birth of the seed. His act of circumcision was a public acknowledgement of this, a cutting off of part of his body that was as good as dead. It was a sign for him of a greater cutting off, an abrogation of self-will, and this was known by Israel from the beginning. Consider these words of Moses to the generation about to enter the land.

> "And now, Israel, what does the LORD your God require of you, but to fear the LORD your God, to walk in all his ways and to love him, to serve the LORD your God with all your heart and with all your soul, and to keep the commandments of the LORD and his statutes which I command you today for your good? Indeed heaven and the highest heavens belong to the LORD your God, also the earth with all that is in it. The LORD delighted only in your fathers, to love them; and he chose their descendants after them, you above all peoples, as it is this day. Therefore circumcise the foreskin of your heart, and be stiff-necked no longer." (Deuteronomy 10:12-16)

It was this, said Paul (Romans 2:28), which defined a true Jew, a true descendant of Abraham – one whose heart was touched by the grace of God, whose faith in the promises was that of Abraham and who did not depend on the Law. How ironical that in the days of the New Testament, Jews were proud of circumcision not humbled by it. It was a sign of their superiority over the Gentiles; they were God's people, physically descended from their father, Abraham, and their salvation was assured by their lineage. How wrong they were!

Abraham, Sarah and Ishmael

Sarah's name was also changed by God. No longer was she Sarai and the change involved the same additional letter and spiritual meaning as the change to her husband's name. For the first time she too was blessed by God and would become the mother of kings.

At this Abraham fell prostrate again before the Lord and laughed in sheer wonder at what had been said. This was not a laugh of incredulity for "he staggered not at the promises in unbelief" but one of absolute joy at what he had been told. What God had said was beyond human comprehension yet it must be true for it was Almighty God who had spoken.

Furthermore the connection between his laughter and the naming of Isaac is such that this must be an act of faith. He laughed (*tsachaq*) and so his son would be called Isaac, 'he laughs' (*Yitschaq*).

Yet Abraham's joy was tempered with sadness that Ishmael was not the chosen seed. God's command to Abraham had been "walk before me" and the man now echoed this in his plea, "O that Ishmael may live before you". Was there an understanding that this boy, now thirteen years old and approaching manhood, had listened to his mother rather than his father and would never develop the spiritual mind essential for those who would be part of the covenant?

Nevertheless he would become a great nation and the twelve princes he begat are mentioned in Genesis 25.

Once again we see Abraham as a man of action, faith put into practice without delay for it was the self-same day when he and all the men of his household were circumcised. It is a remarkable comment on his authority and powers of persuasion that this occurred. He had taken 318 trained men north after Lot; all of these and all of the male children were now circumcised in obedience to him and God's reaction to this is shown in chapter 18.

24 |

The visit of the angels

CHAPTERS 18-19 of the book of Genesis conclude the record of Abraham and Lot. Abraham brought Lot out of Ur to the Promised Land, brought him out of Egypt back into the land, rescued him from Chedorlaomer and brought him back to Salem.

However, God would not now allow him to rescue Lot from Sodom.

These chapters are presented as a contrast between Abraham and Lot, between Abraham's household and Lot's, between Sarah and Lot's wife, between the reactions of the two households to the Gospel and the visiting angels.

The events took place very soon after the circumcision of Abraham's household; he was ninety-nine years of age when that happened and he was one hundred when Isaac was born. Yet now, at the fall of Sodom, Sarah was not yet pregnant. Furthermore, everything we see in these two chapters occurred within a twenty-four hour period.

Once again, laying out events in a chiasmus helps us to focus on the central point.[1]

Abraham's visitors look towards Sodom;
    God tells Abraham about His judgements on Sodom;
        Abraham pleads for Sodom;
            The angels travel to Sodom;

1 Taken from G. Wenham, *Word Biblical Commentary, Genesis 16-50*, page 41.

Lot and his visitors suffer at the hands of the evil inhabitants of Sodom who reject his appeal;

The destruction of Sodom is announced.

Lot's sons-in-law reject his appeal;

The angels and people depart from Sodom;

Lot pleads for Zoar;

Sodom and Gomorrah are destroyed;

Abraham looks towards Sodom.

Entertaining angels unawares

> "Do not forget to entertain strangers, for by so doing some have unwittingly entertained angels." (Hebrews 13:2)

When the writer to the Hebrews wrote these words he clearly had the events of these two chapters in mind. But was he thinking about Abraham or Lot or both? Each was a generous host but they welcomed their guests differently.

Lot gave a courteous welcome to the two angels, 'My lords, stay at your servant's house' and the title he used, *adon*, is used only of men in Genesis, Lot was unaware of the true identity of his visitors.

However, Abraham's welcome was different, 'My Lord (*adonai*), if I have found grace in your sight, do not pass by', and the title he used is only ever used of the Lord God. It was the Lord who appeared to Abraham, the Lord who later spoke to him as the Angel of the Lord and there are clues suggesting he was aware of His identity from the start.

- He "lifted up his eyes", the first of the three occasions he did this and the other two clearly have a spiritual significance to them (Genesis 22:4,13).
- He bowed himself towards the ground before them and the text uses a word that is translated nearly a hundred times as "worship" in men's approach to the Lord God.
- Although there were three men, Abraham understood that they had a special leader whom he addressed specifically: "My Lord ... your sight ... your servant."

The meal, prepared by both Abraham and Sarah was incredibly generous. A prize calf was selected out of his herds and slain. Sarah was told to take three measures, about twenty-two litres, of fine flour to make cakes. Elsewhere fine (*coleth*) meal is only ever used to describe that offered to the Lord as part of the sacrifices on the altar – perhaps another clue that the visitors were recognised as angels. This was an enormous amount of meal for three people. To put its size into context, three *seahs*, measures, were equivalent to ten omers and an omer was the amount of manna gathered each day in the wilderness for one adult.

This hospitality was a fellowship meal which bought forth a Gospel message from the angels. It was an example that would be followed by the Lord Jesus Christ in his ministry as he took a blessing and a message of hope into the homes of those who hosted him. The message the angels brought was confirmation that Sarah would bear a son, yet it is clear that the miraculous renewal of vitality that would come upon both husband and wife, and that would restore Sarah's staggering beauty, had not yet occurred, for Sarah still had doubts.

> "Then the LORD said, 'I will surely return to you about this time next year, and Sarah your wife will have a son'. Now Sarah was listening at the entrance to the tent, which was behind him. Abraham and Sarah were already old and well advanced in years, and Sarah was past the age of childbearing. So Sarah laughed to herself as she thought, 'After I am worn out and my master is old, will I now have this pleasure?'"
>
> (Genesis 18:10-12, NIV)

Note the emphasis on the agedness and tiredness of them both. "I am worn out", said Sarah, and her laugh was indeed an incredulous one unlike that of Abraham previously.

It was the Angel of the Lord who replied for the answer came from the Lord with all of His authority behind it.

> "Is anything too hard (*pala*, marvellous, wonderful) for the LORD? At the appointed time I will return to you, according

> to the time of life, and Sarah shall have a son."
> (Genesis 18:14)

"Is anything too hard …?" No, of course not: it's a rhetorical question, the Lord can do anything. But when this word, *pala*, is used of His acts, it is applied in a special way for it is linked to His loving kindness, His covenant love:

> "Ah, Lord GOD! Behold, you have made the heavens and the earth by your great power and outstretched arm. There is nothing too hard (*pala*) for you. You show lovingkindness to thousands … the Great, the Mighty God, whose name is the LORD of hosts." (Jeremiah 32:17,18)

These things are indeed wonderful and should fill us with awe at what He has done for us for when we read of the one who has become our salvation, the headstone of the corner of God's spiritual temple; we are told that this is the Lord's doing and it is marvellous (*pala*) in our eyes (Psalm 118:22,23). The greatest thing ever done by our Lord God began with another miraculous birth, that of the Seed of Abraham through whom reconciliation comes to all who believe as did Abraham.

Intercession for Lot

The angels came with a twofold purpose. The first was now accomplished, a set time had been given for the birth of Isaac. Perhaps from this occasion onwards the renewal of Abraham's and Sarah's bodies began and they would wait with anticipation for the birth of their child.

But the angels had also a more sombre task. The Lord would no longer tolerate the evil of Sodom. Firstly we read of His musing – should He tell Abraham about it?

> "Shall I hide from Abraham what I am doing? … for I have known him, in order that he may command his children and his household after him, that they keep the way of the LORD, to do righteousness and justice, that the LORD may bring to Abraham what He has spoken to him." (Genesis 18:17-19)

Of course the Lord knew that Abraham would behave in this way. He had commanded his children and household to be circumcised and they had done this on the self-same day that the Lord had given him the instruction. In the beginning, man had been put in Eden to "keep" it. When sin entered the world the responsibility for 'keeping' had been taken from man and given to the angels for the Cherubim were placed at the entrance to the Garden to "keep the way to the tree of life". Now the Lord had found a man in whom He trusted. "I know him ... they [will] keep the way of the LORD to do righteousness." Abraham could indeed be trusted with the news now imparted.

> "And the LORD said, 'Because the outcry against Sodom and Gomorrah is great, and because their sin is very grave, I will go down now and see whether they have done altogether according to the outcry against it that has come to me; and if not, I will know'." (Genesis 18:20,21)

The word used here, *zaaq*, almost always means a cry for help in times of distress. Who then cried to God about the wickedness of Sodom? It must have been Lot, daily distressed by the evil he saw, as the Apostle Peter tells us.

Once again we see the conundrum of Lot's life. The wickedness of Sodom was overwhelming, as it had been in Noah's day: "every inclination of the thoughts of [their] heart was only evil all the time" (NIV). And Lot had been unable to do anything to change this. He was a righteous man and we can imagine him trying to share his belief in the Lord. Now he had been utterly rejected and in despair he had cried to God to intervene to stop this godlessness. But he stayed in the city.

As God came down to Babel in judgement, so now He went down to Sodom, acting through two of the angels. But it was the Angel of the Lord who remained and before whom Abraham stood. His actions were those of a priest, interceding with the Lord for his people – the fervent, effectual prayer of a righteous man. It is obvious from what follows that he knew what had happened to Lot and his family over the years. He bargained with God to save Sodom if there were some righteous people (by definition, those who have faith in the covenant promises) in the city. He started with fifty. Was that the number of people who went down with Lot to Sodom originally? He ended at ten, the number of Lot's family, and we can construct this number from the details in chapter 19.

- Lot and his wife (2);
- A married daughter and her husband (2);
- Two unmarried (but betrothed) daughters (2);
- Two married sons with their wives (4).

It is painful to see Abraham's reasoning. He thought that, even if those who went with Lot had turned their backs on the Lord, surely he will have commanded his family to keep God's way.

And of course not all did. In this we see the contrast between Abraham and his family and Lot and his, leading to the disaster that followed.

25

The tragedy of Lot

IT was a journey of about twenty miles from Mamre to Sodom and the two angels arrived in the evening. Whilst Abraham had "lifted up his eyes" when meeting the three who came to him, recognising that his was a meeting with messengers from God, Lot merely saw two men.

He was seated in the gate, a position of authority and power – what a journey he had made. When he first arrived at Sodom he pitched his tent near the city but now he had a house and a position within it. He arrived as a sojourner, a stranger, but was accused by the men of the city; "he must always be acting the judge" (Genesis 19:9, Rotherham). Now he sat in the seat of the scornful, mocked daily for his beliefs and distraught by it. Peter sums it up for us:

> "[God turned] the cities of Sodom and Gomorrah into ashes, condemned them to destruction, making them an example to those who afterward would live ungodly; and delivered righteous Lot, who was oppressed (*worn down*) by the filthy conduct of the wicked (for that righteous man, dwelling among them, tormented his righteous soul from day to day by seeing and hearing their lawless deeds) ..." (2 Peter 2:6-8)

It is difficult to understand Lot's thinking. He had been there many years, long enough to marry a woman of the city, and have children of marriageable age. Daily he suffered because of the evil, yet for economic reasons he would not leave. When they would not accept his teaching he should have left and shaken off the dust from his feet as a witness (Matthew 10:14,15). Even though he was a righteous man, was there a stubborn pride at work? He had made his choice and he would not acknowledge that it had been a mistake. It would have taken an act of humility to accept this and return to the security of Abraham's household and that was a move he would not make.

Now he would lose everything.

The evil of Sodom

The sexual depravity and violence of Sodom is presented to us in chapter 19 but the Bible tells us much more about its inhabitants. Through the prophets,[1] the Lord later warned Israel about its own behaviour; it was becoming like Sodom and from these passages we can construct a picture of the evil that was there. Sodom's inhabitants were:

- Prosperous and proud of what they had achieved;
- Indolent;
- Oppressors of the poor and needy;
- Neglectful of the fatherless and widows;
- Adulterous (as well as sexual perverts);
- Consumed by wickedness;
- Dishonest;
- Worshippers of Baal.

This was no place for a righteous man.

Was Lot alone in the gate or were there others present who were not interested in providing hospitality for the two visitors? He was horrified when his offer was refused and they suggested staying in the street all night; he was fully aware of the risks that entailed. In this he was being tested. Of course the angels knew what Sodom was like; they had been sent there by the Lord because the sins of the people were very grave.

Lot insisted that they entered his house: he *pressed* them – the same word is used in verse 9 of the inhabitants *pressing* to enter his house, suggesting a physical action. He would not take "No" for an answer.

---

1 Isaiah 1:10-17; Jeremiah 23:14; Ezekiel 16:49.

He prepared food for them, unleavened bread, but strangely his wife played no part in this, unlike Sarah's help of Abraham when the angels visited them. This is the first mention of leaven, in any form, in the Bible and it is difficult to see its significance. Perhaps the meal was prepared in haste but when we think of the way unleavened bread was a part of the urgent Exodus from the enmity of Egypt, was there an understanding by Lot that the dangers for the angels were such that they must leave at the earliest possible opportunity?

The scene that follows paints a picture of the absolute evil of the city. Every man was involved; they refused Lot's desperate offer of his unmarried but betrothed daughters. They were intent on homosexual gang rape and Lot was threatened also: "We will deal worse with you than with them." They had completely forgotten that they had been saved by association with Lot fifteen years earlier when Abraham had rescued them from Chedorlaomer. Now they had another opportunity. Abraham had prayed for the city, the angels had come for Lot and whoever he had in the city, yet none of them were interested.

Perhaps the saddest moment in the whole episode is when Lot faced the mob and called them "brethren". "Let there be no strife between us for we are brethren" (Genesis 13:8), Abraham had said to him before they separated after the arguments between their herdsmen. It is a term used throughout the Bible of those who live together in unity (Psalm 133), yet Lot was prepared to call such evil men his brothers and give them his daughters to placate them and buy peace.

Just as Lot had pressed the angels to enter his house and had shut the door, they now do the same, pulling him in, shutting the door and confounding the men outside with blindness.[2]

The event that followed is one of the dramas of the Old Testament. The angels revealed to Lot the imminent destruction of the city. He went out of his house, found the fiancés of his

2 The unusual word for "blindness" is only used one other time in the Old Testament, in 2 Kings 6:18, where God again protected His people by striking their enemies in this way.

daughters and urged them to leave but they ridiculed him. Lot was torn apart by the splitting of his family. He lingered and the angels seized him, his wife and daughters by the hands and led them out. What a picture of the goodness and severity of God this is. The Lord would not tolerate Sodom's wickedness any longer yet, because He remembered Abraham's intercession, He was merciful to Lot in spite of his prevarication. Although he had asked God to spare the city for ten righteous people, thinking that Lot's family would believe, the Lord knew what the outcome would be. Only two angels with four hands were sent for only four people would respond.

Yet even now Lot dallied. It seems that the angels led them out of the city, rescued them from its evil but they then had to make their own escape and strict instructions were given about not looking back, not lingering further. The word "escape", *malat*, is used four times in these verses and is a word play on "Lot".

Lot's response to their urging is remarkable:

> "... your servant has found favour (grace) in your sight, and you have increased your mercy which you have shown me by saving my life." (Genesis 19:19)

What painful honesty Lot showed. Here is his acknowledgement of his error of living in Sodom and his gratitude to the Lord for His compassion in providing a way of escape. He understood that he did not deserve the Lord's mercy, yet like Noah he had found grace in the sight of the Lord.

In these events we finally see why the Apostle Peter laid such emphasis on Lot's righteousness. Lot had never lost his belief in the Lord and in the promises made to Abraham in Ur. Now he believed what the angels said and in faith was obedient to their call. The judgement of his world had come and he was prepared to abandon everything he had worked for, all of the wealth that he had accumulated, and leave immediately with the angels. Faith without works is dead and in the choice he made, leaving all behind, Lot showed that ultimately his faith transcended everything else in his life; all of it was meaningless in the day of the judgement of the Lord.

Lot's wife looked back, not just a glance but a lingering regard for what she was leaving behind, and was destroyed. Like Lot, she was leaving behind her family and her community but she could not make the choice that her husband did.

The days of Noah and the days of Lot

There are many similarities between the description of Noah's day and that of Lot, both societies being unacceptable to God.

Genesis 6	**Genesis 18,19**
Then the Lord saw that the wickedness (*ra*, evil) of man was great in the earth, The earth also was corrupt before God, and the earth was filled with violence.	The outcry against Sodom and Gomorrah was great, and their sin was very grave.
	They did wickedly (*ra*, evil) and were intent on violence.
So God looked upon the earth, and indeed it was corrupt; for all flesh had corrupted their way on the earth.	The whole city was involved in this wickedness.
And God said to Noah, "The end of all flesh has come before me, for the earth is filled with violence through them; and behold, I will destroy them with the earth".	The Lord will destroy this city.
Enter in to the ark, you and all your house.	Lot was told to take his family out of this place.
When they entered the ark, the Lord was there with them; the door was shut and could not be opened.	The angels pulled Lot into the house; the door was shut and could not be opened.
It was done the selfsame day.	When the morning came Lot had to leave immediately.

In Luke 17 the Lord Jesus Christ directs us to these times, the days of Noah and the days of Lot. They were full of wickedness and rejection of the way of the Lord and so it will be in the last days before Jesus returns.

But the Lord's teaching to his disciples emphasised that these days, this period, will be followed by the day in which he will be revealed and he drew the analogy between the suddenness of his coming and the urgency of the calls to both Noah and Lot. Both had to respond the same day that they were called: Noah was called into the ark and the presence of the Lord, Lot was taken out of the wickedness of Sodom by the angels. Both had spent many years beforehand being mocked for their faith, Noah ridiculed as he built the ark, Lot distraught daily by Sodom. God demanded an immediate response when suddenly the day of His judgement, the Day of the Lord came.

This is a type of the call to disciples when the Lord returns. It will come in one day and disciples need to be ready for the summons whenever it comes. The angels will be sent to call the faithful out of the world (like Lot) to be taken that they might be with their Lord (like Noah).

Moab and Ammon

Little need be said about the remaining verses of chapter 19. Lot had refused to return to the household of faith. He lost everything he had and ended up living in a cave. In his actions there is yet another echo of events yet to come at the return of Christ (Isaiah 2:20,21).

Because of this, his daughters were denied access to faithful men as potential husbands and the descendants of Moab and Ammon behave like the men of Sodom, reviling the way of the Lord and are condemned by God for it (Zephaniah 2:8-10).

26 | Abraham and Abimelech

"And Abraham journeyed from there to the South, and dwelt between Kadesh and Shur, and stayed in Gerar." (Genesis 20:1)

ABRAHAM left Mamre where he had settled and now moved south into the Negev, leaving a fertile area for one which was semi-desert. We do not know if he took all of his people with him or why he went. It has been suggested[1] that the impact of God's judgements on Sodom had affected the land quite widely and he needed new pastures. Perhaps he simply wanted to get away from the tragedy of Lot's life. Certainly he went from a settled existence near Hebron where he had been for many years, amongst people who accepted him and knew of his God, to a place where he thought "the fear of God is not in this place".

It was this that led him to tell Abimelech that Sarah was his sister, the same half-truth he had told Pharaoh many years before. She was now ninety years old with her beauty and youthfulness miraculously restored by the Lord in preparation for the birth of Isaac, and Abimelech's desire for her is an undesigned coincidence to the truth of God's promise about this.

Although put into the king's harem, he had no physical relations with her, prevented by the illness which God had brought upon him and all his family.

In these events it was Abimelech who acted honourably and Abraham who showed such a lack of faith.

---

1 Brother H. P. Mansfield, page 242.

The king knew something of the Lord for:

- He prayed to God (Adonai) protesting his innocence, "I did this with clean hands and a clear conscience".
- God acknowledged his integrity and stopped him from sinning (through the imposition of his illness).

The Lord's response to Abimelech was unusual, 'Don't do this for the man is a prophet'. This is the first mention of a prophet in the Bible and we know from the Psalms (Psalm 105:14,15) that Abraham, Isaac and Jacob were protected by God because they were anointed prophets. We are not told at this point why this role of Abraham was the reason for the Lord's intervention and have to wait until we reach chapter 22 to find the answer.

No doubt the king's protestations to Abraham brought him embarrassment and shame:

> "'What have you done to us? How have I offended you, that you have brought on me and on my kingdom a great sin? You have done deeds to me that ought not to be done.' Then Abimelech said to Abraham, 'What did you have in view (*what did you see in me*), that you have done this thing?'"
>
> (Genesis 20:9,10)

What weak excuses Abraham made in response to this. He claimed that this had been his policy wherever they went after leaving Ur, yet he appears to have used it only once before. He was prepared to lose Sarah to a Canaanite king because he was afraid for his life. Yet El Shaddai had promised him that Sarah would bear him the promised seed. Two thousand years later, the night before he died, the Lord Jesus Christ faced the threat of a foreign power and gained strength and comfort from the words of the Psalmist: "The LORD is on my side; I will not fear. What can man do to me?" He prayed to his Father and was heard for his Godly fear. We are not told if Abraham turned to God in prayer at this time; his weakness of wanting to manage the affairs of his life himself was apparent once again.

Abimelech's response to this was remarkable. Instead of dismissing Abraham, as did Pharaoh, he showered gifts upon him including a huge amount of money, 1,000 shekels,[2] and offered him land to dwell in. Only then did Abraham pray, with a conscience pricked by the knowledge that through his actions the king and his family were suffering. God heard him; the disease and barrenness were removed. "I will bless them that bless you" was indeed true in Abimelech's life. We can only guess at Sarah's feelings. Although she had her strength renewed she was still not pregnant, but all the women of Abimelech's household had become wonderfully fertile.

What compassion the Lord showed to Abraham through all of this. He protected both him and his wife in spite of his lack of faith. Yet, although our God is a merciful and forgiving God we have to live with the consequences of our actions in our lives and this was true of Abraham. Repercussions followed, as we shall see.

2 A labourer earned six shekels a year in Babylon.

27

The birth of Isaac

"By faith Sarah herself also received strength to conceive seed, and she bore a child when she was past the age, because she judged him faithful who had promised." (Hebrews 11:11)

"And the LORD visited Sarah as he had said, and the LORD did for Sarah as he had spoken. For Sarah conceived and bore Abraham a son in his old age, at the set time of which God had spoken to him." (Genesis 21:1,2)

EXACTLY a year passed between the words of the angel to Abraham in chapter 17 and the birth of Isaac at the time God had appointed – hence all of the events of Genesis 18-20 occurred within the space of three months. Sarah had laughed at the angel's words but now believed. Her strength and beauty were restored within this short space of time and fertility given her for the first time in her life. It must have been a time of great wonder within the household of faith. The woman whom they had seen grow old and careworn was suddenly, miraculously reinvigorated; the promises at which she, and perhaps others, had laughed in scorn were indeed true.

For the first time the Lord worked directly with Sarah rather than with Abraham. He visited her: this is the first use of this word and it carries the idea of making a visitation to bring about a change in the life of the person involved. God did "as he had said", "as he had spoken"; it was "at the set time of which [he] had spoken". The emphasis is on the certainty of His word, the things He had promised would certainly happen, His word went forth from Him and did not return to Him void.

And so it was Sarah who was the first to speak directly in this account, acknowledging what the Lord had done for her:

> "God has made me laugh, and all who hear will laugh with me." (Genesis 21:6)

She had laughed with incredulity in chapter 17 and had been rebuked for it, now her laughter was of rejoicing and she foresaw that all who heard of this birth, and of the fulfilment of God's word through it, would rejoice with her.

It was this rejoicing at the miraculous power of the Lord that led the Apostle Paul in Galatians 4:27 to apply the words of Isaiah to the birth of Isaac:

> "'Sing, O barren, you who have not borne! Break forth into singing, and cry aloud, you who have not laboured with child! For more are the children of the desolate than the children of the married woman', says the LORD. 'Enlarge the place of your tent, and let them stretch out the curtains of your dwellings; do not spare; lengthen your cords, and strengthen your stakes. For you shall expand to the right and to the left, and your descendants will inherit the nations, and make the desolate cities inhabited.'" (Isaiah 54:1-3)

These words of the prophet follow the picture of the suffering Messiah in chapter 53. He was *the* son of Abraham through whom many would be made righteous for he would bear their iniquities. Through him, the one seed, in faith many would become Abraham's seed and heirs together with him as God had promised.

How marvellous the scriptures are. Through divine inspiration the apostle saw that Isaiah's words were a commentary on this event and on Sarah's faith and understanding of what it meant. She would bear just one son but both she, Abraham, and all who would become his spiritual descendants, understood that through a unique Son of Abraham many would be made righteous: he would see his seed and be satisfied.

So Isaac (*laughter*) was named, circumcised and committed to the covenant made between his father and the Lord.

Perhaps three to five years now elapsed; Sarah's vigour remained so that she could suckle her child and weaning occurred at a later age than is now customary.

Ishmael mocked

Once again the way the text develops draws our minds to the contrast between the true and the false. We have seen Sarah laugh and the Hebrew root, *sahaq*, laughter, is used five times in these opening verses. It is a key word telling of rejoicing and happiness, not just at the birth of Isaac but also at the implications of it for the fulfilment of God's promises.

Now we read that Ishmael, aged about seventeen, mocked. Sarah saw this and was so angered that she demanded that Hagar and her son be sent away from Abraham's household. He would not inherit with her son, Isaac, and without faith in the promised son, he could not remain in the household.

What happened to enrage her so? We are not told directly who Ishmael mocked or what he said but we can deduce it from the text. The word "mocked" comes from the same root, *sahaq*, as does the name Isaac but it is modified to have a profoundly different meaning. It was used to describe the behaviour of Lot's prospective sons-in-law when they ridiculed the warning of God's impending judgements and of Potiphar's wife when she accused Joseph of trying to rape her (Genesis 19:14; 39:14). We saw in chapter 20 how Abimelech took Sarah into his harem and sought to make her his concubine. No doubt Ishmael believed that an intimate relationship had taken place in spite of the king's protestations, and now, in a deliberate parody of Isaac's name, he mocked him, jeered at him – 'Abraham is not your father, we all know that he is old and impotent, Abimelech is your real father'. It was indeed laughter but of a thoroughly unpleasant and cruel sort; it was not just his idea alone but was fed to him by his mother, Hagar the Egyptian. But it was more than this, for Paul tells us that Ishmael persecuted Isaac. It had apparently been going on for some time[1] but now Sarah became aware of it. The NIV catches the force of her words to her husband:

> "Get rid of that slave woman and her son, for that slave woman's son will never share in the inheritance with my son Isaac." (Genesis 21:10, NIV)

"Get rid of her" she demanded. Hagar was no longer her handmaid, given to Abraham that he may have a son. Through her behaviour, and that of Ishmael, she was a slave and those in bondage could never share the inheritance with the free. So the Lord confirmed to Abraham that he should do as his wife asked. There was a tension between man and wife over the issue, it was very displeasing to Abraham; he too was angry but for different reasons from those of Sarah.

Throughout these events Sarah is shown to be a spiritual woman of faith who influenced her husband for good. Ishmael was a threat to the heir and he had to go. Yet, although he had rejected the teaching of his father, something had lodged in his mind for when he was in extremis, facing death in the wilderness, it was he who prayed to God and was heard whilst his mother simply wept. The Lord was very gracious: for Abraham's sake Ishmael would become the father of a nation and the lad was saved.

The covenant at Beersheba

The final section of chapter 21 is presented almost as an aside, "It came to pass at that time ..." and we need to place it in the context of what had just happened. It draws a contrast between Hagar and Ishmael on one hand and Abimelech and his people on the other. Both groups were Gentiles, one rejected any relationship with God's chosen people through faith; the other recognised the importance of them for "God is with you in all that you do" said Abimelech to Abraham and sought a covenant with him.

The king surely knew the words the Lord had spoken when Abraham was first called, "I will bless them that bless you and

---

1 If the 400 years of persecution started at Isaac's birth then Ishmael had been against him from that moment.

curse them that curse you". He recognised that association with Abraham and his God would bring a blessing on him and the land and he asked for an oath to confirm this.

For the third and final time we read that Abraham called upon the name of the Lord. He called Him *El Elyon*, the everlasting God, linking the covenant he had made with Abimelech with the everlasting covenant the Lord had made with him months earlier (Genesis 17:19).

> "Then Abraham planted a tamarisk tree in Beersheba, and there called on the name of the LORD, the Everlasting God."
>
> (Genesis 21:33)

28 |

The allegory of two sons

TWO thousand years later the greatest Son of Abraham faced similar mocking to that of Isaac, as described in the book of Genesis. It is John who tells us of the debates between Jesus and the Jews at Jerusalem when he went to keep the feasts of the Law. At the heart of the discussions was the Lord's relationship with his Father, something the Jews would not accept.

It began at the Passover recorded in John 5:

> "For this reason the Jews persecuted Jesus, and sought to kill him, because he had done these things on the Sabbath. But Jesus answered them, 'My Father has been working until now, and I have been working'. Therefore the Jews sought all the more to kill him, because he not only broke the Sabbath, but also said that God was his Father, making himself equal with God. Then Jesus answered and said to them, 'Most assuredly, I say to you, the Son can do nothing of himself, but what he sees the Father do; for whatever he does, the Son also does in like manner. For the Father loves the Son, and shows him all things that he himself does ...'" (John 5:16-20)

Because of his Sabbath day healing of the disabled man, the Jews began to persecute Jesus (as Ishmael persecuted Isaac) and this miracle still rankled with them eighteen months later on his next visit to Jerusalem as recorded in John 7.

The Lord's response was to affirm his relationship with his Father. His works declared his Sonship. For this they tried to kill him.

The last day of the Feast

So, in John 7 we see Jesus in Jerusalem at the Feast of Tabernacles, six months before his death, dealing with these pressures. It was on the last day of the feast when he stood up in the temple and spoke:

> "On the last day, that great day of the feast, Jesus stood and cried out, saying, 'If anyone thirsts, let him come to me and drink. He who believes in me, as the scripture has said, out of his heart will flow rivers of living water'." (John 7:37,38)

It was one of the most dramatic moments of the Lord's ministry and the ritual of the last day of the feast helps us to understand what was happening.[1]

- A priest went down the steps from the temple to the Pool of Siloam and collected water in a golden pitcher (running, living water that had come through Hezekiah's tunnel from the Gihon spring).
- This was taken to the temple and poured out together with wine at the base of the altar as sacrifices were made.
- Psalm 118 was then chanted by the priests with the whole congregation joining in the words of verse 25 and crying out: "Save now, I pray, O LORD; O LORD, I pray, send now prosperity."
- After this there was a pause during which the Lord Jesus Christ stood and cried out the words quoted above.
- The daily Psalm, Psalm 82, was then read. Its opening words are: "God stands in the congregation of the mighty; He judges among the gods."

The Lord did not interrupt the service, rather he answered their prayers. True living water was present, God's salvation had been sent to them; the full manifestation of the Lord God in the person of the Lord Jesus Christ did indeed stand in the congregation of His people.

---

1 For full details of this see A. Edersheim, *The Life and Times of Jesus the Messiah*, volume 2, chapter 7.

There was such consternation amongst the worshippers that the temple police could not arrest him as ordered. What could the authorities do to stop him? He was being accepted by some as the Messiah, he continued to talk of the Lord God as his Father in a way that infuriated them and they needed to find a way of undermining him. The response of the priests and Pharisees was not seen until the next day when they set about to discredit his paternity.

They were aware of rumours about the Lord Jesus' birth more than thirty years before. His mother had conceived him whilst betrothed to Joseph but not yet married to him. Joseph had denied paternity of the boy but had accepted both Mary and Jesus into his home. No one really knew who the father was. Mary had insisted that her firstborn son was the Son of God, that the Lord was indeed his Father and he had been conceived in a miraculous way. No one believed this.

So they brought to Jesus a woman caught in adultery. If he condemned her, they could use this against his own mother; if he refused to condemn her then he denied the law of the Lord – either way he would be discredited.

The dialogue that followed was all about Jesus' paternity and his relationship with God as his Father and the links back to Ishmael and Isaac are very marked.

The Jews claimed to be the true children of Abraham and free men because of this. They were not born of fornication they said – inferring that Jesus was. They told him he was a Samaritan, a gross insult implying he was of mixed, unknown blood. Their accusations mirrored those made by Ishmael and Hagar against Isaac two thousand years before.

The response of the Lord Jesus was devastating as he called on the teaching of Genesis in his words to them.

He said that he spoke nothing but what his Father had taught him. In this he was truly the Son of God (remember that Abraham had commanded his children to keep the way of the Lord; Isaac had listened, Ishmael had not). Jesus continued by saying that his words were the truth and could bring them freedom from bondage to sin. This was not automatically theirs simply because they were Abraham's descendants, despite their claims. (Sarah's description of Hagar as the bondslave and of Ishmael as the son of the bondslave rather than a son of Abraham showed an acute understanding of that situation.)

Bondslaves do not remain in their master's house forever, only true sons can do this ('Cast out the bondslave and her son – he will not be heir with my son, even Isaac!').

Later in John, the same leaders plotted the death of the Lord Jesus, for "if we leave him alone ... the Romans will come and take away our place and our nation" and in their hearts we see the same spirit of jealousy and self-interest that was present in Ishmael. It was only at the cross that the matter was resolved for, at the sacrifice of the perfect Lamb of God, there were present both Jews and Gentiles who saw and believed, acknowledging that "truly this man was the Son of God".

Old and new covenants

The Letter to the Galatians was the first epistle Paul wrote and it captures his amazement that the Gentiles, to whom he had preached the true Gospel, had been subverted by the Judaisers and had turned from the grace of God to the Law of Moses. The rite of circumcision had been pressed on them so that they could become 'true Jews', and hence offspring of Abraham. As part of his response to this he gave the allegory we read in chapter 4:

> "Tell me, you who desire to be under the law, do you not hear the law? For it is written that Abraham had two sons: the one by a bondwoman, the other by a freewoman. But he who was of the bondwoman was born according to the flesh, and he of the freewoman through promise, which things are symbolic. For these are the two covenants: the one from Mount Sinai which gives birth to bondage, which is Hagar – for this Hagar is Mount Sinai in Arabia, and corresponds to Jerusalem which now is, and is in bondage with her children – but the Jerusalem above is free, which is the mother of us all. For it is written: 'Rejoice, O barren, you who do not bear! Break forth

and shout, you who are not in labour! For the desolate has many more children than she who has a husband.' Now we, brethren, as Isaac was, are children of promise. But, as he who was born according to the flesh then persecuted him who was born according to the Spirit, even so it is now. Nevertheless what does the scripture say? 'Cast out the bondwoman and her son, for the son of the bondwoman shall not be heir with the son of the freewoman.' So then, brethren, we are not children of the bondwoman but of the free."

(Galatians 4:21-31)

How beautifully the Apostle Paul uses both the Genesis record and the events chronicled in John's Gospel to produce this allegory. Without the words of the Lord Jesus Christ our understanding would be incomplete. With them we can see clearly why Paul chose Ishmael and Isaac as types of the old and new covenants.

As Ishmael mocked and persecuted Isaac, so the did Jews to Jesus, even when he hung on the cross: "If you are the Son of God, come down from the cross ... let God deliver him for he said 'I am the Son of God'." And so, just as Ishmael was cast out through unbelief, sadly we also see that the refusal of the Jews to accept Jesus of Nazareth as the Son of God, their Messiah, would lead to their casting out also (Romans 11:15).

This comparison between two sons and two covenants is seen clearly by listing the different aspects of the allegory as follows.

Two...	**Hagar**	**Sarah**
Women	Bondslave	Freewoman
Mountains	Sinai	Moriah
Covenants	The old which brings bondage	The new which brings freedom
Cities	Jerusalem that now is	New Jerusalem

Two...	**Hagar**	**Sarah**
Sons	Ishmael	Isaac
Relationships	Bondslaves	Free heirs – children of God

29 | The sacrifice of Isaac

"And it came to pass, after these things, that, God, did prove Abraham, – and he said unto him, Abraham! And he said, Behold me! And he said – Take, I pray thee, thy son, thine only one, whom thou lovest, even, Isaac, and get thee into the land of Moriah, – and cause him to ascend there, as an ascending-sacrifice, on one of the mountains, which I shall name unto thee." (Genesis 22:1,2, Rotherham)

GENESIS chapter 22 brings us to the climax of the Lord's dealings with Abraham as he was tested to sacrifice Isaac.

The chapter is packed with detail which drives home the solemnity and importance of what is recorded for us. Immediately we see language very similar to that of Abraham's call from Ur by the Lord. We are invited to see that event and this one as 'bookends' enclosing the record of God's dealings with this wonderful man of faith.

Chapter 12	**Chapter 22**
"Get thee"	"Get thee"
"to a land I will show you"	"to a mountain I will tell you of"
Involved a separation from his country, his kindred, his father's house	Involved a separation from his son, his only son, his beloved son Isaac

Chapter 12	Chapter 22
Immediately in faith he departed	Immediately in faith he departed
God's response was the first of the seven promise-blessings	God's response was the seventh and final promise-blessing

The call of Abraham had been to leave all behind and journey in faith, trusting in God. Now he was asked to give up the only son he had left. Ishmael had gone, the children of Keturah and the concubines had gone. Everything God had promised him centred on Isaac and now he was asked to sacrifice him.

Some years had elapsed after the sending away of Hagar and Ishmael. Isaac is described as a "lad" and the same word is used to describe the teenager, Ishmael, when mocking the heir and also the young men who accompanied Abraham and Isaac. He was no child but a youth,[1] old enough to carry the wood and to question his father about what was happening. Abraham must have been around 120-130 years of age and physically unable to resist Isaac if he had struggled and refused to accept what was happening to him. Both therefore were willingly involved. Isaac had been instructed in the way of the Lord and he alone of Abraham's children had accepted it. No doubt he loved his father, as his father loved him, and his actions showed obedience in faith to his father as did Abraham's to the Lord. In this we are reminded of the words of Abraham's greater Son as he left the upper room the night before his death:

> "But that the world may know that I love the Father, and as the Father gave me commandment, so I do. Arise, let us go from here." (John 14:31)

So father and son went together.

We know from the opening words of the chapter that God had no intention of letting Abraham carry out the sacrifice. He was testing him to see if he would withhold his only son, the most

1 One suggestion (for obvious reasons) is that he was aged 33.

precious thing in his life, the one he loved so dearly. This testing is immediately known to readers of the chapter but Abraham did not know of it. Rather, he had been given a commandment to sacrifice his son by the One whom he knew as the only true God, but it was an act followed throughout the region by worshippers of the pagan gods he had rejected.

This is the first use of *nacah*, to test or prove, in the Bible and its further uses show two distinct ideas.

1. When used of the Lord testing people, He tests their faith to see whether or not it will be outworked in obedience to Him. For example:

   "Then the LORD said to Moses, 'Behold, I will rain bread from heaven for you. And the people shall go out and gather a certain quota every day, that I may test them, whether they will walk in my law or not'."

   (Exodus 16:4)

2. When used of men testing God, it shows their faithlessness and consequently behaviour which demonstrates this. For example:

   "Therefore the people contended with Moses, and said, 'Give us water, that we may drink'. And Moses said to them, 'Why do you contend with me? Why do you tempt the LORD?'" (17:2)

But why did the Lord test Abraham in this particular way? Abraham had been on a journey of faith interspersed with times when the weakness of the flesh had brought temporary moments of faithlessness. Like all of us he would have agonised over his human nature, wondering how the exceeding great and precious promises made to him could be enacted. 'How can the Lord share His glory with a flawed man like me?' must have been a question often in his mind. He knew that the wages of sin were death, yet he had been promised a resurrection to immortal life and possession of the land for ever in the ultimate fulfilment of God's purpose with the earth. How could these things be?

The Lord now showed him the answer. A sacrifice was necessary, not of the ineffective blood of an animal such as he had offered since he came into the land but of an only, well beloved son, who in loving obedience to his father, and fully sharing his beliefs, would willingly participate in the giving of his life.

It is clear from Hebrews 11 that Abraham believed that Isaac was this unique son for we read that he offered him accounting that God was able to raise him from the dead.

In His call of Abraham to go to Moriah God used a term He rarely used when making demands of people. In the KJV it is simply the word "now" (*na*), but it is translated as "I pray (or urge) you" in literal versions. God had already used this twice in addressing Abraham:

> "Lift your eyes *now* and look from the place where you are – northward, southward, eastward, and westward."
>
> (Genesis 13:14)
>
> "'Look *now* toward heaven, and count the stars if you are able to number them.' And he said to him, 'So shall your descendants be'." (15:5)

On each occasion the Lord was asking Abraham to do something in faith, something which would have stupendous consequences in his life – and it was an invitation. It needed a willing response and Abraham rose early in the morning and went as requested.

The only son

Isaac was the *only* son and the use of the language in the Hebrew paints a picture of his relationship with his father. The word translated "only", *yachiyd*, carries the meaning of both uniqueness and solitariness, something precious.[2] God sets the solitary in families, wrote the Psalmist, and this was certainly true of Isaac, who was the solitary, only son. Yet God had already told Abraham that "in Isaac would his seed be called", through this one man; this only son would become a great people who would be the family of the Lord God, privileged to call Him Father.

---

2 See, for example, Judges 11:34; Psalm 22:20; 35:17; 68:6.

But the Septuagint gives a completely different slant to this. It uses the word *agapetos*, beloved, and this is applied to the unique, only begotten Son in the Gospels for twice the Lord God spoke from heaven declaring that Jesus was His beloved Son. Indeed, the word is used uniquely of the Lord Jesus Christ before his death, yet through this, and his resurrection, the way back to God was opened up for men and women who believed. So John wrote of them; "Behold what manner of love (*agape*) that we should be called the sons of God ... beloved (*agapetos*) now are we the sons of God".

Isaac was not just the only son but also the one whom Abraham loved. It is the first mention of the Hebrew word *ahab* translated as "love" in the Bible and it is used of a father asked to take his only, beloved son to a place of sacrifice. In a similar manner we see the first use of the word "worship" and twice it is emphasised that they went to do this together, the father and his son united as one in obedience to their God.

All of this language paints a picture of the intimate relationship between Abraham and Isaac and the cost to him of obeying the Lord in this matter.

Into the land of Moriah

Again we see Abraham depicted as a man of action. This time however he did not try to work things out for himself; rather he showed an absolute commitment to obey what God had asked of him. He rose early in the morning to commence the journey. God spoke to him twice and both times his response was the same, "Here am I". One event followed another seamlessly as he and Isaac quietly prepared for the journey.

It was made into the land of Moriah,[3] to one of the mountains that God would show him. The use of the plural is significant; he was shown two mountains but only one of them was suitable for the sacrifice. Mounts Moriah and Zion are essentially two peaks at either end of a ridge: one is the place

3 We meet this name Moriah only twice, here and in 2 Chronicles 3:1 as the place where Solomon built the temple.

of sacrifice where Ornan's threshing floor was, the other is the city of the great King. It was to the place of sacrifice that Abraham went and he had been there before, to the place where he had met Melchizedek, the place where the Lord had made the covenant with him. Moriah means 'seen (*rah*) of the Lord' and there is a play on words for Abraham lifted up his eyes and saw (*rah*) the place afar off. We can imagine the memories that came flooding into his mind, strengthening him for the task ahead. His faith is seen in the words spoken to the two young men who accompanied them: "Stay here ... we will come back to you." If indeed Isaac was *the* sacrifice for sin, then he was absolutely convinced that God would raise him from the dead; together they would go, together they would return.

The journey was one of about fifty miles, taking them three days. When, on the third day, Moriah came into view, the two young men were left behind, the wood was taken off the donkey and given to Isaac who willingly carried it and who asked, "Where is the lamb?" "My son, God will provide himself the lamb for a burnt offering" was the response. We know that Abraham was a prophet and, thinking of him as one who foretold the future, then this is the only recorded prophecy he made.

When no lamb appeared, Isaac allowed himself to be bound and laid down on the altar that Abraham had built.

All of this must have taken some time; there must have been other dialogue between the two. Did Isaac ask if there was an alternative? When it became apparent that there was none, did he say to his father, "Your will be done"?

We get a sense of the tension and emotions that must have been present in both men as the moment came for Isaac to be slain. The following quotation captures something of this for us and is worth reproducing here:

> "There was many a father who lost his child; but then it was God. It was the unalterable, unsearchable will of the Almighty, it was His hand that took the child. Not so with Abraham. For him was reserved a harder trial, and Isaac's fate was laid, along with the knife, in Abraham's hand. And he stood there, the old

> man, with his only hope. But he did not doubt, he did not look anxiously to the right or the left, he did not challenge heaven with his prayers. He knew that it was God, the Almighty, who was trying him, he knew that it was the hardest sacrifice that could be required of him; but he knew also that no sacrifice was too hard when God required it and he drew the knife."[4]

It was to be a whole burnt offering and in such sacrifices, under the law, the last act before the death was that of the offerer who laid his hand upon that offered, leaning heavily upon it and, in type, transferring his sins to the animal. Just as Abraham prepared to do this the Lord spoke, for this was not to be the sacrifice essential for the fulfilment of God's purpose. Previously it had been God, Elohim, who had addressed him, now it was the Yahweh angel, the messenger of the covenant, who called from heaven and who did so with urgency: "Abraham, Abraham!"

> "Do not lay your hand on the lad, or do anything to him; for now I know that you fear God, since you have not withheld your son, your only son, from me." (Genesis 22:12)

For the second time Abraham lifted up his eyes. He had lifted them up to see (*rah*) the place afar off, now he raised them to see (*rah*) the ram provided by the Lord. It was not just physical sight that he had for in these things he saw the fulfilment, afar off in time, of the promises made to him (Hebrews 11:13) and fully accepted them. It was not a lamb that was provided but a ram, an animal sacrificed by Abraham when he had been at Moriah previously as part of the ratification of the covenant between Him and the Lord.[5] Abraham now knew that it was not the fulfilment of the prophecy just made, for it was not the promised lamb but it was a reaffirmation of the certainty of the promises made to him.

In these things Abraham now clearly saw the day of the Lord Jesus Christ, the lamb who would indeed take away the sins of the world: he saw it, rejoiced and was glad (John 8:56). How

---

4 Quoted in A. P. Ross, *Creation and Blessing*, page 399.

5 See Ross, chapter 13, "In this place".

his heart must have been full to overflowing at the goodness of God. There must have been immense relief that Isaac had not suffered death, yet awe that one would come who would be the Lord God's beloved, only Son and that he would be the one to die for sin. Of all men who have ever lived, it was Abraham who could most enter into the mind of the Lord and the cost to Him of the sacrifice of His Son.

The final blessing

The Lord then spoke to Abraham giving him the seventh and final promise and blessing. It was confirmed with an oath and this was absolutely unbreakable for it was given upon the very existence of the Lord Himself. Here were two things in which it was impossible for God to lie, His promise and His oath (Hebrews 6:17,18).

So the promise and blessing that followed were given in words of certainty not used before by God: 'Because you have done these things, I will *really* bless you ... I will *really* multiply your seed.'

When God first called Abraham out of Ur, the call had included His first words of blessing to the man: "I will bless *you*." Now his spiritual journey was complete and the last words of blessing were given to him; through *the* Seed who would come, *all the nations of the earth* would be blessed because Abraham had obeyed God's voice. What began with one man would end with a multitude of those who are Abraham's seed and heirs with him.

The Apostle Paul drew on these words when he wrote to the Romans of the certainty of the promises throughout the ages; whatever happens to us in life, nothing can separate us from the love of our God who is our Father through the death of the Son given for us. The Lord's words of absolutely certain blessings to come for Abraham and his descendants were possible because He has not withheld (spared) His only Son and so Paul wrote:

> "What then shall we say to these things? If God is for us, who can be against us? He who did not spare his own Son, but

> delivered him up for us all, how shall he not with him also freely give us all things?" (Romans 8:31,32)

Abraham's faith was now perfect and complete because it had been shown in his works; so confident was he in the promises of God and the resurrection from the dead that he would have given his only son. And so a new relationship developed between the Lord and Abraham as James tells us:

> "Was not Abraham our father justified by works when he offered Isaac his son on the altar? Do you see that faith was working together with his works, and by works faith was made perfect? And the scripture was fulfilled which says, 'Abraham believed God, and it was accounted to him for righteousness'. And he was called the friend of God." (James 2:21-23)

He became the friend of God, not just because he believed but because that belief was shown in his works. We meet this title of Abraham three times in the scriptures[6] and the two Old Testament passages use a word that we have already met when thinking about Abraham and Isaac in this chapter. Isaac was Abraham's loved (*ahab*) son, Abraham was the friend (*ahab*), the loved one, of God. Isaac was the only son born to Abraham who accepted the word of God and believed the promises. Abraham was the only man in Ur chosen by God, called alone, says Isaiah, because God found him faithful. But this is not simply a pattern of the past, our Lord picked it up as he spoke to his disciples, and through them to us, the night before his death: "You are my friends if you do the things which I command you" (John 15:14).

Blessed in all things

Abraham would live for another fifty to sixty years, dying at the age of one hundred and seventy-five, yet there is no record of God speaking to him again. Is not this strange? He was the Lord's friend, did He not commune further with him? We do not know if this happened but the reason we are not told is found at the

6 2 Chronicles 20:7; Isaiah 41:8; James 2:23.

beginning of chapter 24: "The LORD had blessed Abraham in all things."

The Lord began His revelation to Abraham with the words "I will bless" (Genesis 12:2), now it ended with the confirmation that He had fulfilled His word, "He had blessed". Yet, God had promised eternal life in the Promised Land; this has yet to be fulfilled. But Abraham's faith in taking his only son to die as a sacrifice was such that the Lord spoke of things yet to come as already accomplished, so certain were they. So it is for us, we who believe in the death and resurrection of our Lord Jesus Christ, for "He who did not spare his own Son, but delivered him up for us all, how shall he not with him also freely give us all things?" Truly, we too are blessed in all things, as was Abraham.

The record of his life is partial but contains all things that are necessary for salvation. Through the spiritual journey of this one man, the way had been made possible for all the nations of the earth to be blessed and so the scriptures now become quiet about the relationship between the Lord God and His friend. Concerning his salvation and that of his seed, the Lord had nothing more to tell him, it had all been perfectly and wonderfully revealed.

We have seen the promise-blessings of the Lord to Abraham, seven in all, complete and perfect. They form a pattern, a chiasmus, focusing on the one at the centre of the message they give, that God's glory will fill the earth, manifest in people He has chosen to bear His name.

---

1. Abraham would become a great nation, his name great, all the families of the earth blessed in him (12:2,3).

2. The land would be given to his seed (12:7).

3. The land would be given to him and his seed forever, he would have many descendants (13:14-17).

4. The promise of God manifestation in him and his seed. "I am your shield and exceeding great reward." The promise of a son, faith in these

things brought righteousness. The land given to him and his descendants (15:1-7).

5. The covenant made, his name changed to Abraham, he would have many descendants and the land would be theirs forever. Isaac promised (17:1-9).

6. Sarah would bear a son (the seed) at the appointed time (18:9-14).

7. In *the* seed all the families of the earth would be blessed because of Abraham's faith (22:16-18).

Indeed, the Lord had blessed Abraham in all things!

DIGRESSION: The place for God's name

"And Abraham called the name of that place Jehovah-jireh: as it is said to this day, In the mount of the Lord it shall be seen."

(Genesis 22:14, KJV)

Much has been written about the ambiguity of the Hebrew word *raah* used here. We meet it four times in the chapter.

1. Verse 4: Abraham *saw* the place afar off.
2. Verse 8: God will *provide* himself a lamb.
3. Verse 13: Abraham lifted up his eyes and *looked*.
4. Verse 14: In the mount of the Lord *it shall be seen*.

Abraham's words are linked to his prophecy about God's provision of the lamb. It would be given in this specific place, the place where the covenant had been ratified and where Abraham's faith had been accounted for his righteousness. This is the mountain of the Lord and when Moses spoke of it in Deuteronomy 12 he described it as the place where God had chosen "to put his name, even his habitation". It is the mount where the Lord appeared (*raah*) to David and where Solomon built the temple.

The addition of the words "as it is said to this day" by Moses, the editor of Genesis, lifts it out of Abraham's day and gives it a timelessness – all Israel throughout the generations who waited for the coming of the Messiah understood that it would be there, on Moriah, that he would be seen. So in John's

Gospel we read of Jesus suddenly appearing in the temple, declaring himself to the people at the feasts and being met with puzzlement: 'Is this the Messiah or not? He is from Galilee, this is not the Messiah we expected.'

And Isaiah confirms this in his chapter about the suffering, sacrificed Son of God.

> "Who has believed our report? And to whom has the arm of the LORD been revealed? For he shall grow up before him as a tender plant, and as a root out of dry ground. He has no form or comeliness; and when we see (*raah*) him, there is no beauty (*mareh*, appearance) that we should desire him."
>
> (Isaiah 53:1,2)

But we can deduce more from this description of Moriah. When Abraham went to this mount before, it was called by another name, Salem, peace. If we put the two names together it becomes 'the place where the LORD will provide peace', Jireh Salem, Jerusalem.

What wonderful things these are. We are privileged to be able to look back and see not only Abraham on Moriah but also the Lord Jesus Christ in Jerusalem fulfilling the promise made to him. More than this, with the Psalmist we can look into the future, see the defiling of the city of the Lord by the heathen at the time of the end and echo his cry for the coming of the kingdom that Lord God might be in His city with its new name, Yahweh Shammah, the Lord is there.

> "Help us, O God of our salvation, for the glory of your name; and deliver us, and provide atonement for our sins, for your name's sake!" (Psalm 79:9)

30 | Abraham's last days

AS we read on from chapter 22 we leave behind God's final words to Abraham and the record of the faithful begins to shift from the father to the son. Abraham had returned to his young men and they went back to Beersheba together. However, Isaac is not mentioned as being with them. The son, who in type had been sacrificed, was apparently not there even though Abraham had said to the young men, "We will come again to you". The transition takes us through the events of Genesis 23-24, details which give us biographical information about the patriarchs and their families but which are difficult at first sight to fit into the pattern of promise-blessings which we are considering. However, when we look at them together we see a pattern emerging, one of Abraham taking successive actions to ensure the continuing separateness of his family from the world after he died. His spiritual journey had commenced with the Lord calling him out of his world and he was determined to ensure that his family stayed separate from it in every way. This pattern is now revealed in four parts.

The family of Nahor

For the first time since chapter 11, Nahor, Abraham's brother is mentioned. When Abraham left Ur to travel first to Haran and then to Canaan, Nahor had remained behind. Yet we know that he later made part of this journey with his family and settled in Padan Aram, a region in northern Mesopotamia in which was the city of Haran (Genesis 25:20; 27:43).

News now came to Abraham that Nahor had a family (Genesis 22:20-23). Milcah, his wife, had borne him eight sons and his concubine, Reumah, another four. Sarah had given Abraham one son in his old age yet his brother had twelve. Would there be feelings of regret that this was so? Bethuel, Milcah's youngest son, had borne a daughter, Rebekah. It is yet another fascinating scriptural coincidence that later Jacob's two wives will give him eight sons and his concubines a further four.

More children were born to Bethuel but only Rebekah is mentioned. Immediately we are introduced to Isaac's bride, the one whom the Lord would provide for the man He had chosen to be part of His promises.

When we come to chapter 24, we find a special emphasis on Nahor. Abraham's servant, sent to find a wife for Isaac, goes to "the city of Nahor". Rebekah is described as a descendant of Nahor and then confirms this herself: "I am the daughter of Milcah which she bore to Bethuel, the son of Nahor". It is not until we reach chapter 31 that we understand why this lineage is so important, for Laban said to Jacob:

> "'The God of Abraham, the God of Nahor, and the God of their father judge between us.' And Jacob swore by the Fear of his father Isaac." (Genesis 31:53)

Nahor had come to know something of the Lord as did his granddaughter, Rebekah. The servant's search will bring him to her as a suitable help for Isaac that the promise-blessings might continue in this family.

The death of Sarah

Sarah died aged one hundred and twenty seven and was the first of the family of the faithful to die, not having received the promises but having been faithful to them all the days of her life. We are expressly told that she died in the land of Canaan. The custom of the time was to bury in one's native land but Abraham would have none of that, he was determined to have a burial place for his family in the land God had promised and he bargained with the local Hittites for one:

> "I am a foreigner (stranger) and a visitor among you. Give me property for a burial place among you, that I may bury my dead out of my sight." (Genesis 23:4)

Even though Abraham had now been in Canaan for over sixty years and was a rich and powerful man, he was still only a resident alien with no land rights. He was determined to have ownership, possession of a burial place for both Sarah, himself and his family. And in making this request he used language the Lord had used to him when promising him a son with Sarah:

> "Also I give to you and your descendants after you the land in which you are a stranger, all the land of Canaan, as an everlasting possession; and I will be their God." (Genesis 17:8)

It is wrong to look at Abraham and think of a weakness of faith at this point. Why did he need to buy a burial plot when he had been freely promised the whole land? Sarah had died and Abraham was an old man, he knew that he would die and attain resurrection before the land was his. We have in his actions a desire that his family could be buried in the land awaiting the resurrection day. When it came, they would still be there.

The bargaining that followed is fascinating. Both parties showed the utmost respect for each other. Abraham asked for ownership of a place for a tomb; the Hittites were most reluctant to give up land but offered free access to one of their own burial places. But Abraham insisted on buying a property and having full rights of possession, so ownership of the cave of Machpelah became his.

> "So the field of Ephron which was in Machpelah, which was before Mamre, the field and the cave which was in it, and all the trees that were in the field, which were within all the surrounding borders, were deeded to Abraham as a possession in the presence of the sons of Heth, before all who went in at the gate of his city." (Genesis 23:17,18)

Even in death Abraham was determined to keep his household separate from the Canaanites and eventually six members of his family would be buried in this cave, Abraham and Sarah, Isaac and Rebekah, Jacob and Leah.

A wife for Isaac

Isaac was thirty-six when his mother died and almost immediately Abraham determined to find a wife for his son. He was "old and stricken in years" and this phrase is only used three times in the Bible. On each occasion it is of a man who still has final work to do for the Lord to ensure that His purpose moves forward: Joshua in allocating the land to the tribes of Israel, David in ensuring Solomon took the throne after him (Joshua 13:1; 1 Kings 1:1).

In his purchase of the cave at Machpelah, Abraham had seen the Hittites as people willing to accept him, inviting him to bury his dead with theirs and no doubt they would have welcomed the heir of such a mighty prince into their families – what wealth he would bring. There was a risk here and Abraham faced up to it. He sent his servant (was this still Eliezer?) back to Nahor's family under solemn oath to find a wife for Isaac.

What a contrast there is in the characters we meet in this episode. We see the servant as a man of prayer committing the decision about Rebekah to the Lord, conscious that an angel was with him in all his ways. He was the chief servant of Abraham's household, his steward, and therefore his heir if Abraham had no son. Naturally speaking he had nothing to gain and potentially everything to lose by finding a wife for Isaac. If the son, no longer in his youth, did not marry, had no offspring or died prematurely then the servant would inherit. Yet we see him as a man totally committed to the task in hand. He too worshipped God calling Him: "the LORD, the God of my master Abraham who has led *me* in the right way" and we can be certain that, as one brought up in Abraham's household to know the way of the Lord, he was not just speaking of the direction of his travel. His life too was a pilgrimage in the right way, he too believed in the promises; through his master and his master's son he could have an inheritance greater than any Hittite law could give him. He was, in his behaviour and faith, the first example of a Gentile achieving righteousness through faith in the heir and so being accepted into the Israel of God.

He was a man entrusted with his master's jewels, gold, silver and clothing, given to him to hand over as part of the bride price. He was totally focused on the task in hand. When enticed to stay with the family, after agreement had been reached, he refused and insisted on leaving the next day, perhaps aware of the risks of staying with Laban too long.

We see Laban as the character who would be fully revealed in his dealings with Jacob. His cordial invitation to the servant, "Come, you who are blessed by the LORD" (NIV) was given after he had seen the jewellery given to his sister. He was an avaricious man whose welcome, using the name of the Lord, strikes a hollow tone; pleasantries not fellowship were there. He had a strange pre-eminence over his father, leading the decision making, wanting the servant to stay. Perhaps he thought that there was yet more to be had from the man.

We see Rebekah, immediately introduced to us as a woman exceeding all that the steward had asked of God. Before he had finished praying, she appeared at the well; she hastened to draw water for him at his request, she offered to draw water for his camels (a camel can drink up to twenty-five gallons) and hastened to do so. We are introduced to her as a generous-spirited, decisive woman full of energy and unafraid to take charge of a situation.

But she was also a woman of faith, for when asked if she would leave immediately (and she was given the right of refusal) said "I will go" and left all behind her the same day. In her we see the same obedience in faith that was present in Abraham when asked to leave his country, his kindred and his father's house, for he too went immediately as the Lord commanded him.

The details of the journey back to Canaan are very precise: she followed the man, he took her and went his way (the way of the Lord). How significant it is that the journey ends, not with a description of arrival in Canaan but of her meeting her bridegroom. The wedding took place and she dwelt in Sarah's tent.

Isaiah's fourth servant song in chapter 53 speaks of the sacrifice of our Lord, the Lamb led to the slaughter who through his sacrifice, will make many righteous (Isaiah 53:11). We have already seen how Sarah rejoiced at the promise of the birth of Isaac and how the Apostle Paul was inspired to apply the words of Isaiah's next chapter, chapter 54 to her situation:

> "Sing, O barren, you who have not borne! Break forth into singing, and cry aloud, you who have not laboured with child! For more are the children of the desolate than the children of the married woman, says the LORD. Enlarge the place of your tent, and let them stretch out the curtains of your dwellings; do not spare; lengthen your cords, and strengthen your stakes. For you shall expand to the right and to the left, and your [seed, KJV] will inherit the nations." (Isaiah 54:1-3)

Here we see Isaiah picking up not only Sarah's rejoicing but God's final words to Abraham that all the nations of the earth would be blessed through the special seed. In type, Sarah's tent is to be enlarged, there must be room not just for her special, only son but for all those who will become part of Abraham's family through faith. And so we read that Isaac took his bride and put her in his mother's tent, perhaps enlarged for the family that would inhabit it.

The coming of the Bridegroom

We noted that, when Abraham and Isaac went to Moriah, Abraham said to the young men with him: "The lad and I will go yonder and worship, and we will come again to you", yet Isaac is not mentioned as Abraham returned to the men and they travelled together back to Beersheba. It will help us to understand this by considering the events of the search for a bride in the following way.

- The father and the son went together to worship in the sacrifice of the only, well-loved son with the promise to men of the household of faith that they will "come again".
- After the sacrifice, the son departed elsewhere and did not return to the household.
- A servant was sent to search for a bride for the son; she must come from a family which believed in the God of Abraham and she must share that belief.

- A bride was found, the servant asked her to leave immediately to go to meet the bridegroom. Unbelieving family members tried to make her stay a while; she refused saying, "I will go".
- The servant led the bride to her bridegroom who came from the south. He had now "come again" to claim his bride. He received her, married her and loved her. She was his wife.

In this pattern we see a type of the work of the Lord Jesus Christ. Here is his death and departure to ascend to the right hand of his Father, "as a man going into a far country". When the time comes for the marriage supper of the Lamb the angels will be sent to call the faithful to meet the bridegroom and become his bride. An immediate response will be essential saying, "I will go" and leaving behind all the things of this world that seek to cling to us.

As Abraham returned to the young men, no doubt they asked where Isaac was; he had said he would come again and yet had delayed his coming. We do not know what Abraham told them, but we do know the words of our Lord who drew on this event as he comforted his disciples the night before his death: he would depart; they would not see him again for he had work to do elsewhere. Yet he would return, like Isaac he would come again and they would then be with him forever.

> "I go to prepare a place for you. And if I go and prepare a place for you, I will come again and receive you to myself; that where I am, there you may be also." (John 14:2,3)

Abraham's final act

We next read of the sending away of Abraham's other children and their mothers. All of these children had been born before Isaac but now they were sent away. Abraham was determined that they would not try to impede Isaac's succession as did Ishmael. Sarah was dead, her spiritual influence and mother's protective care was no longer available. Abraham was old and his days nearly spent. All of his thoughts were on Isaac and the succession that would follow him.

The points made above are therefore linked. Twice we read that Abraham gave all that he had to Isaac; it is repeated to emphasise to us its importance (Genesis 24:36; 25:5). We should not just see this as a natural inheritance of material things but that, as God had said, all the promises would pass to Isaac, and to this son only – all others had to depart. We can say of him as the Lord God said of His Son, he had been appointed heir of all things (Hebrews 1:2) and so it was Isaac alone, of all the patriarchs in Genesis, who never left the land of promise, which in type he inherited. But Isaac in turn had to pass on the promises to his sons. To do this he needed a bride and the wonderfully detailed, careful choosing of her has been shown in chapter 24. The Lord sent an angel to direct events, Abraham having sent his most faithful servant to follow his directions.

It was therefore only after these things that Abraham died aged one hundred and seventy-five. His work in every aspect was then complete and the handover to Isaac is confirmed in the words that immediately follow in chapter 25, for he in turn now received the blessing.

> "And it came to pass, after the death of Abraham, that God blessed his son Isaac. And Isaac dwelt at Beer Lahai Roi."
>
> (Genesis 25:11)

At the end of Psalm 5, one which is a morning prayer for disciples throughout the ages, David wrote words that could have been written specifically of Abraham as an epitaph to his life.

He was the man blessed by the Lord, the one who called on His name and rejoiced when seeing the day of the Lord Jesus Christ, the first man to be accounted righteous because of his faith in the promises the Lord made to him.

> "But let all those rejoice who put their trust in you; let them ever shout for joy, because you defend them; let those also who love your name be joyful in you. For you, O LORD, will bless the righteous; with favour you will surround him as with a shield." (Psalm 5:11,12)

SECTION FIVE:
Chosen families – Isaac and Jacob

31 | Isaac and Rebekah

AS we move from one major section to the next we see that they are often joined together as part of the same literary structure. Genesis is a book packed with information, so many events, places, and people that sometimes it is difficult to see the threads linking one chapter to the next. However, exploring these many patterns and structures can often help us to see the overall 'big picture' of how seemingly quite different events are linked spiritually as part of God's purpose and the move from Abraham to Isaac is no exception.

When we look at the following pattern, we are guided to focus on one central point.

The Lord chooses a younger son, Isaac (21:8-19).
- The rejected firstborn son, Ishmael, marries a foreign woman (21:20,21).
  - Strife between the family of the faithful and Abimelech over Abraham's wells, a treaty is made and separateness agreed (21:22-34).
    - The covenant depends on the willingness of a son to give up his life for it (22:1-19).
      - Genealogy of part of the family who are not of the household of faith (22:20-24).
        - The death of Sarah (23:1-20).
          - **The choosing of the bride and the marriage with the son** (24:1-67).
        - The death of Abraham (25:1-10).

Genealogy of part of the family who are not of the household of faith (25:11-18).

The covenant is rejected by a son whose life is more important to him (25:19-34).

Strife between the family of the faithful and Abimelech over Abraham's wells, a treaty is made and separateness agreed (26:1-33).

The rejected firstborn son, Esau, marries a foreign woman (26:34,35).

The Lord chooses a younger son, Jacob (27:1–28:4).

This pattern helps with the questions that are asked when we look at Isaac and his family. Who was faithful, who was faithless? Why did Jacob and Isaac act as they did? When we look at this structure, the Lord directs us to see all of these events as part of His purpose. All are part of the promise-blessings He has given and which will ultimately lead to the coming of *the* Bridegroom with his bride into the promised kingdom. In these events the Lord works with the faithful and the unfaithful are rejected and sent or go away so that His people are not compromised by them.

Most writers see Isaac as a man who put his love for Esau and a desire for venison stew above his faith in the promises. He is accused as a man who "sought to frustrate the purpose of God" or even "one who disappears from the scene, a vessel no longer fit for the maker's use".[1] Yet in the tangled web of relationships between father, mother and sons only Esau is condemned by God in the scriptures. No word of reproof, no accusation of sin is made by the Lord against Isaac, Jacob, Rebekah.

The Letter to the Hebrews gives us key information about the background of the events in Genesis 25-27:

> "By faith he (Abraham) dwelt in the land of promise as in a foreign country, dwelling in tents with Isaac and Jacob, the heirs with him of the same promise; for he waited for the city

1 A. Pink, *Gleanings in Genesis*, page 235.

which has foundations, whose builder and maker is God."
(Hebrews 11:9,10)

Abraham was one hundred and seventy five years old when he died and therefore his life overlapped those of Jacob and Esau by fifteen years. What a lovely picture this is: here is an aged grandfather spending his last years with a faithful son, Isaac, and grandson, Jacob, teaching them of all that God had revealed to him. We can imagine Jacob, spellbound by what he heard, saying to his grandfather, 'Tell me again about how the Lord appeared to you in Ur, tell me again about how you took my father to Moriah ...' Esau was not there; he too had the opportunity to learn of these precious things but he was not interested. It was only Isaac and Jacob who believed and are named in the roll call of the faithful with Abraham and it was the land of promise that was a key part of their faith. The desire to be a part of this promise would greatly influence Jacob's dealings with Esau.

But there is another key point, "Abraham waited ..." and we get a clue about another message he shared with those who would listen. There had been occasions in his life when he had tried to force the pace, work out God's purpose for himself – the taking of Hagar is a prime example of this. Yet through all these events God had moulded his character until he recognised that the Lord alone could fulfil all that he desired and that He would do it at His appointed time. The Bible often links waiting with patience and the words of David comment beautifully on Abraham's teaching:

"Commit your way to the Lord, trust also in him, and he shall bring it to pass. He shall bring forth your righteousness as the light, and your justice as the noonday. Rest in the Lord, and wait patiently for him ... But those who wait on the Lord, they shall inherit the earth ... But the meek shall inherit the earth, and shall delight themselves in the abundance of peace." (Psalm 37:5-11)

As we read these words perhaps Mendelssohn's music echoes in our ears, "O rest in the Lord, wait patiently for Him and He will give thee thy heart's desires".

What response was there to such teaching by Abraham? Son and grandson responded differently: Isaac is shown to be a meek man, willing to let God work out problems he cannot solve; Jacob was like his grandfather and had to learn meekness the hard way.

Isaac

We saw, when we looked at Genesis 22, that the requested sacrifice demanded faith from both father and son. In meek obedience to his father Isaac lay down on the wood accepting, however incredibly difficult it must have been, that this was the will of God. His next recorded act after this chapter is that he went out into the field to meditate in the evening (Genesis 24:63). His father's steward had been away some time on the search for a bride for him. We can imagine Isaac's intense interest in this: what was happening, when would the steward return? Daily he would have prayed that a woman who could share the promises with him would be found. Day by day he waited patiently and his prayers were answered. He lifted up his eyes, camels were coming and Rebekah was there.

It was into his mother's tent that he took her. Sarah had been dead for four years. Apparently her tent had been retained for Isaac's wife, whenever she came and Rebekah was now to take on Sarah's mantle as the mother of Israel. Sarah had fought fiercely for Isaac, demanding that Abraham's other son be sent away. Rebekah would also be faced with a choice – which son would be the heir?

For the first twenty years of their marriage no children were born to Isaac and Rebekah. Isaac's reaction to this stands in sharp contrast to that of Abraham when faced with Sarah's barrenness. He pleaded with the Lord for his wife and the language implies continuing supplication by him, not for a son for himself, but for the heartache suffered by a barren woman. And in due time the Lord answered the prayers of this quiet man who laid the problem before his God as the only possible course of action.

Two sons, two nations

> "... Rebekah his wife conceived. But the children struggled together within her; and she said, 'If all is well, why am I like this?' So she went to inquire of the LORD. And the LORD said to her: 'Two nations are in your womb, two peoples shall be separated from your body; one people shall be stronger than the other, and the older shall serve the younger.' So when her days were fulfilled for her to give birth, indeed there were twins in her womb. And the first came out red. He was like a hairy garment all over; so they called his name Esau. Afterward his brother came out, and his hand took hold of Esau's heel; so his name was called Jacob. Isaac was sixty years old when she bore them." (Genesis 25:21-26)

It was a difficult pregnancy. It was not just that the babies kicked within her womb. The Hebrew word used, *ratsats*, carries a very powerful meaning: the two oppressed, crashed into each other. From conception, these two sons sought not to coexist together. No womb, no family home, no land would be big enough to accommodate both; there was no sibling love between them.

From the beginning, wherever Abraham had camped, he had built an altar at which to worship the Lord and there was one here at Mamre (Genesis 13:18) where he had returned after the death of Sarah. Rebekah went to ask the Lord about the struggle within her and no doubt it was to this altar she went.

The Lord's answer was startling.

- She was carrying twins.
- Each would father a nation.
- Two distinctly separate races would come from her.
- One would be stronger than the other.
- The elder (the one born first) would be subordinate to the younger. The law of primogeniture would be set aside.

The differences between the two sons are shown in the descriptions of their characteristics and we see immediately that these are spiritual as well as physical. Jacob emerged from the womb clutching his brother's heel; from the beginning he was a supplanter wanting to replace his brother as the firstborn.

This would be a contest for dominion between the flesh and the spirit. It is significant that we do not read of Rebekah sharing the angel's words with Isaac and perhaps she kept this revelation to herself. If so, this would be a major problem for her when the time came for the patriarchal blessing of the eldest son.

Esau was a ruddy (*admoniy*) baby who grew to choose red (*adom*) stew rather than the birthright, hence his descendants would be called Edom (*edowm*). All of these words come from the Hebrew root, *adam*, and are a play on words with the name Adam, given to the first man made from the dust of the ground (*adamah*). "The first man is of the earth, earthy" wrote the Apostle Paul and such was Esau, a man of no spiritual values. He was also a "man of the field", the only time in the Bible this phrase is used. Previously in Genesis we have been introduced to the beasts of the field and this link between Esau and animals is made deliberately for, in his complete rejection of the Lord, he became one of whom the Psalmist wrote: "Man who is in honour, yet does not understand, is like the beasts that perish" (Psalm 49:20). He was a skilled hunter, following the pattern set by Nimrod many years before.

But there is a more telling phrase about him: he was a hairy (*sear*) baby, hence he was called Esau, 'covered with hair'. Yet when Jacob described him to Rebekah he called him a hairy (*saiyr*) man (Genesis 27:11) and he used a different word which described his brother as looking like a goat. It is the word used to describe the animals presented as sin offerings under the law or the pagan gods, devils, satyrs,[2] that Israel was commanded to leave strictly alone. When we come to the New Testament, the choice presented in Matthew 25 is between being a sheep or a goat and anyone seeing flocks of both animals in a developing country immediately notes the fundamental difference. Sheep need a shepherd and will follow his leadership; goats do not need one, will not follow one but go their own way wherever they wish. Such was Esau.

Yet the Lord's words to Rebekah do not imply that Esau was rejected by God before he was even born. As we have seen,

2 Isaiah 34:14; 2 Chronicles 11:15.

Abraham had commanded his household and his children to keep the way of the Lord and no doubt the same command was made to both his grandchildren. Both had the same opportunity, but only Jacob responded. He was a mild (*tam*, perfect) man who spent his time in tents with his father and grandfather sharing their faith. Virtually the same word was used by God to Abraham when he finally realised that only the Lord could give him a son: "Walk before me and be perfect (*tamiym*)"; no doubt this was shared with Jacob and made a great impression on him.

The birthright despised

All of the above is detail given to us to aid our understanding of the sad event that followed:

> "Now Jacob cooked (*zwud*) a stew (*nazid*); and Esau came in from the field, and he was weary. And Esau said to Jacob, 'Please feed me with that same red stew, for I am weary'. Therefore his name was called Edom. But Jacob said, 'Sell me your birthright as of this day'. And Esau said, 'Look, I am about to die; so what is this birthright to me?' Then Jacob said, 'Swear to me as of this day'. So he swore to him, and sold his birthright to Jacob. And Jacob gave Esau bread and stew of lentils; then he ate and drank, arose, and went his way. Thus Esau despised his birthright." (Genesis 25:29-34)

We do not know whether it was a coincidence that Jacob was cooking stew as Esau returned or whether it was a planned event. In either case, Jacob took full advantage of the situation that developed.

The language used to describe Jacob's cooking is unusual: literally it is, "Jacob boiled (*zwud*) boiled food (*nazid*)". Whilst *nazid* is commonly used to describe food, this is the only occasion the verb *zwud* is used of food preparation. The other nine times when it is used in the Bible are of people acting proudly or presumptuously.[3]

3 See *Theological wordbook of the Old Testament*, #547, for example, Nehemiah 9:10,16.

Was there a touch of this in Jacob's behaviour? He was a man who loved the promises, yet by birth he would inherit neither the birthright nor the blessing. He passionately desired them. Now he had an opportunity to take the birthright for himself, using his wits to outmanoeuvre his brother, for Esau thought only of his stomach – the birthright meant nothing to him.

Whilst Esau's request was polite, "Please feed me", Jacob was peremptory to the point of curtness: 'Sell me right now', 'swear to me right now'.

What exactly was the birthright?

Although later we read of the right of the firstborn to have a double portion of the inheritance (Deuteronomy 21:17) it is unlikely that Esau would have given up the rights to anything of material gain. His second words were: 'I'm starving, of what value is the birthright to me?' Was he really so hungry that he felt he was dying of starvation? There is another way of reading his words; he was a man who had rejected all of Abraham's teaching, including that of the resurrection. Life for Esau was all about the 'here and now' and with no belief in a life to come, of what use was the birthright? He was hungry and, to him, the birthright was not worth a bowl of soup.

We find a clue about it later in Genesis when we meet another firstborn son who lost his birthright:

> "Reuben, you are my firstborn, my might and the beginning of my strength, the excellency of dignity and the excellency of power. Unstable as water, you shall not excel."
>
> (Genesis 49:3,4)

Because of his immorality this firstborn son, Reuben, lost pre-eminence in two things that should have been his: the excellency of power – the authority by right of being the firstborn son and the excellency of dignity (*seeth*). The first time this word is used is in Genesis 4 when the Lord spoke to Cain: "If you do well, will you not be accepted (*seeth*)?" What Cain, Esau and Reuben lost was the position of being the family priest in the era before the Law, the responsibility to lead worship at the altars built wherever God's people settled. It is a comment on the inability of human nature to bring reconciliation in this way that no firstborn son was accepted by the Lord in the role to which he had been born. When we reach Moses and the Law, the same principle is in place, all the firstborn belonged to God for His service yet they were replaced by those born into the tribe of Levi. Only when we reach the New Testament do we meet *the* firstborn Son, the one provided by the Lord Himself, who would totally fulfil the purpose for which he came into the world.

It was this role that Esau despised, seeing it as worthless, holding it in contempt and so once again, a younger, faithful son took on this responsibility.

Esau is condemned in unequivocal language in the Bible in both Old and New Testaments.

> "'Was not Esau Jacob's brother?' says the LORD. 'Yet Jacob I have loved; but Esau I have hated.'" (Malachi 1:2,3)

It is a fearful thing to be hated in this way, an enemy of the Lord and later in the chapter, as the Lord rebukes the priests of Israel, we see why Esau was mentioned – he and they had much in common:

> "A son honours his father, and a servant his master. If then I am the Father, where is my honour? And if I am a Master, where is my reverence? says the LORD of hosts to you priests who despise my name. Yet you say, 'In what way have we despised your name?' You offer defiled food on my altar. But say, 'In what way have we defiled you?' By saying, the table of the LORD is contemptible." (Malachi 1:6,7)

In his rejection of the priestly role, Esau had despised the name of the Lord and treated the family altar with contempt. He was, wrote the author of Hebrews:

> "... a profane person ... who for one morsel of food sold his birthright. For you know that afterward, when he wanted to inherit the blessing, he was rejected, for he found no place for repentance, though he sought it diligently with tears."
>
> (Hebrews 12:16,17)

These words also look back to Malachi and his use of the Esau / Jacob relationship as he addressed the priests of his day.[4]

> "Have we not all one father? hath not one God created us? why do we deal treacherously every man against his brother, by profaning the covenant of our fathers?" (Malachi 2:10, KJV)

In despising the birthright, Esau profaned the covenant made by the Lord with Esau's forefathers. He and Jacob had a common father, Isaac, yet reacted quite differently to his teaching. In these words we also get a glimpse of the rift between the two sons. Were Esau's actions seen as treachery against the way of the Lord by his brother?

It is absolutely incredible that any man could so completely turn his back on the promises of the Lord for a bowl of lentil soup. Yet it is summed up for us in the final words of the chapter: he ate and drank and rose up and went *his* way; the way of the Lord, in which he had been instructed, no longer figured in his life.

What of Jacob?

He was in many ways like his grandfather, Abraham, full of the right motives yet trying to bring about God's purpose in his own way. He had seen Esau's neglect of his spiritual responsibilities. No doubt he knew that he despised these things that were so dear to him and, in turn, Jacob despised his brother. If he had cared for him he would have fed him without conditions. The family was without an eldest son to lead them in worship and he aspired to take over this task. Did he not take it to God in prayer? In his actions were sown the seeds of resentment and dislike that would flare up again years later over Isaac's blessing of his sons.

4 There is not scope in this book to consider fully the way Malachi looked back to Esau and Jacob. It is well worth a more detailed study by readers.

32 | Isaac and Abimelech

FOR the second time we meet a famine in the land of Canaan. Apparently it was a local one. It is likely that Isaac had returned to Beer-lahai-roi, the well of Lahai-roi, in the Negev where he settled after the events of chapter 22 and it was an area of low rainfall at the best of times. Perhaps this well would now not support all of his family and he had to move. He went north-west until he reached Gerar, a place of good grazing (2 Chronicles 14:14), and stopped there. It is clear from the events that followed that both Esau and Jacob were missing and that some of the family's flocks and herds had also remained elsewhere. But Gerar (it means 'a lodging place') was not Isaac's final destination; he meant to go down into Egypt as his father had done during the previous famine.

For the first time in the Biblical record God spoke directly to him, repeating the promise-blessings given to Abraham but with significant differences:

> "Then the LORD appeared to him and said: 'Do not go down to Egypt; live (*shakan*, settle down, reside) in the land of which I shall tell you. Dwell (*guwr*, sojourn) in this land, and I will be with you and bless you; for to you and your descendants (*zera*, seed) I give all these lands, and I will perform the oath which I swore to Abraham your father. And I will make your descendants (*zera*) multiply as the stars of heaven; I will give to your descendants (*zera*) all these lands; and in your seed (*zera*) all the nations of the earth shall be blessed; because Abraham

> obeyed my voice and kept my charge, my commandments, my statutes, and my laws.'" (Genesis 26:2-5)

Here are echoes back to promises made to Abraham in Genesis 12-15, but Isaac's mind would be filled most of all with memories of the event of chapter 22. It was at the time of his call to sacrifice Isaac that the Lord swore an oath to Abraham, because he had obeyed His voice (Genesis 22:18). Abraham had been entrusted by God with "keeping the way of the LORD" and this had reached its zenith in his offering of Isaac. It was an act of total obedience, described as keeping all of God's laws.

Now the Lord asked of Isaac a continuing trust in Him, as he had at Moriah and, if he showed this, then the Lord would be with him. This is the first time in scripture that God spoke directly to a man saying, "I will be with you". Whatever happened to him, the chosen son was to continue in the same spirit of meekness and obedience that he had shown in the past; if he did this the Lord would be with him, supporting him all the days of his life.

But there is something new in this promise. Not only did the Lord tell him that from him would come *the* seed through whom all the nations of the earth would be blessed, he was also told that to his seed God would give "all these lands" and this must again refer to the *one* seed, the Lord Jesus Christ. For the first time all the peoples of the earth and the countries in which they live are brought together as part of the promises. The kingdom will encompass the whole earth; the Lord Jesus Christ is heir to it all, peoples and lands together, for the Psalmist wrote of him:

> "Yet I have set my King on my holy hill of Zion. I will declare the decree: the LORD has said to me, 'You are my Son, today I have begotten you. Ask of me, and I will give you the nations for your inheritance, and the ends of the earth for your possession'." (Psalm 2:6-8)

But this promise was conditional: 'Don't go to Egypt, settle down permanently in a place that I will tell you of, sojourn temporarily here at Gerar, in this land, and I will bless you.' Two different places are implied and the Lord appeared to him the second time when he reached Beersheba, the place where he was to settle.

In spite of the promise of God's protecting presence with him in Gerar, Isaac behaved just like his father when faced with a Philistine king.[1] Rebekah was introduced as his sister and, like Sarah, she was a desirable woman even in her old age. Again, a king behaved more honourably than the visitor to his country but trouble followed.

We have seen that it was not God's intention that Isaac should remain in the company of the Philistines. His stay there was to be temporary for spiritual danger lay ahead if they became too close, yet we read that Isaac stayed there a long time. What would the Lord do?

Isaac, for the first time, sowed crops and began a settled existence. God blessed him – it was a miraculous crop, a hundredfold yield, far more than any farmer could ever achieve in the land. The language used emphasises the rapid, miraculous growth in his wealth and position. He 'became great, continued to become greater and became very great'. It is the word that was first used when the Lord said to Abraham: "I will make of you a great nation"; now it was used of Isaac's household to portray it as a microcosm of what Israel could become if it too was obedient to the charge God gave them. Many years later, on the border of the Promised Land, Moses reflected on these words to Isaac in his exhortation to his people:

> "Surely I have taught you statutes and judgments, just as the LORD my God commanded me, that you should act according to them in the land which you go to possess. Therefore be careful to observe them; for this is your wisdom and your understanding in the sight of the peoples who will hear all

1 This Abimelech cannot be the same one as in chapter 20 – that was many years before. The name is probably a royal title rather than a proper name. The Philistines came from Caphtor, Crete, and it seems likely that these people were one of the earliest groups to enter the land. Certainly they were not great enough to occupy the pentapolis we meet in the time of Samuel and David.

these statutes, and say, 'Surely this great nation is a wise and understanding people'. For what great nation is there that has God so near to it, as the LORD our God is to us, for whatever reason we may call upon him?" (Deuteronomy 4:5-7)

Through this miraculous greatness, Isaac became a threat to the Philistines and they had to separate, but through it Abimelech also understood that the Lord was with him and had blessed him. He was worried in case the stronger Hebrew turned against him and did him harm. So he went to him and brokered a peace treaty – they would live at peace but separately and leave each other alone. How marvellously the Lord worked out His purpose through both Isaac and Abimelech. His people were guided in this way to keep separate from the world.

But it is Isaac's behaviour that catches our eyes.

- The Philistines blocked his wells and sent him away.
- Isaac moved on and found a spring, living water, a precious source. The Philistines came and demanded it; Isaac gave it to them, called it Esek (contention), and quietly dug another well.
- The Philistines demanded this one also; Isaac gave it to them, called it Sitnah (trouble), and meekly moved on.
- Once away from their territory, Isaac dug another well, Rehoboth (a roomy place), far enough away from the Philistines so that they left him alone.
- From there, recognising that God was working through him, he went to Beersheba and the *very same night* he arrived God appeared to him. He had reached the place where he was to stay. Years before when his father had arrived in the land that God had shown to him, the Lord appeared to him the second time with an amplified promise. Abraham's response had been to build an altar, pitch his tent and call upon the name of the Lord. Now his son responded in exactly the same way.

"Then he went up from there to Beersheba. And the LORD appeared to him the same night and said, 'I am the God of your father Abraham; do not fear, for I am with you. I will

> bless you and multiply your descendants for my servant Abraham's sake.' So he built an altar there and called on the name of the LORD, and he pitched his tent there; and there Isaac's servants dug a well." (Genesis 26:23-25)

Isaac had recognised the reason for the Lord's guidance of him – he was to remain separate from the people of the land. At Beersheba, the spiritual issues were dealt with first: an altar was built, worship instituted, only then are we told of the forming of the encampment and the rebuilding of the well of the oath, Beersheba.

Esau's wives

Ten years passed: Esau and Jacob were forty years old, their father one hundred. Perhaps Esau remembered that Isaac had been forty when he married. He would know the story of how Abraham was adamant that his son should not marry a Canaanite and sent his servant to Haran to find a wife who would share his beliefs. Esau now deliberately married two Canaanite women in defiance of his parents. In this chapter a contrast has been drawn for us between Isaac's separateness and Esau's rejection of it. For one who despised the birthright, separateness was a nonsense. Why bother with it when he had so much in common with the people of the land? Perhaps he had met some of them when out in the field; perhaps his description in Hebrews as a fornicator had some literal, physical background.

These wives were a source of grief to both Isaac and Rebekah – quarrelsome, provoking[2] them, refusing to listen to their teaching or to accept their God.

Here was a son whom Isaac loved once again going against his father's teaching, yet he was the firstborn. How would Isaac deal with him and the problems his primogeniture brought?

---

2 The Septuagint version uses a word translated as "provoking" or "rebellious".

33 | A family torn apart

THIRTY-SEVEN years had now passed since Esau was married. We are told nothing of this time apart from the one aspect we explored at the end of chapter 35. Esau's wives were a source of trouble and bitterness; they made life miserable for Isaac and Rebekah and the family enclave must have been a very unhappy one. Isaac was fully aware that Esau, whom he loved, had rejected his faith but what could he do? Years earlier, Abraham had also loved Ishmael yet, because of his rejection of the Lord and his behaviour towards Isaac, he sent him away at Sarah's demand. If Rebekah had urged a similar action on her husband, he had refused to take it. We have a picture of a polarised family, husband and wife divided in their views of their two sons. Isaac loved Esau, he was a 'man's man', assertive and dominant, everything that his father was not. Isaac had a weakness for game meat and his elder son had won his affections over many years through supplying him with venison; Esau is described as "his son", "my son".

In contrast, Jacob was his mother's favourite, "her son" and he was the one the angel had described, before his birth, as becoming pre-eminent.

Jacob was a strange mixture of the genes of both parents. We see him like Isaac, a meek man who will work twenty years as an indentured servant without complaint, a mature man who will find much trouble because he will obey his mother's commands to do something wrong. But he was also like his mother, his uncle and both wives. He too had inherited a strong streak of deceitfulness that was prevalent in that side of the family.

But transcending these traits, he was the son who had embraced the way of the Lord, and in her protection of him Rebekah was very like Sarah with Isaac. We see her as she was at the well in Haran: energetic, forceful, taking control of the situation and when she prepared Jacob to go in and trick Isaac out of the blessing we read of one curious detail:

> "Then Rebekah took the choice clothes of her elder son Esau, which were with her in the house, and put them on Jacob her younger son." (Genesis 27:15)

What was this garment and why is it described as Esau's 'best clothes'? Furthermore, what was his mother doing with it? Why was it in her tent and not with one of Esau's wives? It appears that, even though it was a special garment, it had been discarded by Esau and Rebekah had kept it. It has been suggested[1] that this was the priestly garment worn by the firstborn as he exercised his birthright responsibilities as the family priest. Just as Esau had laid these duties aside so he had discarded his priestly coat and Rebekah had kept it safe for many years.

Trickery and deception

> "Now it came to pass, when Isaac was old and his eyes were so dim that he could not see, that he called Esau his older son and said to him, 'My son'. And he answered him, 'Here I am'. Then he said, 'Behold now, I am old. I do not know the day of my death. Now therefore, please take your weapons, your quiver and your bow, and go out to the field and hunt game for me. And make me savoury food, such as I love, and bring it to me that I may eat, that my soul may bless you before I die'." (Genesis 27:1-4)

Although Isaac would live for another forty-three years he felt old and was going blind. It was time for the formal blessing of the oldest son, the heir of the family, the one who would inherit

1 J. J. Blunt, *Undesigned Scriptural Coincidences*, pages 11-15.

when his father died. Such events were often preceded by a formal meal and Isaac asked Esau to provide the dish he loved.

Rebekah heard Isaac's words and ordered Jacob to disguise himself, to pretend to be Esau and take the blessing. In this she absolutely dominated him. Three times he was told 'Do as I say'; he was hesitant, seeing only the difficulties but she completely overruled him, prepared to take any consequences upon herself: "Upon me be your curse my son." Jacob understood the seriousness of what he was told to do; the risk was that Isaac would guess who it was before him and see Jacob as a mocker. His actions show the folly of behaving in this way, one lie led to another to assuage his father's suspicions.

"Who are you my son?"

"I am Esau your firstborn."

"How did you find it so quickly?"

"Because the LORD your God brought it to me."

"Are you really my son Esau?"

"I am".

It is amazing that he got away with this. Esau would never have used the name of the Lord; he would have boasted of his prowess as a hunter when asked such a question.

This was a tragedy based on a complete lack of communication in the family. Apparently Rebekah had never shared with Isaac the angel's words about their two sons in her womb. He had never shared with her his plans about the blessing Esau should have. She then misunderstood what he intended to do and reacted badly thinking that her husband was about to do something completely wrong – to give *the blessing*, that of Abraham and Isaac, to a son who deserved none of it at all. Yet this was never Isaac's plan.

How ironical that Jacob now wore the firstborn's special coat as he went in to Isaac, believing with his mother that his father would deliver the Abrahamic promise-blessing, yet he was not given what he hoped for. But he also went in disguised as Esau, pretending to be that hairy man who had despised his birthright! It is a picture of a man so intent on getting what he wanted in life that he laid aside all that his grandfather and father had taught him. He was hopelessly mixed up!

Isaac's blessings of his sons		
To Jacob (Esau) (27:27-29)	**To Esau (27:39,40)**	**To Jacob (28:3,4)**
And he came near and kissed him; and he smelled the smell of his clothing, and blessed him and said: "Surely, the smell of my son Is like the smell of a field Which the LORD has blessed."	Then Isaac his father answered and said to him:	Arise, go to Padan-Aram, to the house of Bethuel your mother's father; and take yourself a wife from there of the daughters of Laban your mother's brother.
Therefore may God give you of the dew of heaven, of the fatness of the earth, and plenty of grain and wine.	Behold, your dwelling shall be of the fatness of the earth, and of the dew of heaven from above.	May God Almighty bless you, and make you fruitful and multiply you, that you may be an assembly of peoples;
Let peoples serve you, and nations bow down to you. Be master over your brethren, and let your mother's sons bow down to you.	By your sword you shall live, and you shall serve your brother; and it shall come to pass, when you become restless, that you shall break his yoke from your neck.	And give you the blessing of Abraham, to you and your descendants with you, that you may inherit the land in which you are a stranger, which God gave to Abraham.
Cursed be everyone who curses you, and blessed be those who bless you!		

It is important to compare the three blessings Isaac gave his sons. In the first, the one intended for Esau, there was nothing of the special promise-blessing. Isaac never meant to give this to Esau, how could he? This son had rejected his priestly responsibilities, he was a profane man who had joined himself to pagan Canaanite women and was utterly unsuitable for such a privilege. Furthermore there was nothing about the land in Isaac's words and the land was an absolutely key part of God's promises. Esau never showed any interest in the land, only in his father's possessions. Yet Isaac loved him and he was his eldest son; by the law of primogeniture his was the rightful inheritance of his father's estate and position as head of the family.

So he blessed the son before him in the following way, thinking it was Esau.

> "Therefore may God give you of the dew of heaven, of the fatness of the earth, and plenty of grain and wine."

In his direct speech to his son, Isaac did not use the covenant name of the Lord, rather it was the *Elohim*, the God who created the Heavens and the Earth, who was asked to give Esau agricultural fertility, an essential requirement for such an agrarian based community. But the words "grain" and "wine" have a hidden meaning for grain (*dagan*) is the same word as Dagon, the Philistine god of fertility and wine (*tiyrowsh*) the same as Tirosh, a Canaanite, Bacchus-type god.[2] Were these the gods that Esau's Canaanite wives had brought with them and which he had dallied with? Was Isaac reminding the son before him that it was only through his God, the God of Abraham, such a blessing could come?

> "Let peoples serve you, and nations bow down to you. Be master over your brethren, and let your mother's sons bow down to you." (Genesis 27:29)

Esau was the firstborn and therefore political supremacy was his: he was to be the secular head of the family after Isaac, acknowledged as such by his relations. With the headship would come the wealth, the flocks and herds with which God had blessed Isaac – they would pass down to Esau. If Isaac was unaware of the angel's words to Rebekah before his sons' birth then this would have been a perfectly natural and correct blessing to give him.

2 Hamilton, 18-50, page 221.

> "Cursed be everyone who curses you, and blessed be those who bless you!"

This is not the same as the words to Abraham in chapter 12. Isaac did not invoke the name of the Lord as the One who was asked to do this. Rather it was a general benediction for his oldest son – a father's desire for political supremacy for him.

The drama of the event is heightened by the next words. No sooner had Jacob left with this blessing than Esau returned, requesting his blessing and Isaac understood what had happened:

> "Then Isaac trembled exceedingly, and said, 'Who? Where is the one who hunted game and brought it to me? I ate all of it before you came, and I have blessed him – and indeed he shall be blessed'." (Genesis 27:33)

The blessing given was irrevocable and Isaac's reaction was extreme: he trembled and the Geneva Bible captures the intensity of what he felt, "he was stricken with a very great fear". But this was not fear of his son, rather that Isaac immediately understood that the Lord had been at work. There is a remarkable picture in Isaiah, a contrast between the man who trembles at God's word, as did Isaac, and the one who is utterly rejected because of his rejection of it, as was Esau:

> "... on this one will I look: on him who is poor and of a contrite spirit, and who trembles at my word ... they have chosen their own ways, and their soul delights in their abominations, so will I choose their delusions, and bring their fears on them; because, when I called, no one answered, when I spoke they did not hear; but they did evil before my eyes, and chose that in which I do not delight." (Isaiah 66:2-4)

Esau begged his father for a blessing with great and bitter crying. He had brought bitterness of mind to his parents by his lifestyle, now he experienced a heartfelt loss as they had. But there was no way back (Hebrews 12:17), Isaac could not reverse what was done. Years later Jacob described Yahweh to Laban as "the God of my father, the God of Abraham and the Fear of Isaac". This last title is unique to Isaac and it must surely have

Psalm 37

We have already looked briefly at Psalm 37 in connection with Abraham and how he learned to be patient. But its teaching goes further: those who are patient, who rest in the Lord and wait for Him will be rewarded with the inheritance.

- Those who wait on the Lord will inherit the land (verse 9).
- The meek shall inherit the land (verse 11).
- The Lord knows the days of the perfect (such as Jacob) and their inheritance will be forever (verse 18).
- The blessed of the Lord shall inherit the land (verse 22).
- The righteous shall inherit the land and dwell in it forever (verse 29).
- Wait on the Lord and keep His way and He shall exalt you to inherit the land (verse 34).

Once again in words of David we see how well he knew the events of the lives of those who received the promises before him. Here is a divinely inspired summary of the things Jacob had to learn in his life, suffering many hard knocks in the process.

arisen at this time as he trembled with a very great fear. "The fear of the LORD is the beginning of wisdom" and Isaac now understood that, as well as physical blindness, he had suffered from spiritual blindness; his delight in his elder son had led him along a path which was not in the purpose of his God.

In the Letter to the Romans, the Apostle Paul drew on the record of Esau and Jacob, using it to make an analogy with natural and spiritual Israel. For Jews who insisted that they were God's chosen people, Israel His firstborn, it had been difficult to accept that Gentiles could play a part in the Israel of God. Being a descendant of Abraham did not automatically make one a child of God for "the purpose of God according to election stands not of works but of him who calls ... as it is written, Jacob have I loved but Esau have I hated".

Living with the consequences

One of the lessons we learn in life is that, although the Lord will completely forgive our sins through our faith in His Son, He does not take away the consequences of the mistakes that we make. It is from them that we learn lessons, seeing the effect of our behaviour on our lives and those of others, often those whom we love. Then we turn to the example of our Lord Jesus Christ and see in him the pattern of conduct that we should have followed and are more determined to go his way in the future.

In Hebrews 12, before the writer turned to the example of profane Esau, he wrote about sonship and the Father's chastening of a son whom he loved:

> "'For whom the Lord loves he chastens, and scourges every son whom He receives.' If you endure chastening, God deals with you as with sons; for what son is there whom a father does not chasten? But if you are without chastening, of which all have become partakers, then you are [fatherless][3] and not sons. Furthermore, we have had human fathers who corrected us, and we paid them respect. Shall we not much more readily be in subjection to the Father of spirits and live? For they indeed for a few days chastened us as seemed best to them, but he for our profit, that we may be partakers of his holiness. Now no chastening seems to be joyful for the present, but painful; nevertheless, afterward it yields the peaceable fruit of righteousness to those who have been trained by it."
>
> (Hebrews 12:6-11)

In the events that now follow in Genesis we shall see the Lord at work moulding the character of Jacob, chastening him, forcing him to confront his failings and He does this for, "Jacob have I loved". It will take many years until Jacob is ready to become a 'prince with God' yet his life is an example to us of the truth of Paul's words that in the lives of all of God's children, "All things work together for good to those who love God, to those who are the called according to his purpose".

3 NKJV, "illegitimate".

Jacob's deceit brought an explosion from his brother: "He is rightly called Jacob (supplanter) for he has supplanted me these two times." Like all of us at times, Esau was full of self-pity and self-justification, forgetting that he had willingly given the birthright away, despising it for food. The consequences of that decision are now laid out before him. Jacob will be his lord, his brethren will serve him. His land will abound with corn and wine.[4] All that Isaac could offer Esau was that:

- Your dwelling will be away from the richness of the earth and from the dew of heaven.
- You will live by the sword and serve your brother.
- When you grow restless you will throw off his yoke (cf. 2 Kings 8:20-22).

The hatred of Esau for Jacob persisted through the lives of their descendants from Old Testament days into the New – the Jews hated cruel Herod who was of Edomite parentage. It is Ezekiel who tells us of it as a perpetual hatred, existing until the return of Christ. As Esau behaved, so did his descendants, despising the Lord, yet they will be forced to acknowledge Him at His Son's coming (Ezekiel 35:5-15).

Ishmaelite wives

Esau's final, bitter act, as Jacob was sent away to find a wife outside Canaan, was to take further wives for himself. He too decided to marry into the wider family and went to the Ishmaelites.[5] No doubt this was an act of provocation to his father. Isaac had made it clear that he saw Esau's Canaanite wives as evil, now his elder son took wives who were descendants of his father's brother, Ishmael who had mocked Isaac, despised the promises and been cast out. When we next meet Esau he will come from Seir where he had gone to live, leaving his father and the household of faith.

---

4 A blessing fulfilled when Israel entered a land, which was "a good land, flowing with milk and honey".

5 If the chronology of Jacob's life used in this book is correct, Ishmael had been dead fourteen years. Cf. Keil & Delitzsch, *Commentary on the Old Testament*, Volume 1, page 180.

34 | The road to Bethel

IT is clear from the end of chapter 27 that Isaac was not expected to live and that Esau planned to kill Jacob when his father died: "The days of mourning for my father are at hand; then I will kill my brother Jacob." Yet Isaac lived another forty-three years and Rebekah acted in haste. One mistake would now lead to another and no prayer for God's guidance is mentioned.

Instead, once again we see Rebekah as a decisive woman of action. Jacob was instructed to flee to Haran and there is a sad play on words here. In Hebrew 'flee' and 'blessing' sound almost the same: Jacob would indeed receive the blessing he wanted but the manner in which he achieved it caused him to flee for his life. He would be away, or so she thought, for a short time; when the dust settled he would be able to return home. Yet she had said to Jacob, "Your curse be upon me" and her words came true for Jacob would be away for twenty years and his mother never saw him again.

Isaac was apparently unaware of Esau's threat and Rebekah sheltered him from this, telling him of a (non-existent) risk that Jacob, like Esau, might marry a Canaanite. It was Isaac therefore, reacting to this risk, who sent Jacob away, finally giving him the promise-blessing that this son craved for.

> "May God Almighty bless you, and make you fruitful and multiply you, that you may be an assembly of peoples; and give you the blessing of Abraham, to you and your descendants with you, that you may inherit the land in which you are a stranger, which God gave to Abraham." (Genesis 28:3,4)

We can imagine how Jacob felt as he left on his journey. Everything he held dear had been left behind, not only his parents but also the land which he had just been promised. From Beersheba to Bethel was a journey of about 70 miles (113 km) and Jacob took an unusual route, travelling through the Judean mountains whereas the two main, much easier routes north were on the east and west of the great central ridge. But Jacob was seeking a particular location, "a certain place" which was important to him. In his journey he retraced his grandfather's route from Haran into the Promised Land. It was near Bethel

The time of Jacob's trouble

In this event at Bethel we see the origins of the phrase, "the time of Jacob's trouble". On a number of occasions as Judah was threatened with invasion and exile, it was to the God of Jacob they looked. He had promised their father that He would be with him in exile and bring him back to the land, and his descendants sought the same reassurance from the Lord in their troubled lives.

Psalm 46: Hezekiah, faced with Assyrian horde and Rabshakeh's invitation to submit to exile, looked back to Jacob at Bethel.

> "God is our refuge and strength, a very present help in trouble (*tsarah*) ... The God of Jacob is our refuge."

Jeremiah 30: The prophet had just foretold the seventy years of captivity: the words were written in a book, the people were terrified at this prospect and the Lord spoke to them of His mercy, likening their problems to those of Jacob.

> "Alas! For that day is great, so that none is like it; and it is the time of Jacob's trouble (*tsarah*), but he shall be saved out of it ... Therefore do not fear, O my servant Jacob, says the LORD, nor be dismayed, O Israel; for behold, I will save you from afar, and your seed from the land of their captivity. Jacob shall return, have rest and be quiet, and no one shall make him afraid."

that Abraham had built an altar and called upon the name of the Lord; now Jacob came to the same spot. Years later, as he returned and came back to this place, he recalled how he had felt. It had been a time when, "God answered me in the time of my distress (*tsarah*, trouble)" (Genesis 35:3).

Much fervent prayer was made that night before he went to sleep and the Lord answered him in a dream:

> "Then he dreamed, and behold, a ladder was set up on the earth, and its top reached to heaven; and there the angels of God were ascending and descending on it. And behold, the LORD stood above it and said: 'I am the LORD God of Abraham your father and the God of Isaac; the land on which you lie I will give to you and your descendants. Also your descendants shall be as the dust of the earth; you shall spread abroad to the west and the east, to the north and the south; and in you and in your seed all the families of the earth shall be blessed. Behold, I am with you and will keep you wherever you go, and will bring you back to this land; for I will not leave you until I have done what I have spoken to you.'" (Genesis 28:12-15)

What reassurance this was for Jacob and how generous was the grace of the Lord. Jacob was probably over seventy years old at this time, yet we have no previous record of him asking God for guidance or of God speaking directly to him. This was a watershed in his spiritual life. Now there was recognition of what he had done and the consequences of it, he knew that he would never be able to return to the land of promise without the Lord's guiding hand. He was first given reassurance that the Lord was ever at work. Even though Jacob was not aware of them, angels were always being sent out to implement God's purpose and returning to Him afterwards.

But this God was Abraham's God and Isaac's God – how that must have touched a nerve with Jacob. This God who now spoke to him was the God of the father whom he had so badly deceived and lied to. Yet it was because of his grandfather's and father's faith, he too would inherit the promises – the land would be his. How ashamed he must have felt about what he did to

Isaac; his father had a special relationship with God and he had treated him in such a way.

For the first time God spoke to man and said, "I am with you",[1] a reassurance to this man who was going into exile. Wherever he was, for the rest of his life God would be with him, a fact on which he reflected to Joseph just before his death telling him that "the God, before whom my fathers Abraham and Isaac walked, is the God who has fed me all my life long to this day".

God told Jacob that the quest before him had divine approval, the land he desired would be given to him and his seed. Three times the Lord spoke of them. He would indeed find a wife with whom he could share the promises, they would return to Canaan and in all of this the Lord would be with him.

The house of God

Jacob's immediate reaction to this theophany was to take a stone (from the remains of Abraham's altar?) and set it as a memorial pillar. We see what this action meant to him when we read of his return to the land, for when Laban pursued Jacob they exchanged vows at Galeed and Jacob raised a pillar there as part of that process (Genesis 31:45). Here then at Bethel, the house of God, God made a solemn promise to Jacob and he then made a vow in return. One writer describes it in this way:

> "His vow underscores how utterly dependant Jacob is upon his God. He who so easily and callously manipulated his own brother and father is now pictured as one who is completely beyond his own resources and at the mercy of another."[2]

Jacob's words echo the promise God made to him and the text in many versions presents a problem for us. It appears as if Jacob's response was conditional. "If God will be with me" sounds as if he would only accept the Lord as his God if He kept His word and continued to be with Jacob as promised. Yet God's promise of support had been unconditional because of Jacob's faith in the promises made by the God of his fathers.

---

1 Not the conditional, "I will be with you" to Isaac.

2 Hamilton, volume 2, page 248.

We see his words therefore as heartfelt imploring of the Lord: 'In spite of what I have done, if you will be with me then I will know that you are the Lord, my God.' What a relief therefore were the Lord's words to Jacob. How his conscience must have pricked him for what he had done. Would the Lord abandon him because of his deceit? The realisation that the Lord had not done this brought forth an outpouring of faith; he fully believed that what God had promised He would do. The Lord would indeed "perform the truth to Jacob" (Micah 7:20) and, just as Abraham had paid tithes to Melchizedek, so too would his grandson give back to the Lord a tenth of what He had given him.

The Lord's blessing of Jacob	**Jacob's response to the Lord**
I am the Lord God of Abraham your father and the God of Isaac; the land on which you lie I will give to you and your descendants. Also your descendants shall be as the dust of the earth; you shall spread abroad to the west and the east, to the north and the south; and in you and in your seed all the families of the earth shall be blessed.	
Behold, I am with you and will keep you wherever you go,	If[3] God will be with me, and keep me in this way that I am going, and give me bread to eat and clothing to put on,
and will bring you back to this land; for I will not leave you until I have done what I have spoken to you. (Genesis 28:13-15)	so that I come back to my father's house in peace, then the Lord shall be my God.
	And this stone which I have set as a pillar shall be God's house, and of all that you give me I will surely give a tenth to you. (Genesis 28:20–29:1)

3 "Seeing" rather than "if" (Rotherham).

35 | Jacob at Haran

ALMOST 500 miles (805 km) lay before Jacob as he set off on the second leg of his journey but now he knew he was not alone, the Lord was with him and he "lifted up his feet" – we might say that there was a spring in his step. Padan Aram is described as "the land of the people of the east" and there is a spiritual warning in this description. Abraham sent his non-believing children away to the east; this was a land of Godless people yet divine providence was at work, directing Jacob to his relatives to find a believing wife.

As we read Genesis 29, we need to keep the record of a previous visit in mind. Years before Abraham's servant had arrived at a well outside the same city of Haran, seeking a wife for Isaac. He had arrived with great wealth, ten camels accompanied him and no doubt he had extra men to tend and guard them. Jacob arrived alone and penniless;[1] he had obtained the blessing by deceit but none of its material wealth that came to the heir.

The Lord will be my God

Jacob left Bethel with absolute confidence that all would work out well for him. The Lord was with him and was his God – what could go wrong? It is strange that, throughout the record of his journey, there is no mention of Jacob in prayer at this time; the name of the Lord is not mentioned by him at all. When Abraham's servant arrived at the well (perhaps the same one)

1 Laban quickly realises this and Jacob has to work for his living.

the first thing he did was to ask God to lead him to the wife the Lord had appointed for Isaac. Now Jacob did no such thing; his natural desire to sort out matters for himself was once more to the fore. All of the detail of his arrival at the well brings out the two sides of Jacob's character. The Lord had wonderfully led him to exactly where he needed to be. It was a well of Haran, the shepherds there knew Laban and, quite amazingly, Laban's unmarried daughter, Rachel, immediately appeared on the scene. His father's command had been very prescriptive. He must take a wife from the daughters of Laban, his mother's brother (Genesis 28:2), and here was one of them. Indeed, he thought, this must be the choice of the Lord and so we read:

> "And it came to pass, when Jacob saw Rachel the daughter of Laban *his mother's brother*, and the sheep of Laban *his mother's brother*, that Jacob went near and rolled the stone from the well's mouth, and watered the flock of Laban *his mother's brother*." (Genesis 29:10)

He apparently disregarded the local custom of ensuring that water was shared equally between all the flocks. The well was uncovered, he watered Rachel's sheep; the other shepherds were ignored. Jacob too was a shepherd, he knew how important these customs were but he was enchanted by a beautiful face and a good figure (verse 17).

The younger serves the elder

As Laban ran to meet his nephew no doubt memories of the earlier visit were in his mind. What riches would come to him this time? How disappointed this avaricious man would be to find a penniless nephew who told him everything that had happened to him. Very quickly Laban's welcome of Jacob changed and he began to take advantage of him.

His initial greeting had been, "Surely you are my bone and my flesh" and Jacob was welcomed into the household as a relative, invited to stay with the family. Yet just one month later it was all different:

> "Then Laban said to Jacob, 'Because you are my relative, should you therefore serve me for nothing? Tell me, what should your wages be?'" (Genesis 29:15)

How ironical this is. The angel had said to Rebekah that "the elder would serve the younger"; Jacob had deceived Isaac to ensure Esau's blessing came to him and that blessing had included lordship over his brother.

> "Let peoples serve you, and nations bow down to you. Be master over your brethren, and let your mother's sons bow down to you. Cursed be everyone who curses you, and blessed be those who bless you!" (Genesis 27:29)

> "Then Isaac his father answered (Esau) and said to him: 'Behold, your dwelling shall be of the fatness of the earth, and of the dew of heaven from above. By your sword you shall live, and you shall serve your brother ...'" (verses 39,40)

Now Jacob found himself in a position of service to his older uncle and the Hebrew *abad*, to serve, is the word used twelve times[2] to define the relationship between Laban and Jacob. For twenty years he would work as a bondservant, serving Laban for wives and cattle. He would find, to his bitter cost, that he had met a greater deceiver than himself; the Lord had led him to years of chastisement to burn deceit out of his soul.

Laban clearly knew of Jacob's increasing love for Rachel, but would be surprised at the bride price he was prepared to pay. There is a clue in the law that this was fifty shekels (Deuteronomy 22:29) but seven years' wages were worth more than double this amount[3] – a rash promise had been made that would cost Jacob dear.

We can imagine his anger and chagrin when he awoke the morning after his wedding night and realised that it was Leah and not Rachel next to him. It is difficult for us to understand how this could have taken place without him knowing. Perhaps a very merry wedding feast had helped!

---

2 It is surely no coincidence that out of this period of servitude, mentioned twelve times, come twelve sons to Jacob.

3 Wenham, 16-50, page 235.

> "And Laban gathered together all the men of the place and made a feast. Now it came to pass in the evening, that he took Leah his daughter and brought her to Jacob; and he went in to her. And Laban gave his maid Zilpah to his daughter Leah as a maid. So it came to pass in the morning, that behold, it was Leah. And he said to Laban, 'What is this you have done to me? Was it not for Rachel that I served you? Why then have you deceived (*ramah*) me?' And Laban said, 'It must not be done so in our country, to give the younger before the firstborn'." (Genesis 29:22-26)

Jacob had tricked his weak-eyed father who told Esau, "Your brother came with deceit (*mirmah*, from *ramah*, to deceive) and has taken away your blessing". Now Jacob had been tricked by a weak-eyed Leah and complained using virtually the same language his father had used. Laban's reply must have struck hard: 'In your country it may be acceptable for the younger to take the place of the firstborn, but we do not behave like that here.'

The Midrash (Jewish story telling about events in the Pentateuch) has the following story about the morning after:[4]

> "All that night she (Leah) acted the part of Rachel. As soon as he arose in the morning, 'and it was Leah'. Said Jacob to her: Daughter of the deceiver! Wherefore hast thou deceived me? Said she to him: And thou – wherefore didst thou deceive thy father? When he said to thee: Art thou my very son Esau? Thou didst say unto him: I am Esau thy firstborn. Yet thou sayest: Wherefore then hast thou deceived me? Thy father, did he not say of thee: Thy brother came with deceit!"

Jacob would still be given Rachel but had to serve another seven years, in effect pay double – a principle that would later be enshrined in the Law of Moses as justice for someone who had taken the property of another (Exodus 22:9), as Jacob had done to Esau.

4 Leibowitz, page 266.

The chosen wife

As we read on it becomes clear that Jacob's choice of Rachel as his wife was not God's choice. Laban had tricked him and Leah became his first wife, yet she seems to be more spiritual than her sister and was the one suited to be a help for Jacob in the household of faith. She was the first person in this chapter to mention the name of the Lord; she both knew Him and worshipped Him. These are her responses to the birth of her sons.

- Reuben: "The LORD has surely looked on my affliction. Now therefore, my husband will love me."
- Simeon: "Because the LORD has heard that I am unloved, He has therefore given me this son also."
- Judah: "Now I will praise the LORD."

This is a picture of a prayerful and spiritual woman who had taken her distress to the Lord in prayer and trusted in Him. She alone in the family would take this action, present her affliction, her misery before Him and He had seen it. He answered her: she hoped that the birth of a son would help her win her husband's affection yet still he did not love her – perhaps resentment at what Laban had done dominated Jacob's mind. Leah's response was to take it to the Lord again, He heard her, another son was given. Levi followed – would she now be joined to her husband? No! Finally a fourth son was born and for the very first time in scripture we meet the words, "Praise the LORD". The word used carries the idea both of confession and acknowledgement of the Lord and His name and also thanks to Him for what He has done. In the birth of Judah, Leah had produced the son of Jacob through whom the promises would come. Was she given some understanding of this? Certainly the birth of this son took away her unhappiness which was replaced with a contentment in her relationship with her God for a while.

36 | A broken family

THE record of the births of Jacob's sons and the strife within his family is one of the saddest pictures in the Old Testament. It was probably the most miserable time in his life: deceived by Laban who continually changed his wages, toiling hard for him as a shepherd out in the fields day and night and coming home to a household dominated by the struggle for pre-eminence between two warring sisters who saw their husband solely as a provider of children.

Yet, as always, we see that the Lord was directing events to fulfil His promises, waiting for these people to call on Him in prayer and then answering them – for the whole episode is bounded by two similar statements:

> "When the LORD saw that Leah was unloved, he opened her womb; but Rachel was barren." (Genesis 29:31)
>
> "Then God remembered Rachel, and God listened to her and opened her womb." (30:22)

Not only was Leah unloved, she was hated by Jacob. His aversion to her role in his deception was powerful indeed, yet she was the wife who knew about the Lord and called on Him. Years later the Law would spell out clearly that a man's preference for one wife over another, hating one and loving another, should not prejudice the rights of the firstborn to a double portion of the inheritance (Deuteronomy 21:15,16). To Reuben would come that double portion and also "the excellency of dignity and the excellency of power", yet like Esau losing both birthright and blessing, he would lose it because of his behaviour.

It appears that Rachel was more stubborn than Leah. Her complaints were laid before her husband rather than in prayer to the Lord: "Give me children or else I die" she said. She may have been the wife whom Jacob loved but even this relationship was soured by her infertility. Some time passed before she prayed and perhaps further time until her heart was right before the Lord and He answered her. Yet amongst this picture of family unhappiness is a glimpse of Jacob's faith:

> "And Jacob's anger was aroused against Rachel, and he said, 'Am I in the place of God, who has withheld from you the fruit of the womb?'" (Genesis 30:2)

What a picture this gives of Jacob's character. Here is a man driven to anger by the demands of his wives, frustrated by the barrenness of his favourite spouse, but he knew that it was the Lord at work and only He could remove the problem. Both his grandmother and his mother had suffered barrenness and it was only through faith and prayer that God removed this curse and gave them children. Yet in his anger he had forgotten that his father had prayed earnestly to the Lord for Rebekah (Genesis 25:21). Could not Jacob now do the same for Rachel? His response was to throw the onus back on her – why couldn't she see this and make her own imprecations to the Lord (Psalm 127:3)?

Eventually she did this for we read:

> "Then God remembered Rachel, and God listened to her and opened her womb. And she conceived and bore a son, and said, 'God has taken away my reproach'. So she called his name Joseph, and said, 'The LORD shall add to me another son'." (Genesis 30:22-24)

Note the precision of her words. God (*Elohim*) had taken away (*acaph*) her reproach – disgrace, scorn, shame. It tells us of the great difficulties she had faced in the family but she understood that it was God who had worked in her life to take these away. She then called her son Joseph (*yowceph*) believing that Yahweh would add (*yacaph*) another son and this was the first time that Rachel used the divine name. Somehow it had been revealed to her by the Lord that, although she had been blessed with Joseph, His purpose required another son and in due time she would bear Benjamin, the son of the right hand.

Love plants

The episode that most illustrates the family dysfunctionality was the bargaining over the mandrakes. The name literally means 'love plant' and it was thought to be an aphrodisiac. They were found by Reuben, brought to his mother and exchanged by her with Rachel for the right to sleep with Jacob that night. Leah's words about this to Jacob were full of meaning: "You must come in to me, for I have surely hired (*sakar*) you with my son's mandrakes". She used the same root word we find back in Genesis 29 when Laban said to Jacob, "Tell me what your wages (*maskoreth*) shall be". Jacob had been prepared to work for seven years to pay for Rachel as his wife but received Leah, whom he hated, instead. Now she had paid for him to spend the night with her and how absolutely humiliated he must have felt.

In all of this, the Lord was moulding Jacob's character. He was still trying to obtain God's blessing by his own efforts, complicit in seeking children not just from his wives but their handmaids also. As he had struggled with Esau for supremacy in Isaac's family, so now he was faced by two sisters struggling for supremacy within his own. Laban had reduced him from being an honoured kinsman to a hired shepherd; now his wives reduced him from the status of a husband whom they could respect to that of a man whose sexual favours were obtained by a commercial contract. One writer sums it up in these words:[1]

> "The family's life is rotten and broken by the dehumanizing atmosphere of service wages."

Their behaviour during this period was so far away from the divine ideal that we may be shocked by it. How would we deal with anything like this in ecclesial life today? Yet the Lord never gave up on Jacob for his faith in the promises, however flawed

1 Waltke, page 413.

at times, sustained his relationship with the Almighty. It would be some years before he finally understood the folly of trying to work out events for himself and learned to leave it all to the Lord. It would require the severest test of his faith, the removal of physical strength from this strong man and the change of his name before he would be ready to re-enter the Promised Land. Yet the transformation would finally be so complete that the Lord, through the Psalmist, exhorts all of us to follow Jacob's example:

> "Be still, and know that I am God; I will be exalted among the nations, I will be exalted in the earth! The LORD of hosts is with us; the God of Jacob is our refuge." (Psalm 46:10,11)

Possible timeline of the births of the Children of Israel[2]

Jacob's age	Leah	Zilpah	Rachel	Bilhah
84	Reuben			
85	Simeon			
86	Levi			Dan
87	Judah	Gad		Naphtali
88	Issachar	Asher		
89	Zebulon			
90	Dinah		Joseph	
97	Return to Canaan			

2 This chronology assumes Jacob was in Haran for twenty years. However there are certain difficulties around the age of Jacob in Haran and the very short period in which all the children were born. An alternative chronology suggests Jacob was in Haran for forty years; he would be much younger when he went there and the births of his children would have been spread over a longer period. However, such a view means that Rachel was, at the very youngest, about sixty-five when she had Benjamin.

DIGRESSION: The Children of Israel

We find the first mention of "the children of Israel" in Genesis 32 where it is linked to the faith of Jacob and the changing of his name to Israel. It is then used over six hundred times throughout scripture, finally in Revelation 21 where the gates into new Jerusalem bear "the names of the twelve tribes of the children of Israel". We read of these gates once more in chapter 22:

> "Blessed are those who do his commandments, that they may have the right to the tree of life, and may enter through the gates into the city." (Revelation 22:14)

Interestingly, this is the very last time the word "bless" is used in the Bible. "Salvation is of the Jews" said Jesus to the woman at the well in Samaria and the ultimate fulfilment of the blessing from the Lord, the giving of eternal life and entrance into His kingdom, comes through this unique people descended from Jacob. The children of Israel began as twelve sons of one father, became twelve tribes coming out of Egypt as descendants of one man and grew into a great nation that never lost its sense of ancestry as people who inherited the promises made to Abraham, Isaac and Jacob.

The Exodus pattern

This way of consistently describing a nation as each individual being a direct descendant of one man has been defined as unique in the history of the nations.[3] The children of Israel is a term so common in scripture that we simply see it as another name for the nation of Israel. Yet it is much more than this for, as we think of Jacob, his sons and the journey they will now commence back to the Promised Land, we see strong parallels with the exodus of the children of Israel coming out of Egypt and journeying to Canaan (see table opposite).[4]

We know that Israel had forgotten almost completely about the Lord during their sojourn in Egypt (see Ezekiel 20).

3 N. Sarna, *Understanding Genesis*, pages 196,197.

4 This pattern is developed in detail in: D. Daube, *The Exodus Pattern in the Bible* and Y. Zakovitch, *And you shall tell your son, the concept of the Exodus on the Bible*.

When Moses began the task of revealing the name of Yahweh to His people, and showing Him to be their redeemer, he declared:

> "Moreover God said to Moses, 'Thus you shall say to the children of Israel: "The LORD God of your fathers, the God of Abraham, the God of Isaac, and the God of Jacob, has sent me to you. This is my name forever, and this is my memorial to all generations."'" (Exodus 3:15)

No doubt as Moses began his work he would expound to the people how God had made promises to their fathers about possession of the land of Canaan. He would tell them of Abraham's exodus out of Egypt, Jacob's exodus from Haran and the affliction he suffered there. The Lord had been faithful to those who had faith in Him and in the certainty of His promises. The record of their lives would be of reassurance to Israel as it suffered under Pharaoh and learned to trust in the Lord. So the record of their exodus from Egypt ends with the phrase, "the people believed in the LORD and his servant Moses".

Jacob's exodus from Haran	**Israel's exodus from Egypt**
Laban warmly welcomed Jacob	Pharaoh welcomed Jacob and his family
Laban was a hard taskmaster changing Jacob's wages ten times	Pharaoh was a hard taskmaster increasing the tally of bricks and not providing straw
Jacob's family increased and became a threat to Laban	Israel increased and became a threat to Egypt
Laban tried to prevent the increase in Jacob's flocks	Pharaoh tried to prevent the increase of Israel
God saw the affliction of Jacob and his family and told them to return to Canaan	God saw the affliction of Israel and told them to leave for Canaan
The family left in haste and with much wealth	The nation left in haste and with much wealth

Jacob's exodus from Haran	**Israel's exodus from Egypt**
Laban was informed of the escape and pursued the family	Pharaoh was informed of the escape and pursued the nation
Esau came out to meet Jacob and to prevent him from taking the inheritance (which included the land)	Sihon and Og tried to stop Israel from going into the land

SECTION SIX:
From Haran to Canaan

37 | Jacob's return to the Promised Land (1)

JACOB now had eleven sons and one daughter. He had also served Laban fourteen years for his two wives. This period was now complete and he wanted to leave, yet his chastening by the Lord in Haran was not yet complete and the Lord would keep him there for another six years.

> "And it came to pass, when Rachel had borne Joseph, that Jacob said to Laban, 'Send me away, that I may go to my own place and to my country. Give me my wives and my children for whom I have served you, and let me go; for you know my service which I have done (served) for you'."
>
> (Genesis 30:25,26)

It is easy to feel sorry for Jacob in this position. He had to request permission from Laban to depart and his father-in-law made it quite clear to him that all he had earned was his two wives – no flocks were Jacob's, no wealth his, he would depart as poor as when he arrived. His position had long been regularised as being only a bondservant in Laban's clan (Jacob mentioned "service" three times in the statement quoted above – would Laban get the message?). Indeed, Laban saw his familial relationship with his daughters and grandsons as more important than Jacob's (Genesis 31:42,43) and was loath to let them go. There was a risk that Jacob would be forced to leave alone, empty-handed, if he insisted on departure.

But Laban also wanted him to stay:

> "'Please stay, if I have found favour in your eyes, for I have learned by experience that the LORD has blessed me for your

> sake.' Then he said, 'Name me your wages, and I will give it'."
> (verses 27,28)

With these words, Laban's character is revealed to us. He had prospered since Jacob took over the shepherding of his flocks and did not want to lose him. There is a hint that Laban was a lazy man for it was Rachel who initially kept his flock (presumably a very small one if she could look after it and water it alone). Later his sons were entrusted with all the removed, piebald animals, yet they did not prosper but complained about Jacob's success.

Laban now recognised that to keep Jacob he would have to pay him and he was prepared to bargain with him. A Middle Eastern shepherd of this time would expect about twenty per cent of the increase in the flocks and herds as his wages – would Laban go that high?

"Experience" is a poor translation of the Hebrew word *nachash* used here and which means divination or soothsaying.[1] Laban had been perplexed by the way his fortunes had changed after Jacob arrived. His flocks had increased dramatically and Jacob had proved hard working and honest, serving him for his wives. Laban had consulted his gods about it but the Lord had intervened and shown him the cause of his prosperity. Yet he was not a believer in Jacob's God. Later Jacob would tellingly describe the Lord as "the God of Abraham and the God of Nahor" (Laban's grandfather) but never as the God of Laban.

Ringstraked and speckled

Laban must have been amazed and perhaps a little contemptuous when Jacob made his offer of further service. His intention to continue looking after Laban's flocks, keeping only the piebald animals for himself, was an offer too good to refuse. Normally this would generate much less than the twenty per cent mentioned above. But it was Jacob's motives that were important.

> "So my righteousness will answer for me in time to come, when the subject of my wages comes before you: every one

1 See chapter 6 – this word is almost identical to that translated "serpent" in the early chapters of Genesis. Laban shows himself to be a true "serpent's seed".

> that is not speckled and spotted among the goats, and brown among the lambs, will be considered stolen, if it is with me."
>
> (Genesis 30:33)

Jacob was a man trying to act with integrity, looking for a contract that would ensure each could see that the other was behaving in a trustworthy way. Yet Laban immediately removed all of the marked animals, which he had agreed should belong to Jacob, sending them far away with his sons. All Jacob was left with were the pure white sheep and the black goats. His integrity had been met by yet more deception.

The passage that follows is one of the most difficult to interpret in all of the patriarchal records. How did Jacob get so many speckled and ringstraked sheep from the pure colour animals left him by Laban?

Perhaps there are two parts to the answer.

1. The God of Isaac had been with Jacob (31:4) and revealed in a dream what he should do. How else could Jacob initially know which pure colour rams were heterozygotes with the piebald gene within them?

   > "And it happened, at the time when the flocks conceived [rather, 'were in heat'], that I lifted my eyes and saw in a dream, and behold, the rams which leaped upon the flocks were streaked, speckled, and grey-spotted. Then the Angel of God spoke to me in a dream, saying, 'Jacob'. And I said, 'Here I am'. And he said, 'Lift your eyes now and see, all the rams which leap on the flocks are streaked, speckled, and grey-spotted; for I have seen all that Laban is doing to you'."
   >
   > (Genesis 31:10-12)

   Divine providence was at work. These rams were single colour ones yet they were selected out of the flock by the Lord and directed to Jacob for the Lord who "knew their inward parts" knew that they could father piebald offspring.
2. Jacob was a very experienced shepherd and knew that within the fresh wood of certain trees were certain

> substances that enhanced the oestrus cycle of the ewes so that they conceived more quickly, having multiple births. These were the rods he put into the watering trough when the stronger animals came to water so that they conceived.[2]

The hand of the Lord, and Jacob's willingness to trust in the revelation given him, brought a miraculous increase in his flocks. Some he was able to sell, hence "he increased exceedingly so that he had much cattle and maidservants and menservants and camels and asses". The Lord had indeed blessed him in this life – but why? Throughout Genesis, God's ultimate purpose in blessing those whom He has chosen is to bring them to His kingdom. In this life, wrote Paul, all things work together for good in the lives of those who are called according to this purpose. Sometimes they are tested with success and riches, but he goes on in the same chapter in Romans to acknowledge that, as part of "all things", tribulation, distress and peril also happen to the faithful. Jacob had experienced drought, frost and sleeplessness looking after Laban's flocks in the fields. Throughout this testing he had been faithful and honest. Now his dramatic increase in wealth was a further part of his testing and we shall see this as we follow him back to the Promised Land.

Jacob leaves Haran

During the six years that followed Laban sought to limit Jacob's wages but was frustrated by the Lord on every occasion until he and his sons turned against the man. In Laban's immediate breaking of the bargain made between the two, in his whisking away of animals that should have been Jacob's, in the constant changing of his wages Jacob experienced the hurtful impact of one who was a deceiver and who could never be trusted. He would come to understand that, as he saw Laban, so Esau saw him. This self-awareness of what he had done to his twin would

2 Cf. N. Sarna, page 212.

The Divine Law

It appears from the record of Jacob and Laban that Leah, Rachel and the children belonged to Laban as the head of the family and that Jacob could be turned off without anything. How much fairer was the Law given to Moses:

> "If there is among you a poor man of your brethren, within any of the gates in your land which the LORD your God is giving you, you shall not harden your heart nor shut your hand from your poor brother, but you shall open your hand wide to him and willingly lend him sufficient for his need, whatever he needs. Beware lest there be a wicked thought in your heart, saying, 'The seventh year, the year of release, is at hand,' and your eye be evil against your poor brother and you give him nothing, and he cry out to the LORD against you, and it become sin among you. You shall surely give to him, and your heart should not be grieved when you give to him, because for this thing the LORD your God will bless you in all your works and in all to which you put your hand. For the poor will never cease from the land; therefore I command you, saying, 'You shall open your hand wide to your brother, to your poor and your needy, in your land.' If your brother, a Hebrew man, or a Hebrew woman, is sold to you and serves you six years, then in the seventh year you shall let him go free from you. And when you send him away free from you, you shall not let him go away empty-handed; you shall supply him liberally from your flock, from your threshing floor, and from your winepress. From what the LORD your God has blessed you with, you shall give to him." (Deuteronomy 15:7-14)

serve him in good stead when he met him on the road home. And through his further years of trials he behaved honestly: there is no hint that his conduct was wrong, rather that the Lord was with him in his actions.

It was now the right time in the Lord's purpose for Jacob to return to Canaan and so He instructed him.

> "The LORD said to Jacob, 'Return to the land of your fathers and to your family, and I will be with you ... I am the God of Bethel, where you anointed the pillar and where you made a vow to me. Now arise, get out of this land, and return to the land of your family'." (Genesis 31:3,13)

How these words would stir Jacob. In a human sense, Canaan was not the land of Abraham and Isaac; they were merely alien residents (the meaning of "sojourners") and Abraham owned no land except that which he bought for the family tomb. Yet so absolutely certain were the divine promises, guaranteed through the divine covenant the Lord made with Abraham, that the land had been described as belonging to him and his descendants: "Unto your seed have I given the land" and so God now reminds the grandson of this, "Return to the land of your fathers".

This is the only occasion in scripture where we meet the phrase "the God of Bethel" and there is a subtle difference between God's words and Jacob's when he described the same place as the "house of God" (Genesis 28:17). He saw it as the place from where angels ascended and descended and so he described it as the "house of the Elohim". But the Lord used the phrase, "the El of Bethel", literally, 'the Mighty One of the house of the Mighty One'. This was Abraham's God, the Lord the Most High El, Almighty El and in using this title, El, the Lord was reminding Jacob of the exceeding great and precious promises made to his fathers and of the absolute power of the One who was the possessor of heaven and earth to perform what He had promised.

Jacob was about to be tested twice more by men who thought they had the power to stop him, yet both were impotent against the divine care that the Mighty God of Bethel would provide. The Lord reminded Jacob of the vow of commitment he had made there twenty years before and commanded him to keep his promise.

It is to Jacob's credit that his wives so willingly agreed to go with him. In spite of all the family tensions, both were united in this. Whatever our views of Jacob's failings, he had steadfastly worshipped the Lord and shared his faith with his family. They saw their future with him and his family in Canaan and not with Laban.

Look at how he contrasted Laban's behaviour with the support of the Lord.

31:5 – Laban has changed his view of me	But the God of my father has always been with me as He promised
31:7 – Laban deceived me and changed his word trying to defraud me	But God would not let him harm me
31:9,10 – Laban constantly changed my wages	But God frustrated him and rewarded me

Just as the Exodus from Egypt is presented as a battle between Yahweh and the gods of Egypt (in each of the plagues an Egyptian god was vanquished)[3] so I suggest that through the Laban / Jacob struggle the Lord is seen as the one true God, greater than the gods of Laban and Jacob's wives accepted this.

It is ironical that Laban was three days' journey away as Jacob set off. Six years previously Laban had taken animals that should have been Jacob's and placed them three days' journey away. Was this where he now was? It would take him another three days to return to Haran by which time Jacob was six days travel ahead.

However there is a problem with these numbers. Laban caught up with Jacob at Mount Gilead which is nearly 400 miles (644 km) south of Haran. It was impossible for Jacob, with all that was part of his caravan, to get there in six days. There must have been a hiatus between Laban's return to Haran and his setting off after Jacob and it has been suggested that the pursuit only commenced when he found his teraphim were missing.

3 See J. J. Davies, *Moses and the Gods of Egypt*.

Teraphim

The images that Rachel stole were *teraphiym*, household idols used for divination (Ezekiel 21:21) and worship.

In Mesopotamia, possession of them passed from the head of the household to the heir, indicating his right in inheritance.

Rachel, angry that bride price paid by Jacob during the years he worked for her had been squandered by her father rather than being kept for his grandchildren, took Laban's teraphim in an attempt to claim the right to his estate for Jacob.

Laban's fury

As Laban arrived at Mount Gilead, full of fury against Jacob, the Lord spoke to him in a dream:

> "But God had come to Laban the Syrian in a dream by night, and said to him, 'Be careful that you speak to Jacob neither good nor bad'." (Genesis 31:24)

Some writers suggest that Laban was commanded to keep silent but this hardly makes sense.[4] The alternative interpretation, 'refrain from threatening Jacob with any harm'[5] seems to miss an essential point. Laban was a man who had spoken honeyed words to Jacob in the past but then schemed in his heart to deceive him and do him harm. The warning from the Lord is perhaps seen as instruction not to behave like this now.

When Laban reached Jacob he recounted God's words to him but with a subtle play on words.

> "It is in my power (*El*) to do you harm, but the God (*Elohim*) of your father spoke to me last night, saying, 'Be careful that you speak to Jacob neither good nor bad.'" (verse 29)

Laban saw himself as a man who had absolute power over every member of his family, almost god-like in his authority. Yet

4 His words in Genesis 24:50 support this.

5 V. P. Hamilton, *Genesis 18-50*, page 296.

he now had to acknowledge a greater power. Even though he did not worship the Lord, his dream had convinced him of the mighty power of this Being that he dare not ignore.

There is no doubt about Laban's anger for he accused Jacob of:

- Stealing away without telling him.
- Taking his daughters by force (he could not believe that they would want to go).
- Being a fool for leaving like this.
- Acting as a homesick boy longing to see his father.
- Stealing his gods.

Jacob, who had never behaved dishonestly to Laban, hotly disputed this and allowed Laban an exhaustive search of his caravan. Note that he started in Jacob's tent. He thought that Jacob may have behaved as he would have done.

The words used for the search tell us that Laban felt his way through every possession in the tents going to Rachel's tent last – he clearly thought that this daughter would never have taken them. Her ruse was very clever. She claimed discomfort because of her monthly cycle; she could not get off her camel and Laban passed her by.

Laban's accusations that Jacob was a thief brought forth Jacob's longest recorded speech. Perhaps for the first time he stood up to Laban in his indignation at the way he had been treated and thought to be dishonest. It is notable that Laban accused him of stealing away with his daughters and stealing his gods but not of stealing his flocks – even he knew what an honest shepherd Jacob had been.

A covenant was made: they would go their separate ways and not interfere with each other, but a greater test lay ahead for Jacob.

38 | Jacob's return to the Promised Land (2)

"So Jacob went on his way, and the angels of God met him. When Jacob saw them, he said, 'This is God's camp'. And he called the name of that place Mahanaim." (Genesis 32:1,2)

LABAN had left and Jacob could now continue his journey, moving south on the east bank of the Jordan. Apparently, he knew that Esau had left Canaan and lived in Seir at the southern end of the Dead Sea. The scriptures tell us of his careful preparation for meeting his brother; Jacob would not cross over Jordan into the land until peace had been made between the two men.

The appearance of the angels must have brought him reassurance. It would remind him of their presence at Bethel and of the Lord's words as he left for Haran:

> "Behold, I am with you and will keep you wherever you go, and will bring you back to this land; for I will not leave you until I have done what I have spoken to you." (28:15)

For twenty years the angels had been with him, unseen yet always present, protecting him from danger. Had the knowledge of this helped him to knuckle down meekly to work for Laban in spite of the deceit shown to him?

Now, as he faced the last hurdle before entering the land, the angels were still there; they would guard him until the danger was over and God had brought him back to Canaan as He had promised. Yet there is more to it than this for "the angel of the Lord encamps (*chanah*) around them that fear him and delivers them" and Jacob saw their abiding presence as they settled around his camp. So he called it Mahanaim (from *chanah*), two camps. What a reassuring picture this is. We do not see two separate camps but Jacob, and all those who had travelled with him, surrounded by a camp of angels. What can Esau do to him?

As we read the record, picking up the details of the events that unfold, we are reminded of a similar picture elsewhere in the scriptures for this is a type of the greater testing seen in the life of the Lord Jesus Christ.

Consider the following view of Jacob.

- He was rejected by his brother who saw him as one who had come to take away his place. He sought to put him to death (John 12:48,53).
- Though Jacob was a son and his father's heir, he took upon himself the form of a servant (Philippians 2:6-8) in his twenty years of service of Laban.
- Through that period he was mistreated and reviled (Isaiah 53:7) yet never raised his voice in judgement (42:3).
- The night before he thought he would face death at the hands of his brother he wrestled with the angel with tears and supplications and finally overcame his nature, placing his life in the hands of God (Luke 22:39-45; Hebrews 5:7).

We see in these events of Jacob's life one of the greatest exhortations of the Old Testament. We all at times make wrong decisions and have to live with the consequences, as did Jacob. Perhaps we then might "kick against the pricks", trying to fight our way through, sorting out matters for ourselves rather than turning to the Lord. When the Psalmist wrote that "God is our refuge, a very present help in time of trouble" he gave us words of comfort. Yet they do not mean that He is always there but that He is instantly found and willing to help if we turn to Him when we are in distress. The Lord waits for us to turn to Him, as He did for Jacob, but when we do this we find there is always grace to help us in our times of need. He never deserts us. Years later, just before his death, as Jacob blessed his sons he interjected his prophecies about them with a personal statement that looked back to his time in Haran and the patience he painfully learned:

> "I have waited for your salvation O LORD." (Genesis 49:18)

Learning these lessons was not easy for Jacob, and it was not until that last night that self was overcome and he was ready for the last test.

A soft answer to turn away wrath

With the assurance that the angels were with him at Mahanaim, Jacob sent messengers to Esau to tell him of his return.[1]

> "And he commanded them, saying, 'Speak thus to my Lord Esau, "Thus your servant Jacob says: 'I have dwelt with Laban and stayed there until now. I have oxen, donkeys, flocks, and male and female servants; and I have sent to tell my Lord, that I may find favour (grace) in your sight.'"'" (Genesis 32:4,5)

This was a message of appeasement, picking up echoes of the blessing he had stolen from Esau:

> "Let peoples serve you, and nations bow down to you. Be master over your brethren, and let your mother's sons bow down to you. Cursed be everyone who curses you, and blessed be those who bless you!" (27:29)

Jacob claimed none of these things as he returned; he addressed Esau as "my Lord Esau"; he was "your servant, Jacob". Later we shall see him abase himself, bowing down before his brother.

In reading about the meeting of the two men we see that the blessing meant different things to Esau and Jacob. To the elder brother it meant wealth, the inheritance of his father's possessions, which would be chiefly herds and flocks. He showed no interest in Canaan as the Promised Land, indeed he had left it and gone south to settle in Seir and I suggest he took Jacob's inheritance of the flocks and herds with him. In contrast, Jacob showed no interest in his father's material wealth but was solely interested in the land; it was a vital part of the promises in which he believed.

1 The same word *malak* is used of the angels and of Jacob's messengers: both were involved in the Lord's business.

Part of his message to Esau was that he had become rich in exile and the inference is that he was not coming back to lay claim to his father's wealth. All he asked for from his brother was grace, an undeserved favour of forgiveness for what he had done to him in tricking him out of the firstborn's blessing.

Esau of course was an earthy man and did not do grace. He believed that Jacob would act as he would have done in similar circumstances, wanting his illegally obtained inheritance. So he came with his militia of 400 men (remember Isaac's words to him, "by your sword you shall live") and Jacob was terrified for himself and his family.

Immediately Jacob's trait of self-reliance emerges:

> "So Jacob was greatly afraid and distressed; and he divided the people that were with him, and the flocks and herds and camels, into two companies. And he said, 'If Esau comes to the one company and attacks it, then the other company which is left will escape'." (Genesis 32:7,8)

How ironical this is! There are already two companies – Jacob's and the angels', yet in his distress he looked to alleviate the threat by his own actions. This was the Jacob of old at work, trying to sort things out for himself.

Yet his fear then brought forth a fervent prayer in which he poured out his heart to God, reminding Him of the promises made to Abraham, Isaac and himself:

> "O God of my father Abraham and God of my father Isaac, the LORD who said to me, 'Return to your country and to your family, and I will deal well with you': I am not worthy[2] of the least of all the mercies and of all the truth which you have shown your servant; for I crossed over this Jordan with my staff, and now I have become two companies. Deliver (*natsal*) me, I pray, from the hand of my brother, from the hand of Esau; for I fear him, lest he come and attack me and the mother with the children. For you said, 'I will surely treat you

2 This is one of a number of echoes of Jacob's return found in the Parable of the Prodigal Son. It is possible that Jesus based his parable in part on Jacob and Esau.

> well, and make your descendants as the sand of the sea, which cannot be numbered for multitude'." (verses 9-12)

Human nature is very strange. Jacob had angels encamped around him and the unbreakable promise that the Lord would take him back to the land and to Isaac. He had prayed to God for deliverance yet what did he do next? He sought to mollify Esau by his own actions. He sent him a present (Hebrew, *minchah*), a freely donated gift, the word used for offerings to the Lord in the Law. Five hundred and fifty animals was a huge gift and must have been a large part of the livestock Jacob brought from Haran. Again, he sought to mollify Esau by reference to the blessing he had received from Isaac, for his father had promised him "the fatness of the earth" and the evidence of this was seen in the size of his flocks. 'Here it is', his actions said to Esau, 'take it, it's not important to me'.

But his message was even more remarkable, for Jacob said:

> "I will appease (*kaphar*) him (*paniym*)[3] with the present that goes before me, and afterward I will see his face; perhaps he will accept me. So the present went on over before him, but he himself lodged that night in the camp." (verses 20,21)

We meet these words in Leviticus for *kaphar* is translated most often in the Old Testament as "atonement" and the seven other occasions when these two words, *kaphar* and *paniym*, are used together like this are of the priest making intercession before the Lord and seeking atonement. Jacob is shown to be a man who was deeply troubled by his past behaviour and sought forgiveness, hoping to mollify Esau's anger by his humility, atoning for his deceit with the offering presented to him.

Wrestling with the angel

A desperately worried Jacob did not sleep that night but crossed over the Jabbok[4] with his family, awaiting the meeting with Esau. He was the man to whom the Lord had shown surrounding

---

3 *Paniym* is used five times in these verses.

4 Jabbok means 'emptying'. As Jacob crossed it, it symbolised the one who was emptying himself and taking on the form of a servant.

angels at Mahanaim (*Machanayim*), 'two camps', yet just in case he met violence from Esau he had divided his caravan into two bands (*machaneh*). He was the man who had prayed to the Lord: "I am not worthy ... deliver me" but just in case of trouble he sent offerings to Esau and took upon himself the role of an intercessor.

How did the Lord react to this? We see Him as a loving Father, guiding His son to overcome self and to leave all to Him. "Lord I believe, help my unbelief" well describes Jacob's troubled mind.

> "Then Jacob was left alone; and a man wrestled with him until the breaking of day. Now when he saw that he did not prevail against him, he touched the socket of his hip; and the socket of Jacob's hip was out of joint as he wrestled with him. And he said, 'Let me go, for the day breaks'. But he said, 'I will not let you go unless you bless me!' So he said to him, 'What is your name?' He said, 'Jacob'. And he said, 'Your name shall no longer be called Jacob, but Israel; for you have struggled with God and with men, and have prevailed'. Then Jacob asked, saying, 'Tell me your name, I pray'. And he said, 'Why is it that you ask about my name?' And he blessed him there. And Jacob called the name of the place Peniel: or I have seen God face to face, and my life is preserved (*natsal*)."
>
> (Genesis 32:24-30)

These are difficult verses to understand and it will help us to list all that we know about the event.

1. This is the fourth and final time Jacob wrestled. Previously he:
    a. Wrestled with Esau in the womb, trying to achieve the primogeniture by emerging first.
    b. Wrestled with Esau when he persuaded him to sell him the birthright.
    c. Wrestled with Esau when he tricked Isaac into giving him Esau's blessing.

    On each of these occasions, Jacob sought to obtain the right thing by the wrong means, using his own strength to do so.

2. Now he wrestled with an angel who appeared as a man to him, just as angels had appeared as men to Abraham.

   "... he struggled with the angel and prevailed; he wept, and sought favour from him." (Hosea 12:4)

   After the event he called the place Peniel, 'the face of God', for he said: "I have seen God face to face and my life is preserved (*natsal*). Was it the Angel of the Lord he saw? In these words he accepted what had occurred as the Lord's response to his prayer made the previous day: "I am not worthy of the least of all the mercies and of all the truth which you have shown your servant ... deliver (*natsal*) me I pray you from the hand of my brother."
3. He wrestled the angel for a blessing and saw one in the change of name that he was given.

   We have already noted a parallel between Jacob's experience and that of our Lord in Gethsemane who "offered up prayers and supplications with strong crying and tears unto him that was able to save him from death". We see Jacob struggling with men – his own will leading him in his plans to face Esau, and with God – knowing and believing that his prayer would be answered and that it was indeed God's will to save him. There was a contest in his mind between these two ways, trust in himself or trust in God. And the angel was there to test him.

   Jacob demanded a blessing from the angel (and hence directly from God) and was tested to see how much he yearned for this. He refused to let the angel go until he had received it. It was essential for him. If he had this then he was ready to trust absolutely in God and forgo all his own preparations for meeting Esau.

Jacob becomes Israel

So why was this blessing so important to Jacob?

Before he left his parents to go to Haran, Isaac had given him the patriarchal blessing, the special one he had reserved for Jacob:

> "May God Almighty bless you, and make you fruitful and multiply you, that you may be an assembly of peoples; and give you the blessing of Abraham, to you and your descendants with you, that you may inherit the land in which you are a stranger, which God gave to Abraham." (Genesis 28:3,4)

In these words, Isaac passed on to his son the blessing that both he and Abraham had received directly from God. However Jacob himself had *never yet received a blessing directly from the Lord*. He now looked for direct confirmation from God that his family would be safe from Esau, for they were the beginning of this multitude of people that God had promised. He looked for God's guiding hand to take them into the land for this too had been promised to him.

Yet the Lord did not complete His blessing of him until he reached Bethel once again; until after his faith was shown in his works, in the way he would face Esau.

The angel said, "they will no longer call you Jacob",[5] yet we often find the man called by his old name throughout the rest of Genesis. However, the old Jacob, the heel-grasper, the deceiver was gone for good; in future when men said "Jacob", they would no longer think of him in this way.

Instead, he had become "Israel" and, when we look at the language of Genesis 32 and Hosea 12, his new name appears to have two meanings. It can mean both 'a prince with God' and 'God prevails'. Perhaps this ambiguity[6] is deliberate for we see both meanings in the life of Jacob. God had prevailed in his heart, the old man had gone and a new man, trusting totally in the divine hand at work in his life, had emerged.

The Lord would deal with the Esau problem. He could not prevail against him by himself; the Lord alone had the power to do this, only the God of Abraham and Isaac could prevail. In believing this, and in unshakeable trust in the promises, he became a prince, like his grandfather whom the inhabitants of

---

5 The idiomatic meaning of the phrase.

6 The ambiguity of the meaning of Israel is explored at length in Hamilton, volume 2, page 333.

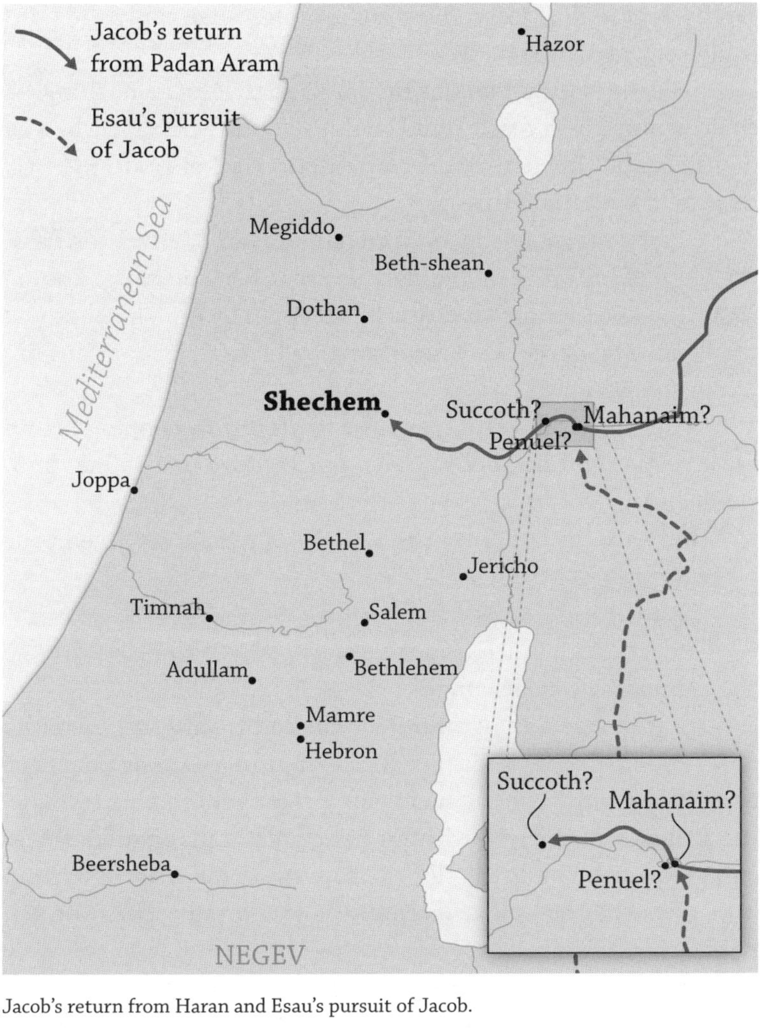

Jacob's return from Haran and Esau's pursuit of Jacob.

the land saw as a mighty prince. From Israel would come a great nation, the people of God, and the kings who would reign over them.

No doubt Jacob's mind was filled with awe at his name change. He was about the same age as his grandfather had been when God changed Abram's name to Abraham. That had happened when he had finally understood that he had no strength or ability to produce the promised heir, only the Lord could rejuvenate his body.

Now his grandson learned a similar lesson: nothing he could arrange by himself could guarantee a safe passage when he met Esau, but his new name contained a title of God, "El" – no one could withstand this!

Faith prevailed. Jacob who had prayed, "deliver me from the hand of my brother" but had also sent Esau offerings hoping that he would "see his face" and be accepted by him, had become the Israel who declared, "I have seen God face to face and my life has been delivered".

The Jacob who sent messages to his brother hoping to find grace in his sight had become the Israel who, when he met him, would say:

"These are the children whom God has graciously given your servant."

And

"God has dealt graciously with me."

But why was he lamed?

Jacob was a man who fled. He fled from Esau (Genesis 35:1) and he fled from Laban (31:21), but now he was unable to flee again from Esau. He had been a strong man, able to move the stone from the well without help, able to manhandle sheep and goats as he built the flocks. Now such things were beyond him; physically as well as mentally he was totally reliant on the Lord.

Yet also through him comes the Israel of God (Galatians 6:16), a spiritual nation knit together by faith in the promises.

Whenever these descendants meet with opposition or trouble in their lives they are able to remember this name, Israel, to which they are called. The example of Jacob who became Israel brings comfort and strength from the knowledge that the angels who guarded him and his family are still present with the children of God today, for they are all ministering spirits sent to minister to those who are heirs of salvation.

The meeting with Esau

No sooner had Jacob been strengthened by his experience with the angel, declaring that his life had been delivered than he looked up and saw Esau coming.[7]

He ordered his family into groups and in turn, led by the patriarch, they approached Esau and made obeisance to him. There was no longer anything of the old Jacob in all of this. His family was exposed and vulnerable; he then came ahead of them and bowed to the ground seven times before Esau. What would his brother have made of this? Before him were four women with twelve young children, with them was his hated brother – but he was now an elderly, crippled man bowing down before him in total submission.

Esau embraced Jacob and kissed him. No doubt Jacob remembered that the last time such an embrace had been given to him was Laban's initial greeting. There would be more than a touch of wariness in the younger brother's response yet Esau would see, with some puzzlement, that Jacob was openly trusting Esau not to harm his family. This was not what he expected.

The dialogue that followed is wonderful.

Esau asked Jacob, "What do you mean by all this company which I met?" Jacob had sent droves of animals but Esau made a crude pun using a word which can also mean an armed host; perhaps his sense was, 'Is this the best you can send against me?'

Jacob's quiet answer: "They are to find favour in the sight of my Lord."

Esau: 'I have a great amount (KJV, I have enough), keep it for yourself.'

There was a warning in this. What Esau had may well have been part of the blessing stolen from Jacob; he had taken it and the warning was that he would not give it back if Jacob wanted it – 'Be satisfied with what you have brother' was the underlying message.

---

7 Compare Jesus' experience in Gethsemane, Mark 14:42,43.

Jacob had seen the face of God at Peniel and now he saw acceptance of his offering in the face of Esau and it encouraged him to go further: "Please, take my blessing that is brought to you, because God has dealt graciously with me, and because I have enough."

He had described the gift of the flocks as an offering, now he called it a blessing, suggesting that this is a giving back to Esau of what he had been tricked. Throughout this, Jacob goes to lengths to show that material possessions were of no interest to him. When he said, "I have enough" he used a different word from that spoken by Esau. Jacob's words literally meant, 'I have totally and absolutely everything'. He had the absolute certainty of the promises and compared to them, everything that was of importance to his brother was of little consequence to him.

In the acceptance of the gift in front of witnesses, the 400 men with him, Esau acknowledged that the debt had been paid, his grievance removed and the matter was closed.

Yet it seems that he still did not quite trust Jacob for he wanted him under his eye in Seir and was prepared to leave some of his men to oversee his brother's journey there. Jacob's heart was set on the land of promise and so the brothers parted, not to meet again until they both attended Isaac's funeral.[8]

At this point in the narrative we should reflect on Isaac for a moment. Twenty years before he had lost his younger son; at some time in the intervening period he lost his elder, favoured son who took what he could and went to live in Seir with his pagan wives and family that were a grief of mind to his father. Isaac would then fully understand that the promises which were so precious to him meant nothing to this son. Rebekah died and we are left with a picture of an elderly man, now nearly 160 years old, blind and lonely, bereft of both sons. Yet the Lord had not

8 Genesis 36:6,7 is difficult to fit into this sequence of actions. Abimelech was willing to share the land with Abraham and his large encampment. We should perhaps see this as the separation between Lot and Abraham, difficulties over water and land rights masking a more fundamental difference in spiritual values.

forgotten him and had commanded Jacob to return to both the land and his kindred – a most poignant meeting was yet to occur.

DIGRESSION: To your descendants I will give the land

As we have looked at Jacob's return to the land of Canaan, and his travels within it, we get a sense of déjà vu. We have seen this pattern before in Abraham's life – and we later come across it again in the Bible, in the days of Joshua.

Abraham:

- Leaves Haran and travels to Canaan.
- Settles at Shechem.
- Builds an altar there.
- Receives the promise-blessing of possession of the land.
- Moves south and pitches his tent between Bethel and Ai.
- Builds an altar there and calls upon the name of the Lord.
- Travels south to Hebron.
- Builds an altar there.

Jacob:

- Leaves Haran and travels to Canaan.
- Settles at Shechem.
- Builds an altar there.
- Moves south and settles at Bethel.
- Builds an altar there.
- Receives the promise-blessing of possession of the land.
- Travels south to Hebron.

Joshua:

- Receives the commandment to go in and possess the land.
- Has his army encamp between Ai and Bethel prior to taking Ai.
- Takes the whole nation north to Shechem; half stand on Ebal, half on Gerizim with Shechem in between.
- Builds an altar on Ebal.
- The Levites give the blessing as Moses commanded that they might possess the land.
- Begins the southern campaign, clearing the land as far as Hebron and Kadesh-Barnea.

The pattern then is unmistakeable. Abraham entered the land and received the promise of inheritance. He was to walk through it as a sign of possession. It was given initially to him but through his faith his seed would inherit also. This faith was in the Lord who called him and hence, at centres of Canaanite idol worship at Shechem and Bethel, he established altars and worship of the one true God.

Jacob followed his grandfather's pattern: it occurred twice showing it was fixed by God, and He would shortly bring it to pass (Genesis 41:32).

These two series of events were a kind of enacted parable, the Lord showing the absolute certainty of His people inheriting the land for He had promised it to their forefathers. But not only this, it would be taken according to this pattern. So Joshua was told:

> "Arise, go over this Jordan, you and all this people, to the land which I am giving to them – the children of Israel. Every place that the sole of your foot will tread upon I have given you, as I said to Moses." (Joshua 1:2,3)

As the land was originally promised to Abraham and through him to his people, so it was now given to Joshua. He personally was to walk through the land; he would take it but share it with his people in turn.

39 |

Shechem and Dinah

THE events that follow in Genesis 34 and 35 tell us of Jacob entering the land and settling there. As he had caused a split in Isaac's family, so fractures now began to appear in his own. We reach the end of this section with the death of Isaac and the same pattern we saw in the lives of Abraham and Isaac is now repeated.

- Abraham died – the focus switched to Isaac's family;
- Isaac dies – the focus will switch to Jacob's family.

But first we are given another insight into the relationship of Jacob and his God.

The God of Israel

> "And Jacob journeyed to Succoth, built himself a house, and made booths for his livestock. Therefore the name of the place is called Succoth. Then Jacob came safely (*shalem*) to the city of Shechem, which is in the land of Canaan, when he came from Padan Aram; and he pitched his tent before the city. And he bought the parcel of land, where he had pitched his tent, from the children of Hamor, Shechem's father, for one hundred pieces of money. Then he erected an altar there and called it El Elohe Israel." (Genesis 33:17-20)

As Esau left, Jacob gathered his caravan and moved back across the Jabbok two miles north to Succoth, travelling in the opposite direction from that of his brother; he had absolutely no intention of going to Seir. We can imagine that he and his family were exhausted by the events of the past two to three weeks. They had fled from Haran, faced the trauma of meeting Esau and needed some rest before they entered the land.

As he arrived at Shechem, his mind was filled with the vow he had made at Bethel before leaving for Haran:

> "If God will be with me, and keep me in this way that I am going, and give me bread to eat and clothing to put on, so that I come back to my father's house in peace (*shalowm*), then the LORD shall be my God." (Genesis 28:20,21)

Poor Jacob, after years of turmoil and potential violence, all he now wanted was peace in the Promised Land, yet there was still trouble ahead. Years later he told Joseph about his return; he proposed to leave to his beloved son an extra portion, that which he took from the Amorite with his sword and bow (Genesis 48:22). Yet we read nothing of this in chapter 33, rather that he bought a piece of land from Hamor for one hundred pieces of silver. Was this how peace finally came?

Now he had safety (*shalowm*), he erected an altar, the first time we see him doing this. His forefathers *built* altars but a different word, *erected*, is used here: it is the same word used of the ladder, "*set up*" on earth, which he had seen in his dream at Bethel.

The altar was for worship of the Lord who was indeed his God for he called it "God, the mighty One of Israel", using his new name in praise of all that the Lord had done for him. He was now back in the land as the Lord had promised and he made a commitment that his life there would be one of faith in Him.[1]

Dinah went out

Dinah was no more than seven or eight years old when they returned from Haran but now she was an unmarried girl past the age of puberty, a teenager. The family therefore had been at Shechem for perhaps five to seven years.

> "Now Dinah the daughter of Leah, whom she had borne to Jacob, went out to see the daughters of the land."
> (Genesis 34:1)

---

1 It is likely that he dug the well mentioned in John 4 at this time.

It is unusual to read of descent from both parents as we see here. We are reminded that Dinah, as a daughter of Leah, was a full sister of Simeon and Levi and also would inherit traits from both parents. She went out and perhaps did this deceiving her family, showing this family characteristic. She "went out to see those of the land". John wrote of those who "went out from us", those who were dissatisfied with the truth of the Gospel, and we have a picture not just of idle curiosity by Dinah but of a desire for something different. We do not know what other teenagers there were in Jacob's camp, whether there was enough social life there for her; we are simply told that she looked outside for companionship.

Those of the land were Hivites, descendants of Canaan, and her grandparents and great-grandparents had seen the dangers in becoming too close to these people who rejected the God of Abraham. Years later, as Israel was about to enter the Promised Land, Balaam prophesied of them:

> "A people dwelling alone, not reckoning itself among the nations." (Numbers 23:9)

Yet immediately after the death of Joshua their assimilation of Canaanite life and Canaanite gods began and remained an abiding problem for all the years ahead until the exile.

Every parent of teenagers will understand Dinah's situation. Our children need friends and social interaction; it is an essential part of their development and if we cannot provide it amongst those who share our faith then they will go out and find it elsewhere.

Tragedy followed, Dinah was taken and raped by Shechem, son of the prince of the territory. He saw her and took her – the same language, saw, took, used of Eve in chapter 3 and the sons of God in chapter 6. In him we see the lust of the eyes, the lust of the flesh and the pride of life. He was the son of a prince, "honoured above all the house of his father" (Genesis 34:19, RV): he believed he could take whatever he wanted. In all that followed there was no apology at all from the Hivites for his actions. It is also clear that Dinah was taken and kept by them (see verses 3,17) which strengthened their position in the bargaining that followed.

Yet after this, Shechem loved Dinah and spoke tenderly to her. He demanded of his father that he get her for him as his wife. He really was a spoilt young man, used to getting what he wanted, impetuous in his offer of whatever bride price Israel wanted. His father, Hamor, however was a duplicitous man with a hidden agenda. Getting Dinah as a bride for his son was just a means to an end. Compare what he said to Jacob with his words to his own people:

> **To Jacob:** "The soul of my son Shechem longs for your daughter. Please give her to him as a wife. And make marriages with us; give your daughters to us, and take our daughters to yourselves. So you shall dwell with us, and the land shall be before you. Dwell and trade in it, and acquire possessions for yourselves in it." (Genesis 34:8-10)

> **To his own people:** "These men are at peace with us. Therefore let them dwell in the land and trade in it. For indeed the land is large enough for them. Let us take their daughters to us as wives, and let us give them our daughters ... Will not their livestock, their property, and every animal of theirs be ours? Only let us consent to them, and they will dwell with us." (verses 21-23)

The lure to Jacob was of peaceful co-existence through which Israel would become rich. The actual plan was to subsume Israel into the Hivite tribe so that everything became their property.

There was terrible danger for Israel in this, its very existence was at risk. Years later the Hivites were identified by the Lord as one of the seven nations to be destroyed by Israel because of this risk. Israel was to make no covenant with them either commercially or through marriage, yet both of these were now on offer to Jacob.

> "When the LORD your God brings you into the land which you go to possess, and has cast out many nations before

> you, the Hittites and the Girgashites and the Amorites and the Canaanites and the Perizzites and the Hivites and the Jebusites, seven nations greater and mightier than you, and when the LORD your God delivers them over to you, you shall conquer them and utterly destroy them. You shall make no covenant with them nor show mercy to them. Nor shall you make marriages with them. You shall not give your daughter to their son, nor take their daughter for your son. For they will turn your sons away from following me, to serve other gods; so the anger of the LORD will be aroused against you and destroy you suddenly. But thus you shall deal with them: you shall destroy their altars, and break down their sacred pillars, and cut down their wooden images, and burn their carved images with fire. For you are a holy people to the LORD your God; the LORD your God has chosen you to be a people for himself, a special treasure above all the peoples on the face of the earth." (Deuteronomy 7:1-6)

Jacob's behaviour in all of this is a mystery. He did not respond to the rape, nor did he send news of it to his sons who were out in the field. Just as Shechem took the lead from his father in the bargaining process, so the sons took over from Jacob, but answered the Hivites deceitfully. The family trait was to the fore yet again. Their offer was that, if the Hivites would agree to be circumcised, then the marriage could go ahead.

The act of circumcision had been given to Abraham by the Lord. It was a recognition by the household of faith that His children were powerless to bring about the fulfilment of the promises themselves, only the Almighty God could do this. Yet it was now used by the brothers as part of a strategy for revenge. The plan was to incapacitate the Hivites through circumcision and then kill all the men. Simeon and Levi went to the unsuspecting city, perhaps presenting themselves as two of Dinah's brothers just coming to check on how she was. The plot worked and Dinah was taken back to Jacob who did not rejoice at her release but was appalled at what had been done. "Their anger was cruel", said their father, "and they did it out of self-will" (Genesis 49:6,7).

Part two of the strategy could now follow and the rest of the brothers then sacked the city taking everything of value. They acted as Shechem had done for they also took the wives for themselves and their idols (Genesis 35:2).

> "You are inexcusable, O man, whoever you are who judge, for in whatever you judge another you condemn yourself; for you who judge practise the same things." (Romans 2:1)

These events brought an estrangement between Jacob and his sons. He was troubled because he had become an abomination to the inhabitants of the land. His personal honour had been affronted because of the duplicity of his sons. Would he again reflect on how Isaac must have felt when he deceived him?

For the sons, family honour was different: "Should he deal with our sister as a whore?" they said.[2]

2 M. Douglas, *Jacob's Tears*, pages 28,29.

40 | Renewed vows at Bethel

IT was never God's intent that Jacob should remain at Shechem. The years there brought riches but also trouble and the family was in need of spiritual renewal. Five times Hamor had spoken of Israel dwelling with his people with the intent of subsuming them into Canaanite life. Now God spoke to Jacob:

> "Arise, go up to Bethel and dwell there; and make an altar there to God, who appeared to you when you fled from the face of Esau your brother." (Genesis 35:1)

The house of God was the place to dwell, the place where Jacob's vows would be renewed and his spiritual authority over his household reclaimed.

Spiritual renewal

Three times in Genesis 34 we read that the rape of Dinah had defiled (*tame*) her.

- Verse 5: Jacob heard of it but he held his peace and did nothing.
- Verse 13: Jacob's sons heard of it and replied deceitfully to Hamor, planning murder.
- Verse 27: Because of it, the city was laid waste.

Although it was Dinah who was defiled yet, in a sense, the whole family was contaminated by its actions against the Canaanites. It too had become defiled and needed cleansing.

> "And Jacob said to his household and to all who were with him, 'Put away the foreign gods that are among you, purify

(*tahar*, cleanse) yourselves, and change your garments'."
(35:2)

Here, at last, was real leadership by Jacob – similar to that of his grandfather who commanded all who lived within his household to keep the way of the Lord. Rachel had brought her family's teraphim from Padan Aram and amongst the loot taken from Shechem were the Hivite's idols. They were to be put away and the language implies not just a physical casting away but also a turning away from considering them as gods. Were the garments they took off also taken from Shechem? Did they have some religious significance?[1]

Such was the authority behind Jacob's words that they gave *all* of these things to Jacob who buried them before the terebinth at Shechem; dead and useless gods buried at the place they had been worshipped, interred at the place where choices were made. Only after this purification could the journey to Bethel begin, protected by the Lord from the anger of the surrounding people.

All that followed shows us the tenderness of the God who so cared for Jacob. He guided him back to "the certain place" where He had appeared to him as he fled from Esau. He reminded him of the faith he had shown in returning to face Esau and the change of his name to Israel. Previously at Bethel Jacob saw angels descending and ascending and God was revealed to him. Now we read:

"God appeared to Jacob again."

And when their interaction was complete:

"God went up from him in the place where he talked with him."

The Lord now revealed himself to Jacob as Almighty God, El Shaddai. This title was used when the Lord gave renewed vigour to Abraham and Sarah so that Isaac could be conceived and the promised nation could emerge through him. In turn, Isaac used this title when, by faith, he blessed Jacob, that he might become a multitude of people and inherit the blessing of Abraham.

1 Compare the actions of Achan in the sack of Jericho, Joshua 7:21.

Of course Jacob would know these things and would remember that circumcision had been demanded by God as the sign that El Shaddai alone had the power to fulfil the promises covenanted to his grandfather. How he would reflect on the misuse of this rite that had just occurred at Shechem.

The Lord then repeated, almost word for word, the patriarchal blessing that Isaac had given Jacob as he left home.

Genesis 28	**Genesis 35**
May God Almighty bless you,	I am God Almighty.
And make you fruitful and multiply you,	Be fruitful and multiply;
That you may be an assembly of peoples;	A nation and a company of nations shall proceed from you, and kings shall come from your body.
And give you the blessing of Abraham, to you and your descendants with you, that you may inherit the land in which you are a stranger, which God gave to Abraham.	The land which I gave Abraham and Isaac I give to you; and to your descendants after you I give this land.

This was the second time that God spoke to Jacob at Bethel and the Psalmist tells us of a significant difference between the two occasions:

> "O seed of Abraham his servant, you children of Jacob, his chosen ones! He is the LORD our God; his judgements are in all the earth. He remembers his covenant forever, the word which he commanded, for a thousand generations, the covenant which he made with Abraham, and his oath to Isaac, and confirmed it to Jacob for a statute, to Israel as an everlasting covenant, saying, 'To you I will give the land of Canaan as the allotment of your inheritance', when they were few in number, indeed very few, and strangers in it." (Psalm 105:6-12)

His word to Jacob, fleeing to Haran was a statute, a divine decree that assured Jacob that the Lord would be with him wherever he was. The Lord's words to Israel who had fully come to believe in this and act upon it were an everlasting covenant. Here, at last, was all the blessing that Jacob could desire.

This would be a wonderful message to his sons. No doubt he had shared Isaac's words with them but now the Lord amplified them. If they remained separate from the people round about, and shared their father's faith, then from them nations (Judah and Israel) would come. Not only would they inherit the land but their descendants would grow to be kingdoms.

These events were an important pattern for Israel in the future. When the nation left Egypt and travelled to Sinai they were told to sanctify themselves, wash their clothes and be ready for the descent of the Lord to speak to them. All of the laws that then followed were given that they might be a separate nation, different from the nations round about – holy because the Lord was holy. The words *tame* (defiled) and *tahar* (cleansed), seen above, are found together a number of times in Leviticus, showing Israel how those defiled by sin could become clean and accepted by their God, a separate people.

And this same pattern was also left for us. We have the example of the one who was holy, harmless, undefiled, separate from sinners. He teaches us how we should behave in the house of God, Bethel, which is the church of the living God, the pillar and ground of the truth and Paul had the example of Jacob at Bethel in mind when he wrote those words. We too have been cleansed with the washing of water by the word. At our baptism we vowed to put off the things of this life and put on those new, spiritual clothes of which the greatest, wrote Paul, is love. Just as Jacob became Israel, finally leaving all the past behind in the rededication at Bethel, with those who hold fast to their faith the Lord will share his own new name at his coming.

The death of Rachel

The Lord had told Jacob to leave Haran to return to the land of his fathers and to his family. Isaac was still alive, living down at Hebron and Jacob, in obedience to God, began the journey

The city of the Great King

When the land was divided by Joshua, the city of Jebus was given to Benjamin. It was on the edge of Judah's territory to the south and the border ran down the valley of the son of Hinnom (Gehenna). David could only take it and rename it Zion when he became king over all Israel and the rift between Judah and the other tribes over the rejection of Saul had been healed.

It was the city of the son of sorrow (Benoni) but became the city of praise (Judah) to the son of the right hand (Benjamin).

south. There was great sadness on the journey for Rachel died in childbirth; she was probably about forty-five years old. When barren she had demanded of Jacob, "Give me children or else I die" and now, receiving what she wanted, her life ended.

Where did this happen? The Revised Version says, "there was still some way to go to Ephrath" (Bethlehem); other versions mention half a day's journey. It has been suggested that she died at Ramah,[2] eight miles (13 km) north of Bethlehem and on the direct route south from Bethel. If this was the case then she died giving birth to Benjamin in territory that would belong to his tribe. It was also the place spoken of by Jeremiah (31:15) in his prophecy about Judah's exile to Babylon (it was the place where Nebuchadnezzar assembled his captives, Jeremiah 40:1).

She lived through the birth for she saw it was a boy and, knowing she was dying and would not live to see him grow, she called him Benoni, the son of sorrow. However, to Jacob he was a delight, Benjamin, the son of the right hand. He was, with this name, an unmistakable type of the Son who would come; the one who would be the delight of his Father and who would ascend to sit at His right hand as the Psalmist prophesied.

2 Wenham, 16-50, page 326.

Reuben's disgrace

On first reading about the events of chapter 35, they seem like disparate incidents with little connection, yet as we look carefully, we see a common theme.

Israel needed to rebuild its relationship with the Lord, which it did at Bethel. There the Lord reconfirmed the promises to Jacob reminding him that his name was now Israel and that he would be the father not just of one nation but of a number of them.

No doubt Jacob had learned previously from Abraham that these promises would ultimately be fulfilled through one special descendant of his. Now, Rachel had died giving birth to a son who was a type of this special offspring and Jacob had acknowledged some understanding of this in the name, Benjamin, given to him.

Yet Reuben was the firstborn and had just heard that nations and kings would come through his father; honour lay ahead for the family and his father's heir. He had just witnessed his father describe his new son as the one who would occupy a privileged position at his right hand. Should this not have been his?

His taking of Bilhah, Rachel's maid, just after Rachel died, was a deliberate attempt to try and lay claim to the blessing and his father's estate, to show he was his father's successor.[3] He was the firstborn son who did indeed seek to grasp at equality with his father and Jacob never forgave him for it.

How ironic it is that this firstborn son disgraced his father at Migdol Edar, the tower of the flock. This was the place where the shepherds were keeping their flocks when the angel appeared to them with the message of the son born in Bethlehem who would be their saviour.

> "Then Jacob came to his father Isaac at Mamre, or Kirjath Arba (that is, Hebron), where Abraham and Isaac had dwelt."
>
> (Genesis 35:27)

---

3 For example, see 2 Samuel 3:7,8 and 2 Samuel 16:21. It was a practice absolutely forbidden under the law (Deuteronomy 27:20).

What a tender moment this was. Isaac was no longer bereft of both sons for the one who shared his faith had returned with twelve sons. Years before God had told him that he would multiply his descendants and now he experienced the beginning of the fulfilment of this promise. We can imagine the words shared between father and son. What comfort Jacob brought as he told Isaac of all that had happened and of God's abiding presence in his life in spite of his deception of his father.

The chapter ends with Esau and Jacob together again at Isaac's funeral.[4] He was buried with his wife and parents in the cave of Ephron at Machpelah where later Leah and finally Jacob would be buried also. The brothers were now aged 120, old men themselves and they had last met twenty-three years before at the Jabbok. All the problems between them were long since over and this was the last time they would see each other.

---

4 Although details of Isaac's death are recorded here, he lived through many events recorded in subsequent chapters. He was alive when Joseph was sold into slavery by his brothers. What would he have made of that?

41 | The generations of Esau

THREE family genealogies are recorded for us in the patriarchal records:[1] Abraham / Isaac / Jacob; Ishmael; and Esau. For both Ishmael and Esau a similar pattern is used, giving us a message about them (see table overleaf).

The records of both Ishmael and Esau are those of sons who had opportunities at the outset to be part of God's purpose yet rejected it. They married faithless wives and their families grew outside the Promised Land which they left. After telling us their genealogies, Genesis shows no further interest in them and immediately moves on to the next stage of the development of the household of faith.

Yet in spite of this we again see the graciousness of God for He listened to Abraham's pleading for Ishmael and promised that he too would become a great nation. Twelve princes would come from him and their names are recorded as confirmation of God's word.

We are told even more about the descendants of Esau. He was hated by the Lord because of his disdain for the promises, yet he was not totally cast off by Him. The Lord warned Moses that Israel was not to meddle with Edom as they passed by for they were their brethren. So the Lord said, "I have given mount Seir to Esau for a possession" (Deuteronomy 2:5) and we read of those who settled there.

1 A fascinating study of the faithful and unfaithful in each generation is given in C. H. Waller, *The Path to the City of Gold*, chapters 1-4.

<table>
<tr><th>Ishmael</th><th></th><th>Esau</th></tr>
<tr><td>Sent away by Abraham</td><td rowspan="8">Esau marries into Ishmael's family (28:9)</td><td>Leaves Isaac</td></tr>
<tr><td>Goes out of the land to Paran (21:21)</td><td>Goes out of the land to Seir (33:16)</td></tr>
<tr><td>Marries an Egyptian</td><td>Marries Canaanites</td></tr>
<tr><td>Record of Abraham's death, buried by both his sons (25:8)</td><td>Record of Isaac's death, buried by both his sons (35:29)</td></tr>
<tr><td>The Generations of Ishmael recorded (25:12)</td><td>The Generations of Esau recorded (36:1)</td></tr>
<tr><td>Nothing more told us of his life in Genesis</td><td>Nothing more told us of his life in Genesis</td></tr>
<tr><td>The Generations of Isaac immediately recorded next (25:19)</td><td>The Generations of Jacob immediately recorded next (37:2)</td></tr>
<tr><td>The record of Jacob immediately begins</td><td>The record of Joseph immediately begins</td></tr>
</table>

Esau's genealogy

This is divided into four parts.

1. **Verses 1-5:** The record of Esau's three Canaanite wives and their sons which were born to him while still in Canaan.
2. **Verses 6-19:** The children and grandchildren born to him in Mount Seir. They became chiefs of the land.
3. **Verses 20-30:** Seir had originally been the territory of the Horites (cave dwellers) led by a chief called Seir. Most were destroyed by Esau but he married a granddaughter of Seir and the remaining Horites were assimilated into Edom.
4. **Verses 31-40:** Further descendants of Esau who became kings in Edom.

Edom and prophecy

Two names stand out in the list of Esau's descendants. They were brothers, grandsons of Esau through Eliphaz.

Amalek was the father of the Amalekites, the first people to attack Israel as they left Egypt (Exodus 17:8) ambushing the rear of the column where the weakest would be. Moses prophesied that there would be war between the Lord and them for generation to generation and this continued until the days of Esther, for Haman was a descendant of Agag, king of Amalek. Amalek therefore represented the perpetual hatred shown by the Edomites to Israel from the beginning to this day:

> "'Because you have had an ancient hatred, and have shed the blood of the children of Israel by the power of the sword at the time of their calamity, when their iniquity came to an end, therefore, as I live', says the Lord GOD, 'I will prepare you for blood, and blood shall pursue you; since you have not hated blood, therefore blood shall pursue you. Thus I will make Mount Seir most desolate, and cut off from it the one who leaves and the one who returns. And I will fill its mountains with the slain; on your hills and in your valleys and in all your ravines those who are slain by the sword shall fall. I will make you perpetually desolate, and your cities shall be uninhabited; then you shall know that I am the LORD. Because you have said, "These two nations and these two countries shall be mine, and we will possess them", although the LORD was there, therefore, as I live, says the Lord GOD, I will do according to your anger and according to the envy which you showed in your hatred against them; and I will make myself known among them when I judge you. Then you shall know that I am the LORD. I have heard all your blasphemies which you have spoken against the mountains of Israel, saying, "They are desolate; they are given to us to consume". Thus with your mouth you have boasted against me and multiplied your words against me; I have heard them'. Thus says the Lord GOD: 'The whole earth will rejoice when I make you desolate. As you rejoiced because the inheritance of the house of Israel

> was desolate, so I will do to you; you shall be desolate, O Mount Seir, as well as all of Edom – all of it! Then they shall know that I am the LORD.'" (Ezekiel 35:5-15)

Yet there will be a remnant of Edom that will be saved and we see a type of this when we look at Amalek's brother.

Kenaz was Amalek's half-brother. From him came Jephunneh the Kennizite and his son Caleb (Numbers 32:12), the proselyte who gained an inheritance in Judah and was the faithful spy who accompanied Joshua. Hence, even from the worst of Israel's enemies would come those who turned to the Lord and who could have an inheritance in His land.

Isaac had told Esau: "By your sword you shall live, and you shall serve your brother" and this came true in the days of David who extended the boundaries of the kingdom from the river of Egypt to the river Euphrates, encompassing Edom, putting garrisons there so that all the Edomites became his servants (2 Samuel 8:14). It is this kingdom territory that will be restored when Messiah returns and once again Edom will be involved for:

> "On that day I will raise up the tabernacle of David, which has fallen down, and repair its damages; I will raise up its ruins, and rebuild it as in the days of old; that they may possess the remnant of Edom, and all the Gentiles who are called by my name, says the LORD who does this thing." (Amos 9:11,12)

Here is a picture of the grace of God at work once more. Esau He hated, his descendants He would perpetually fight against because of their desire to obliterate His chosen people, yet there will be a remnant of Edom, and of Gentiles throughout the world, who will seek Him and call upon His name at the time of the end that they may be part of His kingdom.

SECTION SEVEN:
From Canaan to Egypt

42 | The favourite son

THE final part of Genesis, running from chapter 37 to the end of the book, is its longest. It is often called 'the Joseph story' for it has a more narrative style than previous sections. Once again, the emphasis is on the outworking of God's purpose for when Joseph revealed his identity to his brothers he said:

> "And God sent me before you to preserve a posterity for you in the earth, and to save your lives by a great deliverance. So now it was not you who sent me here, but God; and he has made me a father to Pharaoh, and Lord of all his house, and a ruler throughout all the land of Egypt." (Genesis 45:7,8)

The threat to the household of faith was very great. Without the Lord's intervention Jacob's family was in danger of passing away: "God sent me ... to preserve a posterity for you." Of course, the immediate threat was a physical one, the severity of a very bad famine, but there was also a spiritual danger for these chapters reveal that the separateness of the family from the world of Canaan was at risk from the behaviour of the sons.

There are no further promise-blessings from the Lord in this section but we see the beginning of their fulfilment in the events that unfold before us.

- The family grew so that seventy people went down to Egypt and would become there the great nation promised to Abraham.
- Pharaoh's acceptance of Joseph and his family brought about the unification of Egypt into a great nation. It was a

fulfilment of God's opening words to Abraham: "I will bless them that bless you."

- The Gospel began its journey from the land of Israel through the whole earth for the Psalmist tells us of the work of Joseph as vizier of all Egypt, taking the message of the Lord God of his fathers with him throughout the land.

  > "Blow the trumpet at the time of the New Moon, at the full moon, on our solemn feast day. For this is a statute for Israel, a law of the God of Jacob. This he established in Joseph as a testimony, when he went throughout the land of Egypt." (Psalm 81:3-5)
  >
  > "[The king] made him Lord of his house, and ruler of all his substance: to bind his princes at his pleasure, and teach his senators wisdom." (105:21,22, RV)

Sent to his brothers

Joseph was seventeen years old. From this we know that all his brothers were youths between eighteen and twenty-four years of age and perhaps we should see their actions as those of immature young men. They were the sons of an old man – Jacob was 108 and his influence over his sons had waned. He had yearned to return to the land of promise from Haran; now he was settled, permanently he hoped, at Hebron with no desire to move from it. Isaac was still alive and presumably dwelling with Jacob; he would live there for another twelve years.

All of the tensions between Jacob's two wives now bubbled up again in the relationships of their sons. Reuben was the oldest and by birth should have inherited both birthright and blessing, yet he lost these because of his immoral behaviour with Bilhah. Jacob gave the birthright to Joseph, increasing the family problems, and Judah would emerge as the natural leader of the brothers in the events that followed.

> "Now the sons of Reuben the firstborn of Israel – he was indeed the firstborn, but because he defiled his father's bed, his birthright was given to the sons of Joseph, the son of Israel, so that the genealogy is not listed according to the

> birthright; yet Judah prevailed over his brothers, and from him came a ruler, although the birthright was Joseph's."
> (1 Chronicles 5:1,2)

Yet, shining through all of these troubled relationships is the behaviour of Joseph as the saviour of his people, one of the greatest types of the Lord Jesus Christ in all the Old Testament. The Lord will use Joseph, and his example of willing sacrifice for the brothers he ultimately loved, to change the lives of this dysfunctional family so that they were prepared and fit to be the fathers of the nation.

The talebearer

> "This is the history of Jacob. Joseph, being seventeen years old, was feeding the flock with his brothers. And the lad[1] was with the sons of Bilhah and the sons of Zilpah, his father's wives; and Joseph brought a bad report of them to his father. Now Israel loved Joseph more than all his children, because he was the son of his old age. Also he made him a tunic of many colours." (Genesis 37:2,3)

Joseph was working with Dan, Naphtali, Gad and Asher. The sons of the handmaids, originally servants, were at the bottom of the pecking order of Jacob's sons; now his favourite son had been sent out into the field with them, perhaps by the sons of Leah.

Immediately, we see him both a shepherd and a servant, foreshadowing the Lord Jesus Christ. He was the beloved son, yet he became a bondservant for the salvation of his brethren.

However, there is a contrast between how Joseph should have behaved and what he initially did. As a shepherd, a sheep feeder like his father, and in the tending of his flock, he should have learned to be a son who cared for and looked after his brothers.[2]

He brought a bad report, and the language means one of evil whispering or defamation, to his father.[3] Joseph was a

---

1 Hebrew *naar*, translated as both "lad" or "servant".

2 Cf. Jesus in John 10.

3 The same language is used of the ten spies who brought back a false report to Moses in Numbers 14.

Joseph

> "Then God remembered Rachel, and God listened to her and opened her womb. And she conceived and bore a son, and said, God has taken away my reproach. So she called his name Joseph, and said, the LORD shall add to me another son."

Although the Lord had answered Rachel's distress and opened her womb, one son was not enough for her. She did not pray for many sons as Leah had but for one more. In faith she called her firstborn Joseph, "he shall add", understanding that it would only happen if it was the Lord's will. Indeed it was for she bore Benjamin, "the son of the right hand". Joseph was a great type of the Lord Jesus Christ but he was not the promised seed, another son would be added, the one who would ascend to the right hand of his Father to be an intercessor for his brethren.

Rachel's words are a remarkable prophecy of the special son, the one whom the Lord would indeed add.

talebearer and there was nothing good or true in what he said. This was not the work of a son who cared for his brothers. Many years later the prophet Jeremiah was wrongly accused of similar actions, bringing false reports, and was hated by those in Jerusalem. "Perhaps he will be deceived; then we can overcome him and take our revenge on him" (Jeremiah 20:10, ESV), they said, and in Joseph's actions we see the cause of the hatred of him that developed. He was the favourite son who told tales about his brothers to their father.

Jacob had deceit burnt out of him through the actions of Laban, a greater deceiver, and so understood the hurt such behaviour brought. Joseph the talebearer would meet a worse talebearer in Potiphar's wife and through that experience understand how his brothers had felt about him.

He is described as the son of Jacob's old age yet so were all the brothers, but he was the son of Rachel, the wife Jacob had loved and so he loved her son more than his other children and the rest hated Joseph for this, knowing how their father had hated Leah. Once again, partiality would tear the family apart.

Joseph had a special coat and it defined his role in the family. With the birthright came priestly responsibilities. It was a coat (*kettoneth*) of many colours and the word describes a long-sleeved, full robe. It was first used of the covering of skin provided by the Lord for Adam and Eve (Genesis 3:21) and it is next found in the description of the priestly garments under the Law.

> "And these are the garments which they shall make: a breastplate, an ephod, a robe (*kettoneth*), a skilfully woven tunic, a turban, and a sash. So they shall make holy garments for Aaron your brother and his sons, that he may minister to me as priest." (Exodus 28:4)

But why is it described as a coat of many colours? Perhaps this aspect looks back to the covenant the Lord made with Noah after the Flood. The word "covenant" is mentioned there seven times and its sign in the heavens was the multi-coloured rainbow.[4]

And we have seen such a special coat in this family before. Jacob had grown up listening to his grandfather and father as they told him of the promises. His brother, Esau, had the same opportunity but rejected it, lost the birthright and ultimately the special, priestly coat that came with it. He had been tricked out of the blessing and the inheritance that came with it and, even worse, had been told that he would serve his brother for Isaac had been deceived into telling Jacob:

> "Let peoples serve you, and nations bow down to you. Be master over your brethren, and let your mother's sons bow down to you." (Genesis 27:29)

Because of this Esau hated his brother, declared he would kill him and Jacob left his family for many years.

When we read Genesis 37 with this in mind we get a strong feeling of déjà vu. Here is a special coat, a son claiming

4 Such garments were also worn by the king's daughters, 2 Samuel 13:18.

that his brothers would bow before him, sibling hatred – history is repeating itself!

Dreams and hatred

> "Now Joseph had a dream, and he told it to his brothers; and they hated him even more. So he said to them, 'Please hear this dream which I have dreamed: There we were, binding sheaves in the field. Then behold, my sheaf arose and also stood upright; and indeed your sheaves stood all around and bowed down to my sheaf'. And his brothers said to him, 'Shall you indeed reign over us? Or shall you indeed have dominion over us?' So they hated him even more for his dreams and for his words. Then he dreamed still another dream and told it to his brothers, and said, 'Look, I have dreamed another dream. And this time, the sun, the moon, and the eleven stars bowed down to me'." (Genesis 37:5-9)

These are the first dreams in Genesis in which God does not speak directly to the recipient, yet they are still divinely inspired prophecy. All six of Joseph's dreams came in pairs and, as he told Pharaoh, this doubling was because "the matter was established by God". These were not the words of a braggart, younger brother as his brothers thought!

Twenty times in chapter 37 we meet the words "brother" and "brethren". This was the household of faith and a shared belief in the promise-blessings should have bound Jacob's sons together in unity (cf. Psalm 133) as spiritual brethren. Indeed, when Abraham sought to bring peace between Lot and himself, his plea was "Are we not brethren?" However, Joseph's brothers do not appear to be spiritually minded men at this stage. Had they neglected the teaching of the promises as their uncle had done a generation earlier?

Like Esau, they turned against their brother and hated him.

- When his brothers saw Jacob loved Joseph more than them they hated him and could not even say "Shalom" to him (verse 4).

- When Joseph told his dream to his brothers, they hated him even more[5] (verse 5).
- They hated him yet more for his dreams and his words (verse 8).

Of course they did! Their younger brother had been favoured with the birthright and now he claimed to have had two dreams which showed him with the blessing: "Shall you indeed reign over us? Or shall you indeed have dominion over us?" they said. Yes indeed! Twice Joseph dreamed of his brothers bowing before him and three times they would later do this in Egypt.

Jacob saw the second dream as involving himself and Rachel: "Shall I and your mother indeed come to bow ourselves before you?" Yet there is no record of Jacob bowing before Joseph and Rachel was dead by this time.[6] The envy of his position in the family was now added to the brothers' hatred of Joseph. It seems that they really thought that Jacob's preference for him would lead to a role of leadership and it was this that led them to sell him into slavery (Acts 7:9).

These things take us forward to the time of the Lord Jesus Christ. He was the beloved son of his Father, the one given the birthright, born to be a priest to intercede for his brethren, but also sent to reign over them. It is likely that when Jesus spoke the Parable of the Tenants in the Vineyard in Mark 12 he had the example of Joseph and his brothers in mind:

> "Therefore still having one son, his beloved, he also sent him to them last, saying, 'They will respect my son'. But those vinedressers said among themselves, 'This is the heir. Come, let us kill him, and the inheritance will be ours'. So they took him and killed him and cast him out of the vineyard."
>
> (Mark 12:6-8)

---

5 There is a play on words in the second and third statements of their hate. They "added more hate" using the same word when Rachel named Joseph for, said she, "God will add to me another son".

6 It has been suggested that this must therefore look forward to the resurrection day.

Joseph sent to Shechem

> "Then his brothers went to feed their father's flock in Shechem. And Israel said to Joseph, 'Are not your brothers feeding the flock in Shechem? Come, I will send you to them'. So he said to him, 'Here I am'. Then he said to him, 'Please go and see if it is well with your brothers and well with the flocks, and bring back word to me'. So he sent him out of the Valley of Hebron, and he went to Shechem." (Genesis 37:12-14)

Shechem is sixty miles (97 km) north of Hebron. Why would the brothers make such a journey? It was only two to three years since Simeon and Levi had killed all the men of Shechem and made Jacob's name to stink amongst the inhabitants of the land. It is unlikely that they went on Jacob's instructions. A possible reason was to find water in a dry season for Jacob's well was there and it was a special well. It was not just a cistern, dug out of the ground on a hillside with channels leading to it to collect rainwater. It collected living water from a constant source, a natural spring.[7] Furthermore, Jacob had bought land there (Genesis 33:19) and it is likely the well was on this. Yet John's Gospel also tells us that the land had been given to Joseph by his father (John 4:5)! What would the brothers think of this?

Jacob was worried about his sons: "Go and see if all is well with your brothers" was his request of Joseph. Was he worried about their physical safety or was there another concern? The idols and teraphim brought back from Haran and those looted from Shechem by the brothers were buried there. Did he think that his sons might have dug them up and were using them?

When Joseph arrived at Shechem, the brothers were not there, yet he did not give up. Like the Lord many years later, he had gone to seek and search out those who were lost and so he journeyed north to Dothan.

What role did Jacob expect of Joseph? He went in his special, priestly coat and perhaps it was this that caught his brothers' attention as they recognised him afar off. This coat was

7 See the two different words used for "well" in John 4, which explain this.

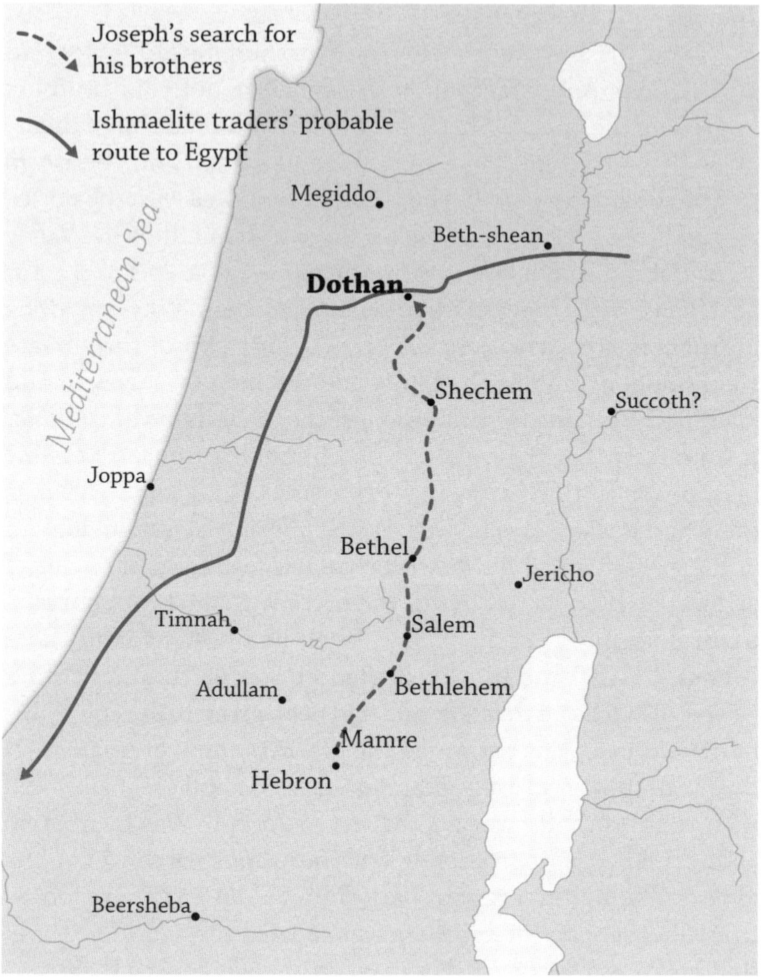

Joseph's travels to his brothers and into Egypt.

used later in their deceit of Jacob. The idea of an envied and hated younger brother, with a reputation for tale-telling, coming to spy on them was more than they could stomach but their response was extreme.

Yet in spite of all that would follow, from the sending of Joseph to the end of Genesis is a theme of divine providence. We see the machinations of men, the enmity of the brothers and the hurt of Jacob, a string of seemingly unconnected events. But in all that took place the hand of the Lord was at work through Joseph, healing the family and reuniting them as brethren together.

Dothan

The name Dothan means 'two wells'; possibly it was those that drew the brothers there further north from Shechem even though it meant leaving the living water of Jacob's well. However, at least one of Dothan's cisterns was dry for they threw Joseph into it.

The prophet Jeremiah alludes to this incident when he wrote of the way Israel had turned aside from the Lord. They had looked to Egypt and Assyria for help and had turned to their gods; he described these powers as two broken cisterns that could not hold water:

> "For my people have committed two evils: they have forsaken me, the fountain of living waters, and hewn themselves cisterns – broken cisterns that can hold no water ... Have you not brought this on yourself, in that you have forsaken the LORD your God when he led you in the way? And now why take the road to Egypt, to drink the waters of Sihor? Or why take the road to Assyria, to drink the waters of the River? ... you have forsaken the LORD your God, and the fear of me is not in you, says the Lord GOD of hosts." (Jeremiah 2:13-19)

The brothers had returned from Haran, saved from the threat of Esau and well knew the promises that meant so much to their father. Yet, in their behaviour they appeared to be drifting away from these things, refusing to have anything to do with the son who had the priestly, birthright role.

Even before Joseph arrived, having seen him coming, they had decided to kill him – their envy and hate boiling over: 'Behold this master of dreams is coming, let's kill him and throw him into a pit.' He had shared with them the dream of his dominance and they made a mockery of it; to them he was indeed a master, but just in his dreams.

Divine providence at work

Joseph was sent by Jacob to see if all was well with his brothers.

- They were not at Shechem but he met a man who told him they were at Dothan (on a main trade route to Egypt).
- Reuben refused to let the brothers kill Joseph, he let them put him in a dry cistern but then departed.
- An Ishmaelite caravan passed by.
- In Reuben's absence, the brothers sold Joseph into slavery.
- In Egypt he was sold to Potiphar.
- Through Potiphar's wife he was cast into prison.
- In prison he met Pharaoh's butler and impressed him with his ability to interpret dreams.
- Pharaoh dreamed, no one could interpret and the butler remembered Joseph.
- Joseph was released from prison, became vizier of all Egypt saving the country from the famine.
- Joseph's family came down to Egypt, were saved from the famine and were given the best of the land in Goshen for their flocks.

Joseph was sent by God to save their lives by a great deliverance.

> "God meant it for good, in order to bring it about as it is this day, to save many people alive."

Thrown into the pit

It was Reuben who prevented murder and suggested that Joseph was thrown into the dry pit (cistern) with the intention of rescuing him later (the design of cisterns is such that it would be impossible for Joseph to get out without help).

They had agreed all of this beforehand so that immediately Joseph arrived he was accosted, stripped of his coat and thrown into the pit. Once again they could not even say "shalom" to him. But, for an unspecified reason, Reuben went away and in his absence Midianite[8] traders passed by on their way to Egypt.

For the first recorded time in scripture Judah spoke, appealing to his brothers not to kill Joseph but to sell him for "he is our brother and our flesh". The fact that he was "made like unto his brothers" finally touched their hearts sufficiently that they agreed not to kill him but to sell him into slavery.

How ironical that the Midianites carried embalming ointments as they took Joseph into Egypt for we shall leave him at the end of Genesis embalmed, in a coffin, awaiting carriage back to Canaan.

There are clues later about further details of these events. When Jacob first sent the brothers down into Egypt Joseph accused them of being spies and put them in prison for three days. Had he, in turn, been incarcerated in the pit for three days? When he released them, he bound Simeon and threw him back into jail. Was Simeon, who was described by his father as cruel, a ringleader in wanting to kill Joseph? This later experience brought back memories of the events at Dothan and shows us how much the brothers later regretted what they had done.

> "Then they said to one another, 'We are truly guilty concerning our brother, for we saw the anguish of his soul when he pleaded with us, and we would not hear; therefore this distress has come upon us'. And Reuben answered them, saying, 'Did I not speak to you, saying, "Do not sin against the boy"; and you would not listen? Therefore behold, his blood is now required of us'." (Genesis 42:21,22)

All that remained was to soak Joseph's priestly coat in blood and present it to Jacob as proof that a wild animal must have taken and killed him. Once more the family trait of deceit emerges and what hypocrisy they showed as they said to their father: 'We are not really sure if this is his coat. Can you identify it?' Of course they knew; it was the hated garment of their hated brother.

---

8 They are also called Ishmaelites and this appears to be a general name given to any mobile, trading peoples in the land.

So Jacob, the erstwhile deceiver, was deceived once again. He had put on Esau's coat and taken the skin of a kid. Now his son's priestly garment, soaked in the blood of a kid, was used to deceive him and he could not be comforted.

For over twenty years the brothers lived with this lie, daily looking at their father and his grief. We leave them at this point in serious spiritual danger, corroded by what they had done. Their treatment of Joseph was not just hatred of him but also rejection of what he stood for and they showed contempt for his role in the way they mistreated his priestly coat. In the years ahead friendship with the world and intermarriage with Canaanite women would creep in. The household of faith was in real spiritual danger until the Lord saved them through their despised and rejected brother.

43 | Judah and Tamar – deception again

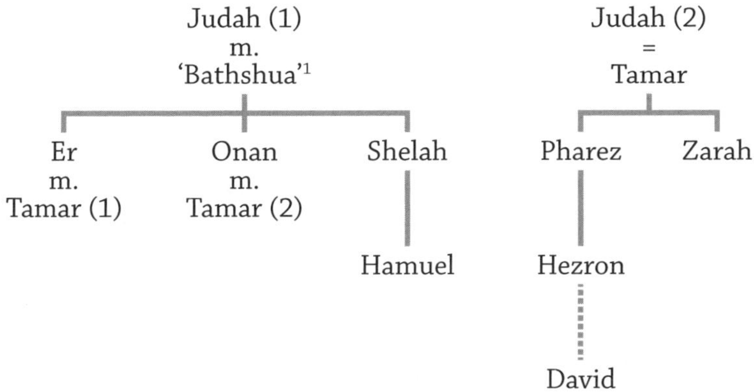

AS we turn to Genesis chapter 38 it is difficult to see how it fits into the Joseph narrative. Indeed, if it were not in the text we would read smoothly on from chapter 37 to chapter 39 without realising that a vital piece of God's purpose had been omitted.

From the beginning, the Lord's command was "Be fruitful and multiply and fill the earth". This was the first blessing and was the foundation on which all the other promise-blessings in Genesis were given. Yet the record is one of barren women: Sarah, Rebekah and Rachel struggled with their infertility, pleading with God that they might have sons. They were driven by a desire to be part of this process of being fruitful and multiplying, faithful

1 Bathshua is a title meaning 'the daughter of Shua'; her real name is unknown.

women who believed in the Lord and who wanted to be part of His purpose; child bearing was an essential part of this. We now see this desire again in Tamar.

There are two quite different women in this record. The first, a Canaanitess (1 Chronicles 2:3) daughter of Shua, had no problems in childbearing; three times we read that she conceived, yet the sons she bore were unacceptable to God and He killed two of them because of their wickedness. The second woman, Tamar, was the first Gentile woman to join the household of faith. She worked hard to have a son and so be part of the divine promises. She prefigured Ruth: "Your people will be my people and your God my God." Her faithfulness is seen in the genealogy of the Lord Jesus Christ for, as the mother of Pharez, she was an ancestor of his.

Chapter 38 also tells us of Judah, the son who led the sale of Joseph into slavery and was then involved in the deceit of his father. Tamar would now deceive him in turn.

Jacob was already worried about the spiritual health of his sons when they went north to Shechem; now a time of testing for Judah followed:

> "It came to pass at that time that Judah departed from his brothers, and visited a certain Adullamite whose name was Hirah. And Judah saw there a daughter of a certain Canaanite whose name was Shua, and he married her and went in to her." (Genesis 38:1,2)

Judah's departure from Jacob's household happened immediately after the brothers returned to their father and deceived him about Joseph. Was Jacob's grief so overwhelming that Judah could not bear to stay? It is significant that he "departed from his brothers", not from Jacob. Perhaps there had been an argument between them all about what they had done. We know from their later appearance before Joseph that their consciences had troubled them for many years (Genesis 42:21,22).

Judah went down from Hebron and travelled north-west about ten miles to Adullam, a royal, Canaanite city (Joshua

12:15), and visited Hirah. Twice in this chapter this man is called Judah's friend and Judah was in spiritual danger for "friendship with the world is enmity with God" wrote James (4:4). He was at risk of making a similar mistake to Lot, leaving the faithful and joining the inhabitants of Canaan.

These events must have occupied most of the twenty years between Joseph's departure to Egypt and his brother's journey there,[2] for Judah's first three sons were born, grew to adulthood and married in this period.

For the first time a faithful descendant of Abraham married someone outside the family. Judah saw, desired and took, as his wife, an unnamed Canaanite woman.

We learn very little about the marriages of Jacob's sons during this time. The option of going back to Haran to find a wife, as did Isaac and Jacob, was unavailable to them. Jacob and Laban had made an agreement that neither would trespass on the other's territory and, with his twenty years of service seared into his mind, Jacob must have actively discouraged his sons from going back there. It seems likely that marriage with other tribes must have been common, yet there is no record of their wives' names.

Bathshua bore Judah three sons in quick succession: Er whom he named; Onan and Shelah whom Bathshua named. Is there a progression in this subtle change? Did her Canaanite influence dominate the household after a time?

Shelah was born at Chezib, near Adullam, reminding us that she and her sons never joined Jacob's enclave or accepted the way of the Lord.

When his sons grew to adulthood, Judah chose another Canaanite, Tamar, as wife for Er, his oldest son. Perhaps the influence of his Canaanite mother outweighed anything his father said for Er was wicked and God took away his life. Judah, however, knew the family need to keep the bloodline alive and

2 "After a long time" (Genesis 38:12, NIV).

gave Tamar to his second son, Onan, who refused to give her a son[3] and God slew him also.

It is significant that we do not read that Judah mourned in any way for the deaths of his two sons. Was he heartless (as some writers suggest) or did he see their wickedness and accept God's judgements that such men would play no part in His purpose? Whatever the reason, Judah was not willing to risk his third son, Shelah, in another levirate marriage and told Tamar to return to her father's house under the pretext that Shelah was not yet old enough to marry her. Even though she was formally betrothed to Shelah we know that Judah had no intention of keeping his word, for verse 12 tells us that many years passed and he had still not given her to his son.

It was then that Tamar acted the role of a prostitute, enticing Judah and becoming pregnant. His route from Adullam to Timnath for the sheep shearing led him past Enaim and Tamar, dressed and veiled as a prostitute, sat by the gate of the city waiting for Judah to pass by. A brief, commercial conversation followed: she would have sex with him in exchange for a young goat. He left his staff and seal with her as surety, intending to send the kid later. No doubt Judah was mystified when Hirah went to pay the kid and retrieve the staff and seal on Judah's behalf, for the woman could not be found.

> "And it came to pass, about three months after, that Judah was told, saying, 'Tamar your daughter-in-law has played the harlot; furthermore she is with child by harlotry'. So Judah said, 'Bring her out and let her be burned!'" (Genesis 38:24)

She was accused of prostitution and an indignant Judah condemned her to death until the truth was revealed: he was the father.

> "When she was brought out, she sent to her father-in-law, saying, 'By the man to whom these belong, I am with child'. And she said, 'Please determine whose these are – the signet and cord, and staff'. So Judah acknowledged them and said,

3 There was a forerunner of the Levirate marriage law given by Moses.

'She has been more righteous than I, because I did not give her to Shelah my son'. And he never knew her again."

(verses 25,26)

Judah's final words, "She is more righteous than I" seem strange until we relate them back to the promises. Abraham had believed them and God accounted him righteous because of his faith. Judah did not forgive Tamar because he discovered that he and not some other man had been her sexual partner. He saw her as more committed to continuing the household of faith than he had been; because of her faith she was more righteous and through her faith Judah would become an ancestor of both David and his greater Son.

44 | From slavery to prison

"Now Joseph had been taken down to Egypt. And Potiphar, an officer of Pharaoh, captain of the guard, an Egyptian, bought him from the Ishmaelites who had taken him down there." (Genesis 39:1)

AFTER the description of Judah's behaviour in chapter 38, the record returns back to Joseph. Chapter 37 ended with the selling of Joseph in Egypt to Potiphar. Chapter 39 reconnects to this, beginning with the reminder that Potiphar bought him.

Twice we read that he was "taken down" and this emphasis suggests something more than the physical journey from Canaan to Egypt. The boy who had been elevated above his brothers had to learn the lesson of humility before he was fit for the Lord's purpose with his family. Such humility is a lesson many others have had to learn throughout the ages, one that the Apostle Peter understood for his Lord had told him: "When you are converted, strengthen your brothers" and before he was ready to achieve this he understood:

> "Servants, be submissive to your masters with all fear, not only to the good and gentle, but also to the harsh. For this is commendable, if because of conscience toward God one endures grief, suffering wrongfully. For what credit is it if, when you are beaten for your faults, you take it patiently? But when you do good and suffer, if you take it patiently, this is commendable before God. For to this you were called, because

> Christ also suffered for us, leaving us an example, that you should follow his steps: who committed no sin, nor was deceit found in His mouth; who, when he was reviled, did not revile in return; when he suffered, he did not threaten, but committed himself to him who judges righteously ..." (1 Peter 2:18-23)

Such behaviour was now asked of Joseph.

Potiphar was an important man, an officer of Pharaoh who would attend at court, the head of his guard and in charge of the special prison for the king's prisoners. The same title was given to Nebuzaradan who served Nebuchadnezzar and who was in charge of the sacking of Jerusalem for his master. But there is a more sinister meaning to this title for it is translated by some writers as "chief of the executioners".[1] This was a powerful and potentially dangerous man.

Previously Jacob had been separated from Isaac for twenty years, in the form of a servant, serving Laban; now Joseph, his son, was separated from Jacob, serving others as slave and prisoner for thirteen years.

He was to meet Potiphar's wife, a talebearer greater than himself and then the butler, a man who promised to remember him but promptly forgot all about him. Yet Joseph's behaviour in all of the following events is remarkable. No doubt his father had told him of the events at Bethel and Mahanaim, how the Lord was with him and looked after him wherever he was. Joseph also had the same divine protection for, like bookends around this chapter, we read:

> "The LORD was with Joseph, and he was a successful (prosperous) man; and he was in the house of his master the Egyptian." (Genesis 39:2)
>
> "... the LORD was with him; and whatever he did, the LORD made it prosper." (verse 23)

Not only was the Lord with him, as He had been with his father and grandfather, but in all that he did in Potiphar's house and in prison, he prospered. Many years later the Lord made a

---

1 For example, Genesis 39:1 (Rotherham).

similar commitment to Joshua, a descendant of Joseph, as he prepared to lead Israel into Canaan:

> "This Book of the Law shall not depart from your mouth, but you shall meditate in it day and night, that you may observe to do according to all that is written in it. For then you will make your way prosperous, and then you will have good success. Have I not commanded you? Be strong and of good courage; do not be afraid, nor be dismayed, for the LORD your God is with you wherever you go." (Joshua 1:8,9)

The name of the Lord is mentioned eight times in this chapter and then just once more in the rest of Genesis – in Jacob's personal statement in chapter 49.

The Lord was with Joseph, all he did flourished and those associated with him found their affairs blessed by God – yet the Lord's name was not directly spoken by him. Joseph was a man who, despite dreadful things happening to him, trusted in God whatever happened. After his period of testing, the events that followed were all driven by him; he was the one who did nothing but what God showed him and the Lord's purpose was worked out through him.

He was a highly talented man with supreme administrative skills.[2] He was a charismatic leader who could outline a course of action and inspire people to follow him; a man of total integrity who inspired trust for he was entrusted with all of Potiphar's affairs including his accounts. He became not only his overseer but his special attendant, his minister involved in his business (as was Joshua to Moses). And, as if this was not enough, he was a man of fine figure and handsome face (exactly the same language was used of his mother, Rachel). No wonder his brothers had been jealous of him.

Potiphar's wife

Potiphar's wife was a bored woman whose husband was not at home (like the woman of Proverbs 7). Her desire for Joseph

2 As was his descendant, Joshua.

was one of lust. He was only a Hebrew slave and her words were peremptory, "Come to bed with me". Day after day she demanded this of him and he steadfastly refused her. Not only would it be a betrayal of the master who trusted him so much, it would be "a great wickedness and sin against God" and she, as well as Potiphar, was aware of Joseph's beliefs. Joseph's words should have struck a chord with Potiphar's wife. Throughout the Middle East adultery was known as a great sin because of the hurt and anger it caused; if committed, both she and Joseph would face Potiphar's wrath. Yet for Joseph there was another, more compelling reason why he would not agree to her demands: it was a sin against God,[3] breaking the divinely given union between husband and wife, which had been established in the beginning. Many years later the greatest king of Israel would commit adultery and would confess to God, "Against you only have I sinned and done this evil in your sight".

The day came when the woman's desires boiled over. She and Joseph were alone in the house and she seized him, grabbing his tunic and he fled without it, leaving it in her hand. As lust turned to hate and a sense of panic, 'What if he tells Potiphar?", she worked out her only course of action. Note what she told her husband compared to what actually happened.

What took place:

- She seized his garment in her hand;
- Joseph fled without it;
- She understood her predicament, called out for the other slaves of the house;
- She accused Joseph of attempted rape and showed them his tunic, left with her.

What she told Potiphar:

- Your Hebrew slave came in to rape me;
- I screamed out;

3 This is the first time that Joseph mentions God. It is noteworthy that he did not use His name or title when telling of his dreams but from this time forward, in almost every speech he made, he mentioned Him. He acknowledged that it was God who is at work, controlling all things.

- He dropped his tunic (having taken it off) and fled.

There is a particular emphasis on the garment. Was it uniquely Joseph's, one that showed his rank in the household? If so, Potiphar would identify it immediately. Once again Joseph had been stripped of a special coat and thrown, not into a pit, but into a special prison, where the king's prisoners were bound.

Yet, even in Potiphar's anger there is a hint that he was not quite sure of Joseph's guilt. This was a capital offence, attempted rape by a slave of his master's wife, and he was the chief of the executioners. Yet, instead of death, Joseph was imprisoned and treated initially most cruelly:

> "He sent a man before them – Joseph – who was sold as a slave. They hurt his feet with fetters, he was laid in irons. Until the time that his word came to pass, the word of the LORD tested him. The king sent and released him, the ruler of the people let him go free. He made him Lord of his house, and ruler of all his possessions, to bind his princes at his pleasure, and teach his elders wisdom." (Psalm 105:17-22)

The butler and the baker

Joseph was kept in chains on Potiphar's instructions. Yet once again his outstanding gifts and the Lord's divine providence come to the fore in his life and we find him running the prison as he ran Potiphar's household.

Sometime later there was trouble at Pharaoh's court and two of the king's high officials, his butler and his baker were thrown into the king's prison. They had sinned against Pharaoh and this brought about a violent and angry outburst from him. It was the captain of the guard (was this still Potiphar?) who gave them into Joseph's care. He had been Potiphar's personal assistant, now he served these two men in a similar capacity.

Each had a dream but had no access to the priests who would normally interpret for them. Joseph's response to this was telling: "Do not interpretations belong to God?" and the Lord was with him, giving him instant understanding of what had been dreamt.

Release was foretold for the butler, execution for the baker, yet the released man forgot Joseph's plea that he ask Pharaoh to intervene in his incarceration. Perhaps he felt it unwise to risk annoying his master again. Two more years of prison lay ahead of Joseph, yet his faith never wavered; his trust in the Lord was absolute.

45 | Vizier of all Egypt

PHARAOH'S dreams were the third pair of dreams linked to Joseph. One night the king dreamt, awoke, went back to sleep and had a second dream. These dreams troubled him (the same language used of Nebuchadnezzar in Daniel 2). He knew they carried an important message but did not know what it was.

The dreams

The Nile valley is only a few kilometres wide yet runs about 1,000 kilometres from the first cataracts north to the delta and all of Egypt's agriculture is within it. The annual floods were measured as they rose and when a height was reached which guaranteed the harvest, the country celebrated. Herodotus wrote:

> "No men in the whole world gain from the soil with so little labour, the river rises and sinks back, each man sows his field and waits for the harvest."[1]

We can understand from this how any dreams about the river would perturb the king; his country's existence depended on it.

The two dreams were different and spoke of a double disaster. For seven years the Nile would flood to a level perfect for agriculture.[2] The marsh reeds and grasses, essential for cattle

1 Herodotus, Book II, paragraph 14.

2 Too low a level and the crops would not flourish; too great a flood and the villages would suffer.

Egypt the gift of the Nile

The stability of Egyptian civilization arose from a unique set of circumstances centred on the ecology of the Nile valley. The land had virtually no rainfall of its own. The water for its irrigation came down the Nile in annual floods, most of which originated in summer rains in the Ethiopian mountains. With the floods came silt, and the combination of fertile soil and ready water could produce yields of crops three or four times those from normal rain-fed soil. As important as the wealth of water and soil was the regularity with which the floods came. The Nile started to rise in May, and from July to October was high enough to flow out over the floodplain of the valley. This was akhet, the time of inundation. Four months later, by the beginning of November, the waters had begun to fall. The land could be marked out and ploughed and sown. This was peret, the time 'when the land reappeared'. The final four months of the year, shemu, from March to June, brought the harvest (C. Freeman, *Egypt, Greece and Rome*, page 14).

The nilometer on an island in Cairo used to measure the height of the annual flood. When the Aswan dam was built, these annual floods were smoothed out and the nilometer no longer used.

Photo of the Nile valley showing fertility next to the river and then desert beyond.

grazing, would flourish, the animals would grow fat and herds would increase. Cereal crops would be superabundant, the land would overproduce in a way not seen before.

This would be followed by seven years when the river did not flood, cattle grazing would be poor; herds would diminish. Not only would there be the problem of the Nile, the climate would change and the Sirocco, the dry scorching wind from the desert, would blow each year shrivelling up whatever crops had been sown and irrigated by hand from the river. In the dream the undernourished cattle consumed the fat ones, the withered ears of corn the full ones; the memories and benefits of the good years would soon disappear as disaster overtook the land.

A saviour arose

None of Pharaoh's magicians could interpret his dreams and suddenly the chief butler "remembered" his experience with Joseph. He had kept quiet about what happened two years previously and his careful language was designed to divert any anger from the king against him; he had suffered Pharaoh's anger before, he did not want to face it again. He was "reminded of his shortcomings" by Pharaoh's words, yet he did not recount the event accurately. In prison he had been greatly troubled, ignorant about what it meant yet he did not tell Pharaoh this, neither did he tell him that it was Joseph's God who had shown the meaning. The butler was a man looking to gain some advantage with his master by telling him of Joseph.

The boy of seventeen had presented himself to his brothers as the one to rule over them. Yet his character was in no way ready for this and thirteen years of slavery had been a necessary time of training. It was a tribute to his spiritual development that now, at the age of thirty, the Lord saw him ready to become the second in the land to Pharaoh, the vizier of all Egypt and the man through whom God would preserve his family.

We can imagine his feelings as he was whisked out of prison, shaved and washed[3] and presented with new clothes so that he could stand before the king. In all he then said there was nothing of Joseph and no recriminations about what had happened to him. 'I have heard that you can understand and interpret dreams' said the king. 'It is God who will give Pharaoh an answer of peace'[4] replied Joseph and, when he had been told the dream: "It is the God who has showed Pharaoh what he is about to do." In describing the Lord as "the God", Joseph made a clear statement that the Egyptian gods of the magicians were helpless in this situation but his God was *the* God, in control of all things.

Divine inspiration took Joseph beyond the interpretation and into advice about how Egypt should respond to the news:

> "Now therefore, let Pharaoh select a discerning and wise man, and set him over the land of Egypt. Let Pharaoh do this, and let him appoint officers over the land, to collect one-fifth of the produce of the land of Egypt in the seven plentiful years.

3 Unlike the Jews, Egyptians were usually clean-shaven men who had a reputation for cleanliness, priests in particular washing daily and their clothes every two days.

4 Not necessarily an answer that will take away Pharaoh's concerns but one which will take away his anxiety that he does not know what the dreams mean.

> And let them gather all the food of those good years that are coming, and store up grain under the authority of Pharaoh, and let them keep food in the cities. Then that food shall be as a reserve for the land for the seven years of famine which shall be in the land of Egypt, that the land may not perish during the famine." (Genesis 41:33-36)

Joseph did not proffer himself in these words but God was at work presenting him as the man whom Pharaoh needed and there was a warning in what was said. The famine would be so severe that, if no action was taken, the land would perish (*karath*) and this word carries another meaning – of being cut off.[5] Joseph's words were not advice from God but a mandate; Pharaoh must accept what was said or else the Lord would cut him off; there would be no further divine help and the land would be destroyed by the famine.

Fortunately, Pharaoh recognised that God was speaking through this man and that both the interpretation and the advice were true:

> "And Pharaoh said to his servants, 'Can we find such a one as this, a man in whom is the Spirit of God?' Then Pharaoh said to Joseph, 'Inasmuch as God has shown you all this, there is no one as discerning and wise as you. You shall be over my house, and all my people shall be ruled according to your word; only in regard to the throne will I be greater than you'. And Pharaoh said to Joseph, 'See, I have set you over all the land of Egypt'." (verses 38-41)

Once again, Joseph's outstanding abilities were on display, but now with recognition that they were God given. It is beyond credibility that the greatest potentate of his time would haul a foreign slave out of prison and immediately make him the second in the land unless divine providence was at work.

Many years later a similar pattern was enacted. The Lord told Moses to take Joshua, "a man in whom is the spirit" (Numbers 27:18), and make him his successor. Joshua was

---

5 For example, Leviticus 7:20.

chosen, as was Joseph, because he already had a mind tuned to the purpose of God. The Lord then strengthened him and he was given some of Moses' honour so that no man could stand before him, for God was with him.

Yet there is a greater Bible echo than this. The spirit of God was on Joseph and he was discerning (*biyn*) and wise (*chakam*). Isaiah wrote of the Lord Jesus in virtually identical language: "The spirit of the LORD shall rest upon him, the spirit of wisdom (*chokmah*) and understanding (*biynah*)" (Isaiah 11:2). Both men began their work aged thirty, both were sent to be saviours of their people, men suited for the tasks ahead of them because their minds were attuned to the purpose of God.

Earlier, Joseph had a priestly coat which was ripped from him by his brothers, then a special coat as Potiphar's assistant, pulled from him by Potiphar's wife. Now he was given robes fitting to his new position as vizier of all Egypt. Pharaoh went to lengths to bind Joseph to Egypt and Joseph understood this.

There was a three stage formal investiture of him by Pharaoh.

Then Pharaoh said to Joseph	"Inasmuch as God has shown you all this, there is no one as discerning and wise as you. You shall be over my house, and all my people shall be ruled according to your word; only in regard to the throne will I be greater than you."
And Pharaoh said to Joseph	"See, I have set you over all the land of Egypt. Then Pharaoh took his signet ring off his hand and put it on Joseph's hand; and he clothed him in garments of fine linen and put a gold chain around his neck. And he had him ride in the second chariot which he had; and they cried out before him, 'Bow the knee!' So he set him over all the land of Egypt."
Pharaoh also said to Joseph	"I am Pharaoh, and without your consent no man may lift his hand or foot in all the land of Egypt."

With these high offices went the king's ring, possibly the royal seal, and the chain of office. Furthermore, Joseph was given a new, Egyptian name, and an Egyptian wife. His name, Zaphnath-paaneah, means 'the god (Pharaoh?) has spoken and he (Joseph) shall live'. His wife, Asenath, was the daughter of Potipherah, the High Priest of the god On, a man who held the title "greatest of the seers".[6]

Yet, in all that followed neither Joseph's Egyptian name nor that of his wife is mentioned again – even Pharaoh referred to him as Joseph.[7]

In all these events there is a tinge of sadness for when Joseph's first son was born he was called Manasseh, because "God has made me forget all my toil and all my father's house". It appears that Joseph had given up all hope of seeing his family again. He was fully embedded in Egypt and second only to the king. What more could a man want? Yet, when Joseph went through the land collecting and storing food he took with him the word of God, "a law of the God of Jacob established in Joseph as a testimony, when he went throughout the land of Egypt". In addition, when his second son, Ephraim, was born he acknowledged that it was God who had made him "fruitful in the land of his affliction". Joseph's life had changed beyond all recognition but the Lord was ever with him – and he never lost his faith in Him.

Years of plenty and of famine

The book of Leviticus (chapter 25) tells us of Sabbath year laws. God instructed Israel not to worry in the sixth year about what they should eat the following year if they did not sow for a harvest. "I will command my blessing upon you in the sixth year and it will bring forth fruit for three years", He said. Although a period of three years is mentioned, just one harvest was lost which had to last through until the harvest of the eighth year.

As Israel obeyed this law in faith, they could look back to the wilderness journey and see its precursor. Every week their fathers had gathered enough manna on the sixth day to last for two days and in doing this had learned that "man does not live by bread alone but by every word of God".

6 N. Sarna, page 221.

7 Just as Daniel was renamed Belteshazzar but is consistently referred to as "Daniel".

The same principles are seen in the years of plenty and famine that occurred in Egypt. God now commanded His blessing upon Egypt and the harvests of the first seven years were so plentiful that a twenty per cent tax laid aside enough food for the seven famine years that followed:

> "... and the seven years of famine began to come, as Joseph had said. The famine was in all lands, but in all the land of Egypt there was bread. So when all the land of Egypt was famished, the people cried to Pharaoh for bread. Then Pharaoh said to all the Egyptians, 'Go to Joseph; whatever he says to you, do'. The famine was over all the face of the earth, and Joseph opened all the storehouses and sold to the Egyptians. And the famine became severe in the land of Egypt. So all countries came to Joseph in Egypt to buy grain, because the famine was severe in all lands." (Genesis 41:54-57)

These words emphasise the extent of the famine. It was very severe, throughout the land of Egypt, over all the face of the earth, in all lands. Only in Egypt was there bread and in Egypt only one man could help the starving people of all lands who came to him. "Go to Joseph; whatever he says to you, do", said the king and many years later, at a wedding where the wine had run out, the mother of our Lord used similar language to his disciples and water was changed to wine as they drew it out of the pots (John 2:5).

The phrase, "whatever he says do", ties together the work of Joseph with that of the Lord Jesus. The king commanded Joseph to save the lives of men from all nations by providing bread to those who came in faith, believing that there was corn in Egypt. Yet wonderful though this was, it was merely an echo of the greater salvation to come. The one who was the bread of God was the living bread which, "if a man ate, he would live forever" and in Jesus' words there was an allusion back to the promises of resurrection and eternal life first given to Joseph's great-grandfather. But, at this point the type breaks down. Joseph could never provide bread for eternal life; that reward demanded the sacrifice of the Lamb that God alone could provide. How salutary it is that the very first miracle our Lord enacted pointed forward to this as he changed the water into wine, that symbol of his poured out blood.

"Whatever he says do", said the king and Joseph provided bread to save lives.

"Whatever he says do", said Mary and Jesus provided wine as the symbol of his blood shed to bring eternal life.

46 | Corn in Egypt

THE famine afflicted the whole world, yet this is a picture of the Middle East world, the countries around Egypt. However, two passages throw a different light on it, putting Canaan at the centre of the troubles:

> "Moreover He (God) called for a famine in the land (Canaan); He destroyed all the provision of bread." (Psalm 105:16)
>
> "And the patriarchs, moved with envy, sold Joseph into Egypt: but God was with him, and delivered him out of all his afflictions (*thlipsis*), and gave him favour and wisdom in the sight of Pharaoh king of Egypt; and he made him governor over Egypt and all his house. Now there came a dearth over all the land of Egypt and Chanaan, and great affliction (*thlipsis*): and our fathers found no sustenance." (Acts 7:9-11, KJV)

Joseph called Egypt "the land of my afflictions" and Stephen picked this up in his speech to his accusers. The Lord focused the famine on Canaan and brought affliction upon Jacob's family there because of what they had done to Joseph. The Lord had tested (Psalm 105:19) and afflicted Joseph for twenty years, now his brothers were to be tested and afflicted. They had lived with guilty knowledge about their treatment of their brother and now providence would force them to face the truth about this and seek reconciliation with Joseph.

Go down and buy for us

The healing of this fractious family could now begin. The news that there was corn for sale in Egypt had spread through many lands. Jacob heard of it and, with some irritation, said to his sons: "Why are you just standing about talking to each other about the seriousness of the situation? Go to Egypt and buy corn for us or else we will die.'

Jacob still had a favourite son, Benjamin, described as Joseph's brother. Twenty years had not healed his pain and he would not entrust Benjamin to his other sons lest he be hurt. Did he still have suspicions about what happened to Joseph? Did he think that the sons might harm Benjamin in another spirit of envy? If so, what a poor opinion of them he had.

But the brothers were changing and the way they are described in chapter 42 changes also.

His (Jacob's) sons (verse 1);
    Joseph's ten brothers (verse 3);
        The children of Israel[1] (verse 5).
    Joseph's brothers (verse 6);
His brethren (by Joseph) (verses 7,8).

Through these events, Jacob's sons became Joseph's brethren. Relationships were healed and this new unity brought them together as the children of Israel.

Joseph was the vizier of all Egypt and it is unlikely that he would personally deal with everyone who came to Egypt to buy corn. Yet divine providence was at work and for some reason the ten brothers found themselves in front of him.

> "Now Joseph was governor over the land; and it was he who sold to all the people of the land. And Joseph's brothers came and bowed down before him with their faces to the earth. Joseph saw his brothers and recognized (*nakar*) them, but he acted as a stranger (*nakar*) to them and spoke roughly to them. Then he said to them, 'Where do you come from?' And they said, 'From the land of Canaan to buy food'. So Joseph recognized (*nakar*) his brothers, but they did not recognize

1 The Hebrew is the same as that consistently translated "children of Israel". See Digression in chapter 36 (page 268).

> (*nakar*) him. Then Joseph remembered the dreams which he had dreamed about them, and said to them, 'You are spies! You have come to see the nakedness of the land!'" (Genesis 42:6-9)

Joseph had left behind his slavery and his father's house yet now, as his brothers stood before him, it all came flooding back into his memory. His words and actions recalled the awful events of twenty years before and brought the brothers to an acknowledgement of their evil deeds.

The Hebrew word *nakar*, to know or recognise, is used four times in the exchange. Jacob recognised his brothers but acted as a stranger, an unrecognised one, to them. They did not recognize him. How could they? He stood before them clean shaven (they would be bearded), dressed in an imperial garment as Pharaoh's right-hand man and speaking Egyptian.

This same Hebrew word, *nakar*, had been used in the exchange between the brothers and Jacob when they brought Joseph's bloodstained coat back to him:

> "So they took Joseph's tunic, killed a kid of the goats, and dipped the tunic in the blood. Then they sent the tunic of many colours, and they brought it to their father and said, 'We have found this. Do you know (*nakar*) whether it is your son's tunic or not?' And he recognized (*nakar*) it and said, 'It is my son's tunic. A wild beast has devoured him. Without doubt Joseph is torn to pieces'." (Genesis 37:31-33)

What irony! They had pretended not to recognise Joseph's coat, now they did not recognise him in the imperial garment he wore.

Three times Joseph accused them of being spies, "come to spy the nakedness of the land". This is highly unusual language, mainly used elsewhere to describe the nakedness of a person. Did the brothers strip him naked when was thrown into the pit without his coat? He had indeed been a spy when he was with the sons of Bilhah: he took an evil report about them back to Jacob and no doubt he had a reputation as a spy from that day forward. However, when he went to see the brothers at Dothan, he was sent by his father to look after their welfare, wearing his priestly garment, but he never had an opportunity to explain his mission before they took him, stripped him and threw him into the pit.

The brothers' response to all of this was one of alarm and protestation. 'We are all true, honest men and your servants, the sons of one man. We have a youngest brother back in Canaan and one who is no more.' Yet they were not true and honest, for twenty years they had lived a lie.

It must have been a terrifying situation for the brothers. From the outset of their interrogation Joseph had spoken harshly, cruelly to them, accusing them. They were in serious trouble and poured out information to him yet used a euphemism to describe what had happened to the brother who "was no more".

And Joseph wanted to know about Benjamin:

> "But Joseph said to them, 'It is as I spoke to you, saying, "You are spies!" In this manner you shall be tested: by the life of Pharaoh, you shall not leave this place unless your youngest brother comes here. Send one of you, and let him bring your brother; and you shall be kept in prison, that your words may be tested to see whether there is any truth in you; or else, by the life of Pharaoh, surely you are spies!' So he put them all together in prison three days." (Genesis 42:14-17)

This was a solemn vow, the most serious he could make and a test of the brothers. Joseph wanted to see his younger brother and to know if he had been mistreated by the others as he had been. Woe betide them if this had been the case!

They were incarcerated for three days. Had they left Joseph in the pit for this period? Were they put in the same prison where he had been? It was retributive justice.

Joseph's exalted position had now brought him two roles: he was governor over the land and it was he who sold to the people. Did he now understand why he had two dreams? The stars had bowed before his star (foretelling his position as ruler) and the sheaves had bowed before his sheaf (foretelling his position as the one who could supply corn).

Something then changed Joseph's mind and he released them because he feared God – had he received a warning in another dream? The brothers were allowed to return to Canaan but were commanded to return with Benjamin. As surety for this, Joseph kept Simeon in prison and bound him before their eyes. He did not forget the years he had spent chained up in jail.

All of the above exchanges led the brothers to a remarkable confession to each other:

> "Then they said to one another, 'We are truly guilty concerning our brother, for we saw the anguish (*tsarah*) of his soul when he pleaded with us, and we would not hear; therefore this distress (*tsarah*) has come upon us'. And Reuben answered them, saying, 'Did I not speak to you, saying, "Do not sin against the boy"; and you would not listen? Therefore behold, his blood is now required of us'." (Genesis 42:21,22)

How this burst forth from them! Perhaps this was the very first time they had openly acknowledged their guilt to each other and it began the healing of the family for, unknown to them, Joseph understood and was reduced to tears.

There is a principle here, met many times in scripture: the Lord desires truth in our inward parts and forgiveness can only follow confession and repentance.

> "He who covers his sins will not prosper, but whoever confesses and forsakes them will have mercy." (Proverbs 28:13)

The return to Canaan

The brothers departed laden with corn and food for the journey and with their purchase money put secretly in their sacks; once again they were tested. In the past they had accepted twenty shekels for the sale of Joseph and kept quiet about it; they were heartless when enriched by his suffering. What would they now do about the money they found?

> "Then their hearts failed them and they were afraid, saying to one another, 'What is this that God has done to us?'"
>
> (Genesis 42:28)

There was a dawning recognition that, somehow, in a way not yet understood, the Lord was at work in their lives. They returned to Jacob and told him *all that had happened to them*.

What a contrast with the earlier occasion when they had returned to their father with lies and prevarication over the disappearance of Joseph.

Jacob was adamant that he would not entrust Benjamin to his sons; he would not let them take him to Egypt. Indeed, he blamed his sons for the loss of both Joseph and Simeon, "You have bereaved me: Joseph is no more, Simeon is no more". He firmly rejected Reuben's offer of his two sons as surety for Benjamin's life; he knew he was an unstable man. Jacob's words show us once again how little he thought of his sons – how much he had loved Joseph and now loved Benjamin.

> "My son shall not go down with you, for his brother is dead, and he is left alone. If any calamity should befall him along the way in which you go, then you would bring down my grey hair with sorrow to the grave." (42:38)

47 |

The brothers return

THERE was no intention by father and sons for the family to return to Egypt, yet Joseph knew they would have to go back. The famine was only in its second year, another five years of crisis lay ahead and matters grew worse. Previously the famine had been sore, *chazaq*, strong, but now it was *kabad*, strong, heavy. It lay as a great burden across the land of Canaan and all the corn bought in Egypt had been consumed. There was no other choice, the brothers had to return to Egypt and so Jacob told them, "Go back, buy us a little food".

A family debate

Jacob meant, of course, return without Benjamin and the brothers refused to go. It was Judah who spoke. We last heard from him at the end of the episode with Tamar when he said 'she is more righteous than me' and saw there the beginning of a change of heart. Her desire for a child was driven by a strong faith in the promises, a concern that the family of faith did not die out. Now Judah shared the same worry.

> "And Judah said unto Israel his father, Send the lad with me, and we will arise and go; that we may live, and not die, both we, and thou, and also our little ones." (Genesis 43:8, KJV)

The shortage of food was a matter of life and death and the only solution was corn in Egypt. What a quandary for Jacob. He was desperate to keep Benjamin at home; the thought of losing Rachel's second son was more than he could bear. He would rather abandon Simeon to jail in Egypt than send Benjamin there. Yet he was prepared to entrust him to Judah even though he had flatly refused to do so to Reuben. There was really no choice: Joseph had made it clear that he would not give them an audience, and access to corn, unless Benjamin went with them.

Judah's words to his father show another echo back to the interaction with Tamar:

> "I will be surety (*arab*) for him; of my hand shalt thou require him: if I bring him not unto thee, and set him before thee, then let me bear the blame for ever." (Genesis 43:9, KJV)

When Judah had bargained with Tamar about the cost of sex with her, he had left his staff and seal as a pledge, *arabown*, of his honesty. Yet he had not been honest with her; he had broken his word and would not give her to Shelah in a levirate marriage. Now a changed Judah promised that he would accept full responsibility for Benjamin's safety – if necessary he would pledge himself to preserve the lad's freedom.

Jacob's response to this showed the two sides to his character. 'Take a present for the man' he said (just as he had sought to appease Esau) but he also said:

> "And may God Almighty give you mercy (*racham*) before the man, that he may release your other brother and Benjamin. If I am bereaved, I am bereaved!" (verse 14)

This is a marvellous expression of Jacob's faith. He invoked the title of the Lord revealed to Abraham at the time when Jacob's grandfather became totally dependent on Him for the birth of a son to Sarah and himself. He may have sent a present to appease the vizier but he knew that only God could resolve the matter and show mercy. This is the first time this particular Hebrew word is used in the Bible and it carries the meaning of pity and love, particularly of a father to a son.

> "As a father pities (*racham*) his children, so the LORD pities those who fear him." (Psalm 103:13)

Jacob was a father unable to hold his family together and keep them safe; he saw no human solution to the dilemma before him. Yet he drew strength from his memory of the covenant confirmed by El Shaddai to his grandfather that He would give the land of Canaan to Abraham and his descendants and that He would be their God (Genesis 17:8). Jacob had experienced this in his own life; the angels had been with him all the years he had spent out of the land, now in faith he looked for the same divine care in the lives of his sons.

In all that now followed it was Judah who led the brothers along the path of reconciliation with Joseph as they returned to Egypt.

Invited to a feast

It is clear that Joseph had given instructions to his household to keep a lookout for the brothers' return and his steward was well briefed. The brothers poured out their explanations to this man about finding their money in their sacks. They had brought it all back, their integrity was intact, their first test passed and the steward acknowledged it:

> "He said, 'Peace be with you, do not be afraid. Your God and the God of your father has given you treasure in your sacks; I had your money'. Then he brought Simeon out to them."
>
> (Genesis 43:23)

How unusual this must have sounded to them as the steward invoked a title of the Lord, "the God of your fathers". Jacob had prayed for God's mercy that Simeon would be released and Benjamin kept unharmed. Now, the Lord answered that prayer through the words of an Egyptian steward. "I had your money", he said, the books had been balanced, someone else had paid the debt; the money in their sacks was a present, 'please see it as coming from your God'. Then Simeon was released to them.

Joseph was almost overwhelmed at the sight of Benjamin and a feast followed. The brothers were dumbfounded that this strange potentate apparently knew the ages of them all and seated them accordingly. Benjamin's plate was heaped higher than that of everyone else – would they be jealous? Joseph watched for their reactions.

The final test

It was a very merry occasion and no doubt there were sore heads the next morning. Joseph was keen to put the brothers to a final test and they were sent away at daybreak, leaving Egypt with their asses laden with grain – far more than they had paid for. Would they be prepared to stand by Benjamin when he faced slavery in Egypt or would they abandon him as they had Joseph?

> "And he commanded the steward of his house, saying, 'Fill the men's sacks with food, as much as they can carry, and put each man's money in the mouth of his sack. Also put my cup, the silver cup, in the mouth of the sack of the youngest, and his grain money'. So he did according to the word that Joseph had spoken." (Genesis 44:1,2)

The cup was a special bowl used for divination.[1] It would have stood on Joseph's table at the feast and it would have been almost impossible for the brothers to steal it unnoticed. They were greatly indignant when the steward reached them and accused them of theft. They said, 'If you find it, put to death the thief and enslave us' but the steward knew his master's purpose and replied:

> "Now also let it be according to your words; he with whom it is found shall be my slave, and you shall be blameless." (Genesis 44:10)

What a dramatic picture this is. The steward knew exactly where the cup was but he started with Reuben and searched every man's animal in turn, finally ending with Benjamin.[2] We can imagine the brothers growing relief as nothing was found and then their absolute horror as it came out of Benjamin's sack; they rent their clothes in anguish. They could have taken the steward at his word, claimed their own innocence, abandoned Benjamin to slavery in Egypt and carried on back to Canaan, yet they spoke no word against the lad and all returned to Egypt to stand before Joseph.

1 J. Currid, *A Study Commentary on Genesis*, volume 2, page 309.

2 Would they remember a similar search made by Laban many years ago?

His words to them were full of innuendo:

> "And Joseph said to them, 'What deed is this you have done? Did you not know that such a man as I can certainly practise divination?'" (Genesis 44:15)

Joseph did not say that he practised divination but that a man in his position in Egypt would be able to do so. This would make sense to the brothers: Joseph was married into a priestly family, he had an uncanny prescience, he knew the relative ages of them and he knew where the cup was. However there is irony in his words, he did know the future for the Lord had revealed it to him in dreams. As his dreams had told him, his brothers had bowed before him in obeisance; now they were prostrate, lying in the dust. Previously they had shown deference to the vizier of Egypt, now they grovelled before him in desperation and Joseph waited to see how they would respond to his offer: 'You can go in peace to your father but Benjamin must remain as my slave.'

Judah's speech

It was Judah who stood up and spoke on behalf of the family. His speech is the longest in Genesis and one of the finest in scripture. One writer sums it up in these words.[3]

> "Judah would have none of it (leaving Benjamin behind in slavery). Instead, he launched into a sustained entreaty on Benjamin's behalf. The Old Testament has no intercession to compare with it. This persevering appeal is in a class of its own. Judah was a mediator for his brethren long before Levi was!"[4]

The brothers were of one mind in making the appeal but it was Judah who spoke for them and his mind was full of regrets for past events.

He was the brother who had suggested selling Joseph into slavery and had seen his father's misery over the loss of his favourite son during the past twenty years. He had experienced the premature deaths of two of his sons and now would do

3 Brother H. Whittaker, *Joseph the Saviour*, page 66.

4 Hebrews 7:14.

anything he could to prevent the loss to Jacob of a second son – he knew how his father would feel. In his speech he mentioned Jacob as a "father", fourteen times; the whole thrust of his argument was about the fact that enslaving Benjamin would kill their father, Jacob.

His initial words to Joseph were very unusual.

> "What shall we say to my Lord? What shall we speak? Or how shall we clear ourselves (*tsadaq*)? God has found out the iniquity of your servants; here we are, my Lord's slaves, both we and he also with whom the cup was found."
>
> (Genesis 44:16)

The cup was *found* in Benjamin's sack: in the eyes of Joseph, Benjamin alone was guilty of the theft yet Judah said that God had *found* out their iniquity, the perversity of their behaviour. This cannot refer to the theft of the cup but must refer to the sense of guilt carried by Judah through so many years. By now, the brothers must have seen the analogy of what was happening to them with their sale of Joseph into slavery.

"How can we clear ourselves (*tsadaq*)?", he asked and spoke the same word he had used of Tamar, "she is more righteous (*tsadaq*) than I". There was no self-justification, no explanation of what had occurred. There was no plea from the brothers for their own safety. Judah spoke only of their father, Jacob, and the certainty that he would die of grief if Benjamin did not return to him. The brothers would feel the responsibility of this:

> "... it will happen, when he sees that the lad is not with us, that he will die. So your servants will bring down the grey hair of your servant our father with sorrow to the grave."
>
> (verse 31)

With a certain boldness Judah stood up, approached Joseph uninvited and pleaded with him that he would take Judah as his slave instead of Benjamin.

I am Joseph

Chapter 45 unrolls before us as a great drama. The heartfelt plea of Judah touched the heart of Joseph in a way he had not expected and a wave of emotion overwhelmed him. All his staff were quickly dismissed. "They did not tarry" wrote one translator: it is a vivid picture of startled servants rushing out as Joseph broke out in such loud weeping that it was noted throughout Pharaoh's palace.

"I am Joseph" he said and the brothers were terrified (were they still prostrate before him?). Had this great man gone mad, what would he do next? "Come near", he told them and as they stood and approached him, they understood that this was indeed their brother.

Joseph's dreams had shown him his brothers bowing before him and it had happened. Yet they had not prepared him for this outcome. Submission to his power would not heal the family but grace, love and forgiveness now prevailed and brought a healing.[5]

It was all the work of the Lord:

> "But now, do not therefore be grieved or angry with yourselves because you sold me here; for God sent me before you to preserve life ... And God sent me before you to preserve a posterity for you in the earth, and to save your lives by a great deliverance. So now it was not you who sent me here, but God; and he has made me a father to Pharaoh, and Lord of all his house, and a ruler throughout all the land of Egypt."
>
> (Genesis 45:5-8)

What wonderful words these are. Joseph was a man always aware of God's guiding hand, yet he believed that his destiny was in Egypt and that he should forget his father's house (Genesis 41:51). Now he saw that everything that had happened was part of the divine purpose with the household of faith. The Lord had delivered him and he understood that the same grace extended to him was being extended through him to his brethren; the Lord had sent him to be a deliverer and not a judge.[6]

---

5 K. Matthews, *The New American Commentary on Genesis*, volume 1B, page 807.

6 A lesson Moses had to learn also.

Three times he told them, "God sent me", yet he and his brothers had always thought they did it! He had been sent to preserve their lives (from the famine) but also to preserve a posterity (to ensure the family of faith survived).

The brothers' rejection of their saviour had begun when they saw how much their father loved him:

> "But when his brothers saw that their father loved him more than all his brothers, they hated him and could not speak peaceably to him." (Genesis 37:4)

Now they saw how much their brother loved them and reached out to them:

> "Moreover he kissed all his brothers and wept over them, and after that his brothers talked with him." (45:15)

It would be a very excited group that set off on the return journey to Canaan, yet as they approached home they faced another moment of truth. When they revealed to Jacob that Joseph was not dead but the ruler of all Egypt, they "told him all the words of Joseph that he had said to them" and these must have included details of their initial treatment of him. They told "Jacob their father" but it was Israel who said, "It is enough; Joseph my son is still alive". In these words, the healing was complete, their father drew a line under all that had happened before. It was the purpose of God, forgiveness had been sought and given and the family would relocate into Egypt.

48 | Israel in Egypt

"So Israel took his journey with all that he had, and came to Beersheba, and offered sacrifices to the God of his father Isaac. Then God spoke to Israel in the visions of the night, and said, 'Jacob, Jacob!' And he said, 'Here I am'. So he said, 'I am God, the God of your father; do not fear to go down to Egypt, for I will make of you a great nation there. I will go down with you to Egypt, and I will also surely bring you up again; and Joseph will put his hand on your eyes'." (Genesis 46:1-4)

JACOB yearned to see Joseph again but was cautious about going down to Egypt. He had overcome his problems with Esau and Laban, he had returned to the Promised Land and settled there (Genesis 37:1); his desire was never to leave it again.

Yet now, in his old age, he faced another exile. His grandfather, Abraham, had gone down into Egypt at a time of famine and it brought him nothing but trouble. Isaac also had intended to make a similar journey at a time of famine but God had forbidden it. Jacob needed to know the Lord's will before he was prepared to leave Canaan.

He travelled south to Beersheba and he took all that he had. The famine was such that he could not stay any longer at Hebron – his future lay either at this new location or in Egypt. Beersheba was the place where both Abraham and Isaac had dug wells and claimed rights to them from Abimelech. It was the place where Abraham had called upon the name of the Lord and now, in turn, Jacob sought guidance from Him: should he go to Egypt or should he look for water in this place?

The Lord's answer was immediate: Jacob should not be afraid of going into Egypt. Just as the Lord had promised him that He would be with Jacob all the time he was away at Haran, now He promised that He would be with him in Egypt. In these words we have the final promise given by God in the book of Genesis.

- The Lord would be with him and his family in Egypt.
- They would become a great nation there.
- At some future time the Lord would lead them back to Canaan.
- Jacob and Joseph would be together until the patriarch died.

The numbering of Israel

For the first time in scripture, we find the numbering of the children of Israel. Many people must have travelled to Egypt in the caravan. Abraham's household contained at least 318 trained men, yet no such retainers are mentioned here. Instead, the numbering is very specific, telling us only of Jacob's children, grandchildren and great-grandchildren (Genesis 46:26).

- Jacob plus sixty-six family members travelled to Egypt. As well as his sons, one daughter (Dinah), one granddaughter (Serah) and four great-grandsons are listed.
- The total number of the family was seventy and included Joseph, Ephraim and Manasseh. We have already seen the significance of this number[1] and the details of the names given here emphasise the importance of it in the purpose of God.

Yet there is another number of this family recorded elsewhere:

> "And the second time Joseph was made known to his brothers, and Joseph's family became known to the Pharaoh. Then

1 Chapter 14, *All the Nations of the Earth*.

Joseph sent and called his father Jacob and all his relatives to him, seventy-five people." (Acts 7:13,14)

Ephraim and Manasseh had five sons[2] bringing the tally of Israel up to seventy-five, but why did Stephen use this number? What lesson was he trying to teach the Jews of his day and what do we learn from it?

The Lord would indeed make a great nation of Israel; they would return to Canaan as He had promised Abraham and Jacob, yet many years later they would leave it again as slaves to Nebuchadnezzar and Babylon because of their rejection of the Lord and His ways. In Jeremiah's final words, as he wrote of the destruction of Jerusalem and the temple, he gives a list of those who were taken to Riblah and slain before the king of Babylon. Seventy-four souls are listed but the prophet had not quite finished for in his final words he wrote of the king kept in exile, Jehoiachin, "until the day of his death". Many more than these were killed by Nebuchadnezzar but these seventy-five people were a representative number telling of God's rejection of His people for their wickedness.

The implication of Stephen's words is very clear. Those who saw themselves as Abraham's seed and hence the Lord's chosen Israel, no matter how they behaved, should look back to their fathers and see how physical descent was not enough. As their fathers had been rejected so would they unless they repented and their refusal to do this brought the day of judgement in AD 70.

Herein is a lesson for us also, for the Apostle Paul wrote that those who are the Israel of God are members of the household of faith and hence the number of the elect.

Why Egypt?

This record of Joseph's life is a drama leading to Israel's settling in Egypt. But why did the Lord want this move? Why orchestrate the relocation away from the Promised Land?

---

2 Numbers 26:28; 1 Chronicles 7:14.

- Dinah had gone out to have social interaction with the girls of Shechem, a marriage had been suggested with the Hivites hoping to integrate Jacob's family into their own.
- Judah had gone out and married a Canaanite woman; their first two sons apparently followed her ways, not those of the Lord.
- Simeon had multiple wives including one who was a Canaanite.

Joseph went to great pains to settle his family in Goshen away from the Egyptians. Perhaps he understood that the danger to them was a spiritual one. They had begun to intermarry with other tribes in Canaan, the Lord had brought them out, away from that temptation, and Joseph sought to minimise any risk when in Egypt.

Yet by the time of Moses, Israel had completely forgotten the name of the Lord and worshipped the gods of Egypt (Ezekiel 20:5-10). When they left, a mixed multitude went with them and contributed to the call to return to that land (Numbers 11:4).

It is ever thus with God's people. When faced with open hostility to their faith, they find strength to remain faithful but when the world seeks subtly to squeeze them into its mould, they are so easily seduced away by it.

In the land of Goshen

Joseph used his position to give his family special favours during the intense famine that continued for another five years. He directed them to Goshen, his dwelling was nearby and he promised to nourish them. His decisions were rubber-stamped by Pharaoh. Five of the brothers were presented to the potentate, carefully coached by Joseph as to what they should say. They were shepherds; they had come to sojourn for the duration of the famine, which was very bad in Canaan (the implication was that they would return there once it was over). Pharaoh's response was generous: they could have the best of the land and he wanted to know if any of them had special ability. Were there any more like Joseph with his astounding talents? His herds and flocks were kept in Goshen, would this special family look after them?

Once again, we return to the theme of blessing. "I will bless them that bless you" the Lord had told Abraham. Pharaoh had dealt favourably with Israel and now Jacob blessed him in return.

But, was Joseph wise to favour his family in such a way? The narrative that follows in Genesis 47 is an inclusio, contrasting the state of the Egyptians with that of the family and is bounded by these two verses:

> "And Joseph situated his father and his brothers, and gave them a possession in the land of Egypt, in the best of the land, in the land of Rameses, as Pharaoh had commanded."
> (Genesis 47:11)

> "So Israel dwelt in the land of Egypt, in the country of Goshen; and they had possessions there and grew and multiplied exceedingly." (verse 27)

Between these two verses we learn that "Joseph provided his father, his brothers, and all his father's household with bread, according to the number in their families" but for the Egyptians "there was no bread in all the land; for the famine was very severe".

The family had told Pharaoh that they had come to sojourn there, implying that they would return to Canaan after the famine was over, but Joseph settled them in Goshen and gave them property in the best of the land. The language used is of "inalienable property received from a sovereign or at least from one who has the power to release land".[3] We then read how, in progressive stages through the famine, Joseph acquired all the money, livestock, land and people of Egypt for Pharaoh in exchange for corn. Jacob's blessing of the king was fulfilled; Egypt became a united kingdom in which the land belonged to the king and the people were, in effect serfs, tenant farmers upon their lord's land and a national twenty per cent tax was levied upon them every year. Due to the famine, the Egyptians

---

3 Hamilton, volume 2, page 613.

lost their flocks and their land to Pharaoh; due to the famine Pharaoh gave Israel free possession of land for their flocks and, in addition, asked them to look after his animals – perhaps some of those that came to him through Joseph's work.

This was clear favouritism and was perhaps unfair. In any case, it stored up long term problems for the family, for many years later another king arose who did not remember Joseph and his remarkable work for Egypt (Exodus 1:8). How ironic that, at a time when all Egyptians had become servants of Pharaoh, Jacob's family had settled as free, land owning men but their descendants would become slaves to Pharaoh, resented by all Egypt.

Ephraim and Manasseh

The famine ended and another twelve years passed, Jacob was now 147 and approaching the end of his life. Two things occupied his mind, he wanted to be buried back in Canaan and he wished to pass on the patriarchal blessing to Joseph's two sons, Ephraim and Manasseh. Jacob was nearly blind, like Isaac had been when he had blessed his sons, and Joseph guided his hands. Once again, guided by the Lord, the younger received more honour than the firstborn, Ephraim more than Manasseh.

SECTION EIGHT:
Final blessings

49 |

Jacob's blessing of his sons (1)

"And Jacob called his sons and said, 'Gather together, that I may tell you what shall befall you in the last days: Gather (assemble) together and hear, you sons of Jacob, and listen to Israel your father'." (Genesis 49:1,2)

"All these are the twelve tribes of Israel, and this is what their father spoke to them. And he blessed them; he blessed each one according to his own blessing."[1] *(verse 28)*

JACOB was dying. He had blessed Ephraim and Manasseh, leaning heavily upon his staff (reminding us again that he was a lame man) and it had been an act of worship (Hebrews 11:21). Now he summoned all twelve of his sons to him for the final promise-blessing of the patriarchal age.

They came and stood before him as an assembly, one body, the children of Israel, now mature men in their sixties. They were called as the sons of Jacob but he spoke to them as Israel. This was an inspired message delivered by the prince with God and he spoke as a prophet. For the first time they are described as "the twelve tribes".

Jacob knew his sons' strengths and weaknesses and he was concerned about how each tribe would develop. Would the descendants carry the characteristics of their fathers? What he desired above all was that each son and each tribe would have

1 ESV, "blessing suitable to him".

Names of the Children of Israel

Much has been written about the meanings of the names of Jacob's sons and the different orders of them in the four lists in the Bible. Some writers have constructed a statement showing the whole purpose of the Lord in His Son, using these meanings.

Jacob blessed his sons in an unusual order. All six of Leah's sons were addressed first, but not in birth order, then the sons of the handmaids, then those of Rachel.

What stands out is the message from the names of the first and the last.

- Reuben: 'See a son'
- Benjamin: 'The son of the right hand'

When we turn to the Lord Jesus Christ in the Gospels, we read of the beginning of his ministry aged thirty, baptized by John. His commitment to his Father's work was acknowledged in the voice from heaven, "This is my beloved Son".

When that work was completed, the Gospels end with the picture of his ascension: "he was received up into heaven and sat on the right hand of God."

an inheritance in the eternal age to come and his prophecies are linked to this hope. He spoke of the last days and this is the first time that this phrase is used. Whilst many commentators translate it as "the coming days", the majority of uses are of the days before the return of the Lord.[2] One writer sums it up in these words: "Here (the last days) embraces the entire history of Israel from the conquest and distribution of the land to the consummate reign of Jesus Christ".[3]

We can imagine what the brothers thought about as they obeyed their father. They knew the family history about the

2 For example, Ezekiel 38:16.

3 Waltke, page 605.

promise-blessings to Abraham, Isaac and their father. What was now reserved for them?

Their father blessed them not in birth order but according to their mother, the sons of Leah first, then the sons of the handmaids and the sons of Rachel last.

Reuben

> "So Leah conceived and bore a son, and she called his name Reuben; for she said, 'The LORD has surely looked on my affliction. Now therefore, my husband will love me.'"
>
> (Genesis 29:32)
>
> "Reuben, you are my firstborn, my might and the beginning of my strength, the excellency of dignity and the excellency of power. Unstable as water, you shall not excel, because you went up to your father's bed; then you defiled it – he went up to my couch." (49:3,4)
>
> "Let Reuben live, and not die, nor let his men be few."
>
> (Deuteronomy 33:6)

There was sadness in Jacob's words. Reuben had been his firstborn, a son in whom he wanted to delight. He hoped this son would grow to have strength and power like him. Not only this, he should have inherited both the birthright (to become the family priest) and the blessing (heir to his father's estates and possessions).

Yet Reuben inherited neither of these (1 Chronicles 5:1,2) because he had sexual relations with Bilhah, his father's concubine (Genesis 35:22) and defiled his father's relationship with her. Years later in Israel, such behaviour was understood to be a challenge by a son to his father's authority and position.[4] Was this also Reuben's intention?

Jacob's words linked Reuben's loss of the birthright to that of Cain. The Lord had said to him, "If you do well, will you not be accepted (*se'eth*)?" But Cain disobeyed and was rejected. Reuben was given the birthright, "the excellency of dignity (*se'eth*)" and then lost it.

4 2 Samuel 16:20-22; 1 Kings 2:13-24.

From that time onward, his father saw him as unstable, with a lightness of character and not to be trusted. As the oldest brother he should have protected Joseph but he was swayed by the hatred felt by the others finally saying, helplessly, 'What shall I do?' His father later refused his offer to guarantee Benjamin's safety in Egypt. Why should he trust him; he had not looked after Joseph.

It was men from Reuben, Dathan and Abiram, who joined Korah's rebellion in Numbers 16, accusing Moses of wanting to make himself a prince over them. No doubt the tribe suffered badly in the plague that followed, perhaps leading Moses to intercede with God later asking that the tribe be not wiped out.

It was Reuben and Gad who looked at the good pasture land on the east bank in Gilead and asked Moses if they could settle there because they had substantial livestock. Surprisingly, there is no record of Moses approaching the Lord in prayer about this and these two tribes, together with half of Manasseh, were the only tribes who were not given their inheritance by lot under divine guidance. They promised Moses all of their fighting men would accompany the other tribes to conquer Canaan, but then provided less than fifty per cent of the men available.

The many flocks of Reuben's sheep in Gilead were a stumbling block to him in the days of the Judges. Deborah and Barak called Israel to arms to fight Sisera. Amongst those who did not respond was Reuben, for "there was a great searching of hearts but they listened to the bleating of the sheep"; the men of Reuben put their own needs first and stayed in Gilead (Judges 5:15,16), declining to fight with the others.

Although Reuben was the first tribe to settle, its fighting men were the last to do so, only returning home after every battle had been fought and won. Yet, in their vulnerable habitation on the east bank, they were the first to go into captivity. For them, "the first would be last and the last would be first".

Yet, there is a hint of a later change in the hearts of the Reubenites and in Saul's reign they fought the Hagarites; the Lord gave them victory for "they cried out to God in the battle. He heeded their prayer, because they put their trust in him" – hence the name of Reuben is on one of the gates of new Jerusalem and they will return to their inheritance at the coming of their king.

Simeon

> "Then she conceived again and bore a son, and said, 'Because the LORD has heard that I am unloved, he has therefore given me this son also'. And she called his name Simeon."
>
> (Genesis 29:33)
>
> "Simeon and Levi are brothers; instruments of cruelty are in their dwelling place. Let not my soul enter their council; let not my honour be united to their assembly; for in their anger they slew a man, and in their self-will (*ratsown*, pleasure) they hamstrung an ox. Cursed be their anger, for it is fierce; and their wrath, for it is cruel! I will divide them in Jacob and scatter them in Israel." (49:5-7)

Jacob's words to his second and third sons were as scathing as those to Reuben. They had disgraced their father and made his name stink amongst the Canaanites by their slaughter of the Shechemites. They had also cut the Achilles tendons of their animals and done it for their pleasure. Jacob refused to be associated in any way with their actions; they were cruel men whose descendants must be separated for the good of Israel.

What a comment on human nature that, although Simeon had committed murder to stop his sister marrying a Canaanite, he then did exactly the same thing himself (Genesis 46:10)! Years later, in the wilderness, his tribe suffered the greatest losses from the plague following Israel's whoredom with the Moabite women sent amongst them by Balaam, for the only name mentioned of those who died was that of Salu, a prince of Simeon.

Simeon's cruelty had been shown in another way. He was the brother Joseph kept locked up in Egypt whilst the rest of the brothers went back to Canaan for Benjamin. Joseph had particularly bad memories of Simeon's part in his abduction.

Both Simeon and his tribe appear as unlovely and unloved people. Reuben and Gad spent forty years living alongside Simeon yet immediately turned their backs on that tribe as they reached the border of the Promised Land. It was Judah who looked on the diminished strength of Simeon, took pity on them, and said, "Come up with me that we may fight together against the Canaanites". Gradually the tribe of Simeon was subsumed into Judah, scattered in Israel.

Levi

> "She conceived again and bore a son, and said, 'Now this time my husband will become attached to me, because I have borne him three sons'. Therefore his name was called Levi."
>
> (Genesis 29:34)

Simeon and Levi were full brothers with an age difference of no more than about one year. They were very close, sharing the same zeal but Levi's zeal found a very different outlet from that of his brother.

When Moses delayed his return from Mount Sinai to the people, they went back to the gods of Egypt, making and worshipping the golden calf. It was Levi that responded to Moses' call: "Who is on the LORD's side?" and fought against those who had left Him. Because of this, the Lord chose the Levites to be priests in Israel in place of firstborn sons (Numbers 3:6-9) and they were "scattered in Israel" by settling in forty-eight Levitical cities throughout the land. Later this divine choice was expanded when Levi again stood up for the Lord. It was a Levitical priest, Phinehas, who stopped the plague brought on Israel by their worship of Midianite gods at the time of Balaam and, in return, he was given the promise that his seed would be an everlasting priesthood (Numbers 35:12,13). So we read in Ezekiel of this priesthood in his details of the temple yet to be built in the Millennial age for it will be the sons of Zadok, descendants of Phinehas, who minister in it to the nations who come to Jerusalem to worship the Lord (Ezekiel 40:46).

Judah

> "And she conceived again and bore a son, and said, 'Now I will praise the LORD'. Therefore she called his name Judah. Then she stopped bearing." (Genesis 29:35)
>
> "Judah, you are he whom your brothers shall praise; your hand shall be on the neck of your enemies; your father's children shall bow down before you. Judah is a lion's whelp; from the prey, my son, you have gone up. He bows down, he lies down as a lion; and as a lion, who shall rouse him? The sceptre shall not depart from Judah, nor a lawgiver from between his feet, until Shiloh comes; and to him shall be the obedience of the people. Binding his donkey to the vine, and his donkey's colt to the choice vine, he washed his garments in wine, and his clothes in the blood of grapes. His eyes are darker than wine, and his teeth whiter than milk." (49:8-12)

Leah's reactions to the births of her first three sons form a pattern. 'See, a son!' she said when she produced her firstborn (Reuben) for her husband; now he would listen to her (Simeon); she would be joined to him (Levi). However, when Judah was born, her reaction was different: "Now will I praise the LORD: therefore she called his name Judah (praise); and left bearing" (KJV). She saw something special in him. Here was a son whose birth caused her to turn to the Lord with joy. Perhaps this was the son who eventually united her truly with her husband for he too saw in Judah a son worthy of praise. Judah was the son who was willing to offer himself to Egypt instead of Benjamin, the son who was willing to give himself for his brothers.

So Jacob turned to his fourth son: "As for you Judah, *you* are the one whom your brothers will praise."[5] It was almost as if he had turned aside from the first three sons and now blessed Judah with words which foretold the future summed up by the chronicler:

> "Judah prevailed over his brothers, and from him came a ruler." (1 Chronicles 5:2)

5 Matthews, volume 1B, page 891.

The following is a suggested interpretation of Jacob's words.

- Balaam saw all Israel as a great lion that would not lie down until it had eaten of its prey (Numbers 23:24), quoting Jacob's words about Judah. He interpreted this as a prophecy foretelling the inevitability of Israel's conquest of Canaan.
- When the invasion of Canaan began, Joshua asked God, "Who shall go up first to fight against the Canaanites?" and the Lord replied, "Judah shall go up, I have delivered the land into his hand" (Judges 1:1,2). In this we see the beginning of the lion going up and taking its prey; the fulfilment of the promise-blessings about the land commenced, the land was inhabited by Jacob's descendants.
- Yet the land was not taken completely until the time of David. We read of his seven campaigns (2 Samuel 8-10) against the nations round about until, "the fame of David went out into all lands; and the LORD brought the fear of him upon all nations" (1 Chronicles 14:17). His hand was upon the necks of his enemies.
- David was the descendant of Judah and when the tribes came to Hebron to make him king over all Israel, they claimed a familial relationship with him: we are your bone and flesh, they said (2 Samuel 5:1) – so his brothers praised him.

  > "Then all the tribes of Israel came to David at Hebron and spoke, saying, 'Indeed we are your bone and your flesh ... and the LORD said to you, "You shall shepherd my people Israel, and be ruler over Israel"'. Therefore all the elders of Israel came to the king at Hebron, and King David made a covenant with them at Hebron before the LORD. And they anointed David king over Israel." (2 Samuel 5:1-3)

- Yet the promises could not be fulfilled in David. They needed a special descendant who would arise out of Judah, one whose kingdom would be an everlasting kingdom. The rule of Judah with the sceptre and the lawgiver's staff would not be complete until Shiloh ('until he comes') came and the language used is almost identical to that of Ezekiel, "until he comes whose right it is, and I will give it to him" (Ezekiel 21:27).

- When he comes, he will be the promised ruler out of Judah and the nations of the earth will go to Jerusalem to worship him; to him will be "the obedience of the people".

Jacob's words to Judah are precious indeed. In them are seen things already fulfilled, exactly as the patriarch said and so we have absolute confidence in the final fulfilment of them at our Lord's return. At the very end of the scriptures, the Apostle John understood how Jacob had foreseen both David and his greater Son for he wrote of the lion of the tribe of Judah, the root of David, who prevailed to open the book and loose its seals, that the future may be secure.

Zebulun

> "Then Leah conceived again and bore Jacob a sixth son. And Leah said, 'God has endowed me with a good endowment; now my husband will dwell with me, because I have borne him six sons. So she called his name Zebulun'." (Genesis 30:19,20)
>
> "Zebulun shall dwell by the haven of the sea; he shall become a haven for ships, and his border shall adjoin Sidon." (Genesis 49:13)

Jacob now departed from the birth order of his sons and blessed Zebulun, his tenth son, Leah's sixth and last. In his words to Judah, the patriarch had spoken of the Messiah; now in his words to Zebulun he spoke about the part of Israel from which he would come. His message was different from those spoken previously. Zebulun's blessing was not associated with his character but with the territory the tribe would inhabit. There is a problem here for the lot that fell to Zebulun on entry into the land does not appear to include any sea coast (Joshua 19:10-16). Yet Josephus wrote that the tribe had land "as far as Genesareth and that which belonged to Carmel and the sea".[6] We can only surmise that it extended its territory in the years that followed. "Zebulun" means 'dwelling' and when he was born, Leah said, "Now will my husband dwell (*zabal*) with me". Nazareth was in Zebulun, part of Galilee, and it was this region that, on occasions, provided a haven, a safe dwelling place for Jesus when Judea sought to kill him.[7]

But it is Isaiah who provides the strongest link between Zebulun and the Messiah:

> "Nevertheless the gloom will not be upon her who is distressed, as when at first he lightly esteemed the land of Zebulun and the land of Naphtali, and afterward more heavily oppressed her, by the way of the sea, beyond the Jordan, in Galilee of the Gentiles. The people who walked in darkness have seen a great light; those who dwelt in the land of the shadow of death, upon them a light has shined." (Isaiah 9:1,2)

The initial fulfilment of this prophecy was in Hezekiah's days. When he finally came to the throne of Judah as sole ruler he immediately reinstituted the Passover and invited the remnants of the ten tribes left in Samaria after the Assyrian exile to repent and come and share the Passover lamb. The initial response was from some of the tribes in Galilee, "the land of Zebulun ... by the way of the sea" who went south to Jerusalem and worshipped the Lord.

But this was only a partial fulfilment of the prophet's message for Matthew quoted Isaiah's words and applied them to the beginning of the ministry of the Lord Jesus. Immediately after his baptism and his temptations in the wilderness the Lord Jesus Christ began his ministry "in the sea coast of the borders of Zebulun and Naphtali that it might be fulfilled that was spoken by Isaiah the prophet". His message was one of the need for repentance for the kingdom of God was coming, and great multitudes followed him from Galilee, Zebulun at the forefront – a remarkable parallel with the days of Hezekiah.

---

6 Josephus, Chapter V, paragraph 22.

7 Matthew 2:22; 4:12; John 7:1.

Issachar

> "And God listened to Leah, and she conceived and bore Jacob a fifth son. Leah said, 'God has given me my wages, because I have given my maid to my husband'. So she called his name Issachar." (Genesis 30:17,18)
>
> "Issachar is a strong donkey, lying down between two burdens; he saw that rest was good, and that the land was pleasant; he bowed his shoulder to bear a burden, and became a band of slaves." (49:14,15)

The birth of Issachar, Leah's fifth son, was linked to the unsavoury episode of the mandrakes which Leah gave to Rachel in return for a night spent with Jacob. She hired (*sakar*) him, became pregnant and called the resulting child Is-sachar, a reward.[8]

When the men of Issachar settled in Canaan, they were given the best farmland in the country, in the Jezreel Valley: it was pleasant land and they saw it as their reward. However, Jacob's words about Issachar are difficult to understand and two different interpretations are possible.

1. Issachar became a tribe of peasant farmers, content with their lot but who made little effort to subdue and expel the Canaanites and, in time, became their servants.
2. The second view uses the Septuagint version describing the men of Issachar as content with their lot as farmers. This description of Issachar as quiet and contented people is perhaps supported by Moses' words about them: "Rejoice Issachar in your tents." They were 'stay at home' people, happy with their position in life.

   > "Issachar has desired that which is good; resting between the inheritances. And having seen the resting place that it was good, and the land that it was fertile, he subjected his shoulder to labour, and became a husbandman." (Genesis 49:14,15, LXX)

8 As, for example, in Jeremiah 31:16.

50 |

Jacob's blessing of his sons (2)

"And Bilhah conceived and bore Jacob a son. Then Rachel said, 'God has judged my case; and he has also heard my voice and given me a son'. Therefore she called his name Dan." (Genesis 30:5,6)

*"Dan (*dawn*) shall judge (*diyn*) his people as one of the tribes of Israel. Dan shall be a serpent by the way, a viper by the path, that bites the horse's heels so that its rider shall fall backward." (49:16,17)*

Dan

HAVING spoken to all six of Leah's children, Jacob now turned to the sons of the handmaids. Dan was a son born out of envy. Rachel was desperate for a son and gave her handmaid, Bilhah, to Jacob. Her child was born "upon Rachel's knees", a phrase used of formal adoption – he became legally a child of Rachel, the senior of the sons of the handmaids. But the history of his tribe also shows his descendants in another light. Like Ishmael Dan was a son of a handmaid and his descendants would eventually turn aside from the way of the Lord.

The tribe of Dan was the second largest tribe to enter the Promised Land and the last to be given an inheritance by Joshua. Their territory was one of the smallest, bounded by Ephraim to the north and Judah to the south – powerful tribes who could have supported it. All of this was carefully done, inspired by the

Lord for Dan was spiritually the weakest of the tribes and is the last mentioned in the sad list in Judges 1: they were a slothful people, pushed out of part of their territory by the Amorites even though God had said that the time of the Amorites was over.

Yet the Lord's longsuffering is shown once again for out of the weakest of the tribes came the strongest of the judges, Samson. To the spiritually apathetic came a man who was a Nazarite, dedicated to the work of the Lord. He judged not only Dan but Israel for twenty years, binding his tribe with its brothers "as one of the tribes of Israel".

But when Samson died, disaster followed. Dan left its inheritance and went north, to the very edge of the land, looking for a place to settle. They took with them an apostate priest and set up idols, worshipping there in this way until "the day of the captivity of the land" (Judges 18:30).

Worse was to follow for when Jeroboam became king he set up idols in Dan and Bethel. These things became a serpent in the way for those who travelled to them for apostate worship and it was this example Peter had in mind when he warned disciples of all ages:

> "... the time has come for judgment (Dan) to begin at the house (Bethel) of God."

Bethel was in Ephraim and these two tribes, Dan and Ephraim, became the centres of idolatrous worship in the northern kingdom. It is noteworthy that they are both missing from the list of tribes in Revelation 7, perhaps telling us that there is no spiritual example from their behaviour to help spiritual Israel on the way to the kingdom.

Gad

> "When Leah saw that she had stopped bearing, she took Zilpah her maid and gave her to Jacob as wife. And Leah's maid Zilpah bore Jacob a son. Then Leah said, 'A troop comes!' So she called his name Gad." (Genesis 30:9-11)
>
> "Gad, a troop shall tramp upon him, but he shall triumph at last." (49:19)

The birth of Gad highlights the battle fought between Rachel and Leah. Leah had ceased bearing children after Judah, barren Rachel had responded by using Bilhah to have children she would adopt. In retaliation Leah then gave her handmaid, Zilpah, to Jacob to have children for her and Gad was born. In triumph Leah said, "A troop comes!" Did she anticipate more children – whatever Rachel did would Leah always seek more?

Jacob's words in Genesis 49 use this word "troop" four times. We could read it as, "this troop, a troop shall troop over him; but he shall troop at the last".[1]

Yet Gad was one of the smallest tribes!

Gad's name comes first in the list of the three tribes that negotiated with Moses for land on the east bank of the Jordan suggesting it took the lead. Although the land of Gilead was good land, well suited to pastoral farming, it was vulnerable to raids from Ammon, Moab and from the Syrians in the north. Gad made life more difficult for itself as, apparently, it disobeyed a commandment the Lord gave Moses. As Israel travelled up the east side of the Jordan, skirting Edom, Moab and Ammon, the Lord told Moses that they must leave the territories of Moab and Ammon alone. He had given them to the descendants of Lot for a possession (Deuteronomy 2:19).

Israel was allowed to take Amorite territory and overcame Og, king of Bashan. However, Og had previously occupied half of Ammon, including Rabbah (Deuteronomy 3:11), and when Gad took this, it never gave it back to Ammon. Because of this the Ammonites became a perpetual thorn in the sides of Israel. Later they complained to Jephthah about the unjustness of the situation yet he justified the decision (Judges 11). Gad had to build fenced cities in Gilead because of this although there is no record that Reuben and Manasseh had to do the same (Numbers 33:36). Throughout Old Testament times, Gilead was a pawn, fought over by Syria, Ammon and Moab; the tribes living there eventually became subject to Hazael of Syria and then were the

1 C. H. Waller, *Names on the Gates of Pearl*, page 83.

first to go into captivity when Tiglath-Pileser invaded (2 Kings 15:29).

Gad went into isolation for economic reasons and life was one of perpetual warfare: the world constantly sought victory. Yet it will share the triumph of the Lord at his return and receive its territory in the kingdom to be established, triumphing at last.

Asher

> "And Leah's maid Zilpah bore Jacob a second son. Then Leah said, 'I am happy, for the daughters will call me blessed'. So she called his name Asher." (Genesis 30:12,13)
>
> "Bread from Asher shall be rich, and he shall yield royal dainties." (49:20)

When Zilpah, Leah's maid, bore Jacob a second son Leah called him Asher, "for the daughters will call me blessed (*asher*, happy)". What a contrast with the births of her own sons when she had looked to the Lord. Now she sought the approbation of the women of the compound, not the blessing (*barak*) of the Lord. Asher was linked with a desire for happiness rather than promise-blessings of the Lord and his descendants sought such contentment in the land they were given. The tribe settled on the north-west coast of Canaan in a strip running just north of Carmel to just south of Tyre, land which significantly included Sidon.

It appears never to have produced any religious or political leader throughout its history. Deborah had to reprimand it for its unwillingness to participate in the fight against the Canaanites.

Its land was the fertile coastal plain and was noted for its olive groves. Bread from Asher was rich (*shamen*, fat) and Moses used the same word when he prophesied that Asher would dip its foot in oil (*shemen*).

Once again, Judges 1 is vital in understanding the history of the tribe for we read:

> "Nor did Asher drive out the inhabitants of Acco or the inhabitants of Sidon, or of Ahlab, Achzib, Helbah, Aphik, or Rehob. So the Asherites dwelt among the Canaanites, the

> inhabitants of the land; for they did not drive them out."
> (Judges 1:31,32)

This list of towns is the longest for any tribe in this chapter. Asher was content to live alongside *all* the Canaanites and thrived materially, yet this brought disaster.

Many years later, Ahab, king of Samaria, took false worship to a new level. He was not content with following the example of Jeroboam with apostate worship at Dan or Bethel but married Jezebel, daughter of the king of Sidon, and went and "worshipped and served Baal". Yet even this was not enough for he made a grove (*asherah*, a place of happiness) and worshipped Ashtoreth, the consort of Baal (1 Kings 16:30-33).

What irony there is in this: the descendants of a son, born from a focus on human happiness rather than the way of the Lord, ended up seeking happiness in the worship of the false gods of Canaan.

Yet there was still a faithful remnant for when Hezekiah's summons to the Passover went forth, men of Asher humbled themselves and travelled south to Jerusalem.

Naphtali

> "And Rachel's maid Bilhah conceived again and bore Jacob a second son. Then Rachel said, 'With great wrestlings I have wrestled with my sister, and indeed I have prevailed'. So she called his name Naphtali." (Genesis 30:7,8)

"Naphtali is a deer let loose; he uses beautiful words." (49:21) Jacob's words to Naphtali are probably the most obscure of the blessings and many differing translations have been offered, but they give us a wonderful picture of our salvation.

We need to go back to Naphtali's birth. He was the second son of Bilhah and at his nativity Rachel said, "'With great wrestlings (*naphtuwl*) I have wrestled with my sister, and indeed I have prevailed.' So she called his name Naphtali". Naphtali therefore represents not just wrestling but a wrestling that is victorious and this is seen in the tribal life that followed.

Naphtali settled in the Upper Galilee valley on the north-west of the lake. Like so many of the northern tribes it compromised with the Canaanites and lived alongside them in fertile country. Yet in the period of the judges, at a time of peril through the whole of the north when Jabin, king of Canaan reigned, it was a man of Naphtali, Barak, who obeyed the call of the Lord through Deborah and called Naphtali and Zebulun to him to fight Sisera.

> "Zebulun is a people who jeopardized their lives to the point of death, Naphtali also, on the heights of the battlefield. The kings came and fought, then the kings of Canaan fought in Taanach, by the waters of Megiddo; they took no spoils of silver. They fought from the heavens; the stars from their courses fought against Sisera." (Judges 5:18-20)

But, how do we link this with the idea of a hind? We find help in the words of David. He understood his military prowess as a gift from the Lord who gave him tactical nous:

> "It is God who arms me with strength, and makes my way perfect. He makes my feet like the feet of deer, and sets me on my high places." (Psalm 18:32,33)

What a vivid picture of Barak's victory this is. The men of Naphtali were on foot and faced the formidable chariots of Sisera; they could not defeat them face to face on the plains of Jezreel. Yet, fleet-footed as a deer fleeing from danger they withdrew to Mount Tabor, in the heights, and enticed Sisera into the marshes around the brook Kishon.

A victory followed. Jabin the king of Canaan was destroyed and the occasion was marked with beautiful words, the song of Deborah and Barak of Naphtali. "Awake, awake, Deborah: awake, awake, utter a song: arise, Barak, and lead thy captivity captive" (Judges 5:12, KJV).

This phrase was used by the Apostle Paul as he wrote to the Ephesians about the victory won by the Lord Jesus Christ in his death, resurrection and ascension (Ephesians 4:8). He was the one who wrestled with strong crying and tears, fighting against sin and prevailed. He took captive the power of sin which had captured men and women through the ages.

Solomon looked back to Jacob's words and applied them to the beloved one, the bridegroom coming for his bride:

> "The voice of my beloved! Behold, he comes leaping upon the mountains, skipping upon the hills. My beloved is like a gazelle or a young stag." (Song of Solomon 2:8,9)

Jacob's words to Naphtali therefore take us forward to the days of the Lord Jesus Christ, the one who began his ministry in the borders of Zebulun and Naphtali (Matthew 4:13,14), drawing the multitudes to him in a high mountain and speaking beautiful words, "Blessed are the poor in spirit for theirs is the kingdom of heaven ..."

51 | Jacob's blessing of his sons (3)

"Then God remembered Rachel, and God listened to her and opened her womb. And she conceived and bore a son, and said, 'God has taken away my reproach'. So she called his name Joseph, and said, 'The LORD shall add to me another son'." (Genesis 30:22-24)

"Joseph is a fruitful bough, a fruitful bough by a well; his branches run over the wall. The archers have bitterly grieved him, shot at him and hated him. But his bow remained in strength, and the arms of his hands were made strong by the hands of the Mighty God of Jacob (From there is the shepherd, the Stone of Israel), by the God of your father who will help you, and by the Almighty who will bless you with blessings of heaven above, blessings of the deep that lies beneath, blessings of the breasts and of the womb. The blessings of your father have excelled the blessings of my ancestors, up to the utmost bound of the everlasting hills. They shall be on the head of Joseph, and on the crown of the head of him who was separate (naziyr) *from his brothers." (49:22-26)*

Joseph

REUBEN had lost both birthright and blessing because of his behaviour. To whom would Jacob give it? The birthright was the right of the firstborn son and he decided that it should pass from the firstborn of Leah to the firstborn of Rachel – so it was given to Joseph.

Later, Moses made it clear that the firstborn should get a double portion of the inheritance (Deuteronomy 21:17) and it appears that this principle was adopted at the time of Jacob also for he had already told Joseph that he had given him one portion more than his brothers. Instead of the tribe of Joseph, there would be two tribes, Ephraim and Manasseh, "they will be mine" said Jacob, "just as Reuben and Simeon are mine".

Rachel died giving birth to Benjamin and had been buried on the way to Ephrath, 'the place of fruitfulness', not quite reaching it. She would have no more sons and the fruitfulness of many children, given to Leah, would never be hers. Yet fruitfulness is a part of every blessing given by the Lord in Genesis: Adam, Noah, Abraham, Isaac, Jacob were all told that they would be fruitful and multiply, part of God's promise to fill the earth with His people.

Joseph understood that God was at work through him, he would be fruitful and so he called his second son Ephraim, 'doubly fruitful'. Through both Manasseh and Ephraim, Joseph believed that God would continue His work and now he received his father's blessing in his turn:

> "Joseph is a fruitful bough (*ben*, son), a fruitful bough by a well; his branches (*bath*, daughters) run over the wall."

Together, the two tribes of Joseph were by far the largest contingent to enter the land and were given the largest territory. In time Ephraim's position became so powerful that his name is used in the prophets to stand for all of the northern tribes in Samaria. Shechem was in Ephraim and hence Jacob's well; Ephraim was indeed a fruitful son by a well.

It was the daughters of Zelophehad, from the tribe of Manasseh who complained to Moses. The laws of inheritance meant that, if they married men from other tribes, their tribal inheritance would be lost to Manasseh (Numbers 36). They lived in Gilead on the east bank of the Jordan; the daughters of Zelophehad had indeed extended over the God-given boundary of the land, over the wall.

The following verses are difficult to interpret and perhaps verses 23-26 apply to Joseph individually.

It was his brothers who hated him, plotted against him and spoke bitter words about him as the Psalmist said:

> "Hide me from the secret plots of the wicked, from the rebellion of the workers of iniquity, who sharpen their tongue like a sword, and bend their bows to shoot their arrows – bitter words, that they may shoot in secret at the blameless; suddenly they shoot at him and do not fear. They encourage themselves in an evil matter; they talk of laying snares secretly; they say, 'Who will see them?' They devise iniquities: we have perfected a shrewd scheme." (Psalm 64:2-6)

Yet, through all of his affliction, Joseph remained strong, for he relied on the Lord for his strength. His God was:

- The Mighty One of Jacob
- The shepherd, the Stone of Israel
- The God of his father
- The Almighty

God would give him the blessings of fruitfulness, many children would come from him, of the breasts and of the womb.

And it was this God who was his father's God, the One from whom his father's blessings came, blessings that were greater than those of the inheritance such as Mount Gerezim, the mount of blessing in Ephraim or the hill country given to the same tribe.

> "Your father's blessings are greater than the blessings of the ancient mountains, than the bounty of the age-old hills."
> (Genesis 49:26, NIV)

The promise of the everlasting age to come would be on the head of Joseph and also on the head of one who, like him, would be separate from his brothers.

The Nazarene

Joseph was indeed separate from his brothers: he was separated when they threw him in the pit and sold into slavery, separated by his high position in Egypt and separated in his death, buried in a tomb in which no man had laid. He was the beloved son, the firstborn who received a double portion, the son despised and rejected by his brothers yet the forerunner, sent ahead of them by the Lord to be their saviour.

In so many ways Joseph was separate from his brothers and the word used, *naziyr*, is that used to describe the Nazarite (Numbers 6), a man or woman who made a vow of absolute service to the Lord for a period in which his separation unto the Lord was "upon his head". It was a role in which a non-Levite could act in a dedicated role, like a Levite and it was on the head of Joseph and also on the head of the greater one who would follow. Joseph was merely a type of the Lord Jesus Christ, the one who would be called the Nazarene.

He was the beloved Son, the one who was despised and rejected by his brothers who did not believe that the time would come when he would rule over them and they would bow the knee to him. He was separate from them, "holy, harmless, undefiled, separate from sinners". He was the forerunner sent by his father to be the saviour of his people and he, as the firstborn from the dead, received the firstborn's double portion: both peoples and lands will be his for David wrote of him –

> "Ask of me, and I will give you the nations for your inheritance, and the ends of the earth for your possession." (Psalm 2:8)

Benjamin

> "Then they journeyed from Bethel. And when there was but a little distance to go to Ephrath, Rachel laboured in childbirth, and she had hard labour. Now it came to pass, when she was in hard labour, that the midwife said to her, 'Do not fear; you will have this son also'. And so it was, as her soul was departing (for she died), that she called his name Ben-Oni; but his father called him Benjamin. So Rachel died and was buried on the way to Ephrath (that is, Bethlehem)." (Genesis 35:16-19)

> "Benjamin is a ravenous wolf; in the morning he shall devour the prey, and at night he shall divide the spoil." (49:27)

Rachel was over forty years of age when Benjamin was born. At last the Lord fulfilled His word to her, she bore the son that He promised at the birth of Joseph. But the labour was too much for her and, knowing that her death was near, she called her baby, ‘the son of sorrow’. Was this sorrow that she was dying or that she would bear no more children?

In a sense Benjamin was always the baby of the family, fiercely protected by his father and loved by his older brothers. We know nothing of his character; we have no words of his, no actions recorded in Genesis.

How surprising therefore to read that his descendants would be ravenous wolves and yet we read of many examples of such behaviour in the Old Testament.

Ehud was a Benjamite judge in Israel who assassinated Eglon and then led the slaughter of the Moabites so that no man was left of about ten thousand warriors (Judges 3).

The Benjamites of Gibeah acted in such a vicious and brutal way to visitors to their town that the rest of the tribes rose up against them, a civil war followed and only six hundred men of Benjamin were left (Judges 19,20).

Saul, the first king of Israel, was a Benjamite, a man who destroyed the peace that existed with the Philistines; he overcame the Amalekites yet spared the spoil and gave it to the people in direct contradiction of God’s commandments (1 Samuel 15).

When we come to the New Testament, it was Saul of Tarsus, of the tribe of Benjamin (Philippians 3:5), who instituted a pogrom against the disciples of the Lord Jesus Christ, persecuting them, putting them in prison and delivering them to the death penalty (Acts 8:3; 26:9,10).

Yet in the conversion of Saul of Tarsus to become the Apostle Paul, Benjamin the wolf disappeared from the pages of the Bible. In its place we see the man who spent his life seeking to protect his brethren and sisters from grievous wolves who would try to destroy the ecclesias (Acts 20:29).

No doubt Jacob’s words received a mixed reaction from his sons. He only used the word “bless” when speaking to Joseph, and others such as Simeon and Levi may have thought their message was more like a curse. But the gifts and calling of God are irrevocable and Jacob made it clear that all of his sons had a part to play in the Lord's redemptive purpose; the promise-blessings were to every one of them and all received his blessing.

> "All these are the twelve tribes of Israel: and this is it that their father spake unto them, and blessed them; every one according to his blessing he blessed them."
>
> (Genesis 49:28, KJV)

52 | I have waited for your salvation, O LORD

IN the middle of blessing his sons, Jacob broke off and spoke of his own faith in the promises: "I have waited for your salvation, O LORD." We do not know why his words came at this moment, perhaps they burst out of him after the depressing message given to Dan. He was a son who would go seriously astray from the Lord as we have seen in spite of the fact that his father's faith had ever been an example to him of patient waiting for the kingdom.

There are two literary devices used in chapter 49 which help us to see the overall picture.

The chapter is an inclusio, a section of text begun and finished with the same word or phrase telling us that the included words all relate to the beginning and ending. Here it is the word "gather" that is important.

> "And Jacob called his sons and said, 'Gather (*acaph*) together, that I may tell you what shall befall you in the last days':"
>
> "And when Jacob had finished commanding his sons, he drew (*acaph*) his feet up into the bed and breathed his last, and was gathered (*acaph*) to his people."

Jacob was literally dying. This was his last act and we can imagine this aged man, one hundred and forty-seven years old, summoning strength to share these messages from the Lord. His blessing of his sons and his decease are linked; this was the very last thing he did. As he understood the imminence of his death he urgently needed to share with his sons what God had revealed to him.

But another structure is also used, for we can lay out the chapter as follows.

Jacob gathers his sons together;
 He blesses his sons;
  I have waited for your salvation, O LORD.
 He blesses his sons;
Jacob dies and is gathered to his people.

This focuses the chapter on Jacob and his faith and what a moving picture of the patriarch it is. He was a man who had learned patience through the things he had suffered: for twenty long years he had toiled for Laban, meekly accepting that man's constant cheating of him. Now he was dying in faith, not having received the promises but having seen them afar off and the Letter to the Hebrews tells us why Jacob's final words were a plea to be buried in Canaan:

> "These all died in faith, not having received the promises, but having seen them afar off were assured of them, embraced them and confessed that they were strangers and pilgrims on the earth. For those who say such things declare plainly that they seek a homeland. And truly if they had called to mind that country from which they had come out, they would have had opportunity to return. But now they desire a better, that is, a heavenly country. Therefore God is not ashamed to be called their God, for he has prepared a city for them."
>
> (Hebrews 11:13-16)

The children of Israel were sojourners,[1] resident aliens, strangers and pilgrims in Egypt and Jacob was the man who desired the inheritance of the land of promise more than anything else, for it was there that God's purpose would be fulfilled. He had no opportunity to return and would now die in Egypt but he commanded his sons, gave them strict orders, to bury him with his fathers in Canaan.

---

1 Genesis 47:4; Exodus 12:40.

Jacob's words contain the first mention of salvation (*yeshuwah*) in the Bible and the last mention of the name "Yahweh" in Genesis, and it is significant that these two words come together in this way. Jacob's hope was beautifully defined by him: it was of Yahweh's salvation, that revealed to Abraham in chapter 15. He looked for the special seed promised to his grandfather, for the Lamb that the Lord would provide, for the one who would be named Jesus, *Yehowshuwa*, Yah is salvation, for he would save his people from their sins.

When we leave Genesis we find these ideas again at the beginning of Exodus, for the next use of the name of the Lord and of gather (*acaph*) together, is in Exodus 3.

At the burning bush, the Lord revealed to Moses His intentions to lead Israel out of Egypt to Canaan and Moses was instructed to share this information with his people:

> "Moreover God said to Moses, 'Thus you shall say to the children of Israel: "The LORD God of your fathers, the God of Abraham, the God of Isaac, and the God of Jacob, has sent me to you. This is my name forever, and this is my memorial to all generations." Go and gather (*acaph*) the elders of Israel together, and say to them, "The LORD God of your fathers, the God of Abraham, of Isaac, and of Jacob, appeared to me, saying, 'I have surely visited you and seen what is done to you in Egypt; and I have said I will bring you up out of the affliction of Egypt to the land of the Canaanites and the Hittites and the Amorites and the Perizzites and the Hivites and the Jebusites, to a land flowing with milk and honey'"'."
>
> (Exodus 3:15-17)

No doubt, the elders of Israel were the heads of the tribes and what a fine link to the gathering before Jacob this is. The Lord began the revelation of His name to Moses and He emphasised, twice, that he was Yahweh, the same God of Abraham, Isaac and Jacob. The promises would be fulfilled, His people would return to the Promised Land and would inhabit the territories promised them by Jacob in his dying words. When the elders were gathered and heard these words, they bowed their heads and worshipped

(Exodus 4:31). It was the beginning of the reformation of a people who had completely forgotten about the God of Abraham, Isaac and Jacob, and the descendants of Jacob's sons needed to learn afresh of the exceeding great and precious promises made to their fathers before they were fit to leave Egypt and enter into the inheritance foretold by Jacob.

53 | Last things

THE Genesis record ends with the death and burial of Jacob and the death, years later, of Joseph. But more than this, it tells us of the personal examples of both Jacob and Joseph and the influence these had on the brothers.

Jacob's funeral

Jacob was adamant that he wished to be buried in the cave of Machpelah at Hebron; his final words were a commandment to his sons to do this. Abraham and Sarah, Isaac and Rebekah and also Leah were buried there and he wished to be laid alongside them. Interestingly, he did not ask to be buried next to Rachel at Ramah, but with Leah. She had been the one who had given birth to Judah and the Lord had revealed to Jacob that His purpose would be fulfilled through his descendant, not through a son of Joseph. Many years later the Psalmist confirmed this choice: "He refused the tabernacle of Joseph, and chose not the tribe of Ephraim: but chose the tribe of Judah" (Psalm 78:67,68, KJV).

Joseph led the family's mourning: he fell on his father's face, wept and kissed him. Previously Jacob had said that it should be Joseph who would "close his eyes" (Genesis 46:4), a formal phrase telling of the honour, reserved in advance for the descendant who had been closest to the deceased.[1] It was Joseph who commanded the embalming of the body which took forty days and then another thirty days of mourning followed, seventy days in all, the

1 Hamilton, volume 2, page 691.

last number given in Genesis echoing the number of the Children of Israel that went down into Egypt. Joseph needed Pharaoh's permission to leave Egypt and, because he was in mourning, he could not approach the king personally but sent him a message. Pharaoh's response showed the esteem in which Joseph, Jacob and the family were held. It was essentially a state funeral attended by Pharaoh's household and the senior politicians of the land so that the Canaanites saw it as solemn mourning of the Egyptians.

The brothers' concerns

With Jacob's death the brothers felt vulnerable. Would Joseph now turn on them and seek revenge for their behaviour? Their treachery had occurred nearly forty years ago yet it still preyed on their minds. They had heard Jacob bless Joseph with words that described them as men of arrows who had shot at Joseph and who hated (*satam*) him. Now they wondered if he, in turn, would hate (*satam*) them for the evil they did. As Joseph felt unable to approach Pharaoh directly and sent a message to him, now they did the same:

> "Before your father died he commanded, saying, 'Thus you shall say to Joseph: "I beg you, please forgive the trespass of your brothers and their sin; for they did evil to you."' Now, please, forgive the trespass of the servants of the God of your father. And Joseph wept when they spoke to him. Then his brothers also went and fell down before his face, and they said, 'Behold, we are your servants'. Joseph said to them, 'Do not be afraid, for *am* I in the place of God? But as for you, you meant evil against me; but God meant it for good, in order to bring it about as it is this day, to save many people alive. Now therefore, do not be afraid; I will provide for you and your little ones'. And he comforted them and spoke kindly to them." (Genesis 50:16-21)

What remarkable behaviour this was by all concerned.

Jacob, who had been so devastated by the loss of Joseph that he refused to be comforted, left a message for his beloved son to forgive as he had forgiven.

The brothers felt unable to approach Joseph as brothers, calling Jacob, "our father" but said to him "your father ..." almost as if they felt unworthy of claiming a relationship with him. Their own words were, "forgive the trespass of the servants of the God of your father", using language which acknowledged a terrible act of rebellion against the Lord. For the first time they asked Joseph to forgive them for what they had done. Finally they fell prostrate before him and said, "we are your slaves" to the man they had refused as their leader and whom they had sold into slavery.

Joseph wept. He was indeed a man of sorrows and this is the seventh time we find him weeping over his family. His words to them literally were, "I in the place of God". Of course he forgave them because Jacob asked this of him, but there was a greater reason. Joseph was God's man and his God was a merciful and forgiving God whose forgiveness was without reservation to those who came to Him seeking it.

> "He who covers his sins will not prosper, but whoever confesses and forsakes them will have mercy." (Proverbs 28:13)

Through the brothers' actions Joseph had been presented as dead, his blood-covered, torn coat was evidence of that. Then miraculously the news was that he lived, almost as if he had come back from the grave. Those who had 'killed' him had done evil, yet through their machinations the Lord was at work for good to save may people alive, not just Israel but all the peoples who had come to him seeking him at the time of the famine. So he spoke comfortably to his brethren assuring them that their iniquity had been pardoned.

Joseph's death

Joseph lived for another fifty-four years; he saw his great grandchildren including Gilead, the son of Machir, who was the grandfather of Zelophehad, so the record leaves us with yet another link to future events.

Joseph therefore saw the fourth generation from himself and he would be aware of the promise the Lord made to Abraham that Israel would come out of Egypt in the fourth generation (Genesis 15:16). He would hope that he would still be alive when that happened, yet it was not to be and he commanded his sons, as Jacob had given commandment:

> "'I am dying; but God will surely visit you, and bring you out of this land to the land of which he swore to Abraham, to Isaac, and to Jacob.' Then Joseph took an oath from the children of Israel, saying, 'God will surely visit you, and you shall carry up my bones from here'. So Joseph died, being one hundred and ten years old; and they embalmed him, and he was put in a coffin in Egypt." (Genesis 50:24-26)

Like his father, he had waited all his life for the Lord's salvation and now died in faith. He had not received the promise but had seen it afar off and he was absolutely convinced of it. Through his life, he had embraced it and the Lord had directed his steps wherever he had been. Though he became the vizier of all Egypt, one of the most powerful men in the whole of the Middle East, he was a stranger and a pilgrim on the earth, waiting for that better country that the Lord had prepared and for this faith God was not ashamed to be called his God.

APPENDICES

Appendix 1: Blessing

SOMETIMES when we read the scriptures we see words that are so familiar to us we don't stop to think about them and their meaning. It is a good idea to imagine that, after we have read them, we have to explain the passage and the meaning of its words to people who have never come across them before. That certainly gets the grey cells working.

How would we, for example, explain the word "bless"? In modern life its use is vague and ambiguous. When someone says, "God bless you" they probably mean no more than "hope everything goes well". What do we mean when we ask God for a blessing on the food we are about to eat?

Even a concordance does not help too much. It might define the word as "to bless, praise or kneel"; and with this we are no further forward. Furthermore, we would find that not only does God bless people but men also bless Him and sometimes each other.

As with all Bible study, the best solution is to turn to the Bible itself and look carefully at the various passages in which the word is used. By doing this for the word "bless" we can build up a picture of the purpose of God in all of scripture.

Firstly a few comments about the meanings of key words. In this book we have only looked at "bless" in the Old Testament, and in the book of Genesis in particular. When we do this, we find two Hebrew words used.

- *ashar* – to be happy, to bless;
- *barak* – to kneel, bless, praise.

It is the second of these words, *barak*, that we have concentrated on, but it is important to understand the difference between the two.

Ashar basically means to be happy or to make happy. It is never used with God as the subject; He never blesses (*ashar*) anyone, God never *makes* anyone happy. However it is very often found, particularly in the Psalms, of a man who has done something which has brought him a blessing (*ashar*). Generally this action is a positive one; he has trusted in God or acted according to the Lord's commandments and in doing so has found happiness and contentment. For example:

> "Praise the LORD! Blessed is the man who fears the LORD, who delights greatly in his commandments." (Psalm 112:1)

So, the Lord does not use His power to make people happy but provides, through the teaching of His word, all that is needed for happiness in this life.

Barak essentially means to bless and when God blesses, He always uses this word. It is linked to His power and also His loving kindness and mercy. When men bless (*barak*) others they can never do it in their own strength; rather they do it on behalf of the Lord and invoking His name.[1]

> "At that time the LORD separated the tribe of Levi to bear the ark of the covenant of the LORD, to stand before the LORD to minister to him and to bless in his name, to this day."
> (Deuteronomy 10:8)

Generally a blessing was transmitted from the greater to the lesser. For example:

- Father to son (Genesis 49);
- Brother to sister (Genesis 24:60);
- King to subjects (1 Kings 8:14).

These blessings spoke of things that would be given in the future and, as such, are linked to the message of prophecy and the promises of the Lord God.

1 C. W. Mitchell, *The Meaning of brk, "to bless," in the Old Testament*.

However sometimes, particularly when spoken by men to the Lord, they were used as praise and acknowledgment that the One addressed had the power to deliver the things promised in the blessings they had received from Him.

Often when the Lord is addressed in this way, acknowledgment of His power to bless is linked to His character. He is the God of loving kindness and tender mercies and this is shown to His people in the ways that He blesses them, particularly with the promise of life in an age to come:

> "Bless the LORD, O my soul; and all that is within me, bless his holy name! Bless the LORD, O my soul, and forget not all his benefits: who forgives all your iniquities, who heals all your diseases, who redeems your life from destruction, who crowns you with lovingkindness and tender mercies, who satisfies your mouth with good things, so that your youth is renewed like the eagle's." (Psalm 103:1-5)

The Old Testament portrays God as the only source of these things. His presence confers blessing (2 Samuel 6:11-20) and it is only in His name that others can confer blessing (Deuteronomy 10:8). God's name, the manifestation of His nature, is at the heart of all blessing.

The book of Psalms further helps our understanding of men blessing God, for each of its five books ends with a blessing of the Lord.

Book 1:

> "As for me, you uphold me in my integrity, and set me before your face forever. Blessed be the LORD God of Israel from everlasting to everlasting! Amen and Amen." (Psalm 41:12,13)

Book 2:

> "His name shall endure forever; his name shall continue as long as the sun. And men shall be blessed in him; all nations shall call him blessed. Blessed be the LORD God, the God of Israel, who only does wondrous things! And blessed be his glorious name forever! And let the whole earth be filled with his glory. Amen and Amen. The prayers of David the son of Jesse are ended." (Psalm 72:17-20)

Book 3:

"Remember, Lord, the reproach of your servants – how I bear in my bosom the reproach of all the many peoples, with which your enemies have reproached, O LORD, with which they have reproached the footsteps of your anointed. Blessed be the LORD for evermore! Amen and Amen." (Psalm 89:50-52)

Book 4:

"Save us, O LORD our God, and gather us from among the Gentiles, to give thanks to your holy name, to triumph in your praise. Blessed be the LORD God of Israel from everlasting to everlasting! And let all the people say, 'Amen!' Praise the LORD!" (Psalm 106:47,48)

Book 5:[2]

"The LORD is near to all who call upon him, to all who call upon him in truth. He will fulfil the desire of those who fear him; he also will hear their cry and save them. The LORD preserves all who love him, but all the wicked he will destroy. My mouth shall speak the praise of the LORD, and all flesh shall bless his holy name forever and ever." (Psalm 145:18-21)

When we put these together they give us a summary of the promise-blessings, the Gospel revealed throughout the Bible.

- God exists from everlasting to everlasting, He alone is immortal.
- He is the Lord, the God of His people, Israel.
- His name is linked to His blessings.
- His purpose is to fill the earth with His glory.
- He will save His people and hear the cry of all who love Him whilst destroying His enemies.

Hence, whereas *ashar* speaks of happiness in this life, *barak* is associated with the ultimate fulfilment of God's purpose. Together, therefore, they give us a picture of what our lives should be.

2 Taking Psalms 146-150 as an epilogue of praise of the Lord concluding the whole of the Psalms.

God provides for happiness and peace now for all those who commit themselves to Him in a life of discipleship, but He never imposes this on them – it has to be sought in the delights of His word. Yet even the most committed of disciples can do nothing to attain the ultimate blessing of immortality in the kingdom to come. Only the Lord God can do this and from the very beginning of scripture He reveals this to us in the blessings He gives.

Blessings and promises

It should come as no surprise then to learn that God's blessings are intimately connected with His promise. They are given throughout scripture to those whom He chose to play vital roles in His purpose. We see this particularly when we look at the origins of the Lord Jesus Christ. He is revealed gradually to us throughout the Bible; indeed we do not learn of his name until his birth. Little by little God reveals to us the ancestry of His Son in increasing detail, narrowing it down from the whole earth (in Genesis 3), to a tribe (Judah), to a family (Abraham's), choosing a faithful person from many on each occasion, until we arrive at just one person, Mary. And on each occasion it is accompanied by a blessing. The giving of a blessing was an essential part of God's purpose, as we see when proceeding through the book of Genesis.

Appendix 2: Chronologies

NOT everyone is interested in chronology and numbers and so in this book they have been placed in an appendix, which can be skipped over. It is not essential reading. However, these genealogies help us to see the ways in which great ages gave long overlaps of the lives of those who lived before the patriarchs.

Chronology from Adam to the Flood

Years from Adam	Name		Lifespan
	Birth	Death	
0	Adam		
130	Seth		
235	Enos		
325	Cainaan		
395	Mahalaleel		
460	Jared		
622	Enoch		
687	Methuselah		
874	Lamech		
930		Adam	930
987		Enoch	365
1042		Seth	912
1056	Noah		
1140		Enos	905
1235		Cainaan	910
1290		Mahalaleel	895
1422		Jared	962
1558	Shem		
1651		Lamech	777
1656 (The Flood)		Methuselah	969

Chronology from the Flood to Jacob

Years from Adam	Name		Lifespan
	Birth	Death	
1656 (The Flood)			
1658	Arphaxad		
1693	Salah		
1723	Eber		
1757	Peleg		
1787	Reu		
1819	Serug		
1849	Nahor		
1878	Terah		
1996		Peleg	239
1997		Nahor	148
2006		Noah	950
2008	Abraham		
2026		Reu	239
2108	Isaac		
2049		Serug	230
2083		Terah	205
2096		Arphaxad	438
2126		Salah	433
2158		Shem	600
2168	Jacob		
2187		Eber	464

Chronology of Abraham and his family

Event	Terah	Abraham	Isaac	Jacob	Joseph
Abraham born	130				
Leaves Ur **(430 years to exodus)**	200	70			
Leaves Haran	205	75			
Marries Hagar		85			
Ishmael born		86			
God gives promise of Isaac		99			
Isaac born **(400 years to exodus)**		100			
Isaac offered (?)		133	33		
Sarah dies aged 127		136	36		
Isaac marries Rebekah		140	40		
Jacob born		160	60		
Abraham dies		175	75	15	
Jacob takes birthright (?)			90	30	
Esau marries Canaanite women			100	40	
Ishmael dies aged 137			123	63	
Jacob takes the blessing			137	77	
Jacob marries Leah and Rachel			144	84	
Joseph born			151	91	

Event	Terah	Abraham	Isaac	Jacob	Joseph
Jacob returns to Canaan			157	97	6
Rachel dies (~44 years old)			166	106	15
Joseph goes into Egypt			168	108	17
Isaac dies			180	120	29
Joseph before Pharaoh				121	30
Seven years of plenty end				128	37
Israel goes into Egypt				130	39
Famine ends				135	44
Jacob dies				147	56
Joseph dies					110
EXODUS					

Scripture index

Exodus

Leviticus

Numbers